# Treasures of
# Utah

by William Faubion

*a part of the Morgan & Chase Treasure Series*
*www.mcpbooks.com*

# Morgan & Chase
### Publishing inc.

*Published by:*
Morgan & Chase Publishing, Inc.
531 Parsons Drive
Medford, Oregon 97501
888-557-9328
www.mcpbooks.com

*Printed by:*
C & C Offset Printing Co., Ltd. - China

First edition 2006

ISBN: 0-9754162-7-8

I gratefully acknowledge the contributions
of the many people involved in the writing and production of this book.
Their tireless dedication to this endeavor is inspirational.
—Damon Neal, Publisher

*Editors:*
Cindy Tilley Faubion
Mary Beth Lee
Chris McCrellis-Mitchell
Brenda Rosch
Jennifer Strange

*Contributing Writers:*
Stacey Adams
Dusty Alexander
Mark Allan
Sterling Carmichael
Jennifer Coles
Larry George
Scott Honeywell
Angela Martindale
Maggie McClellen
Susan Vaughn
Todd Wels
Emily Wilke
Dellene Vincent-Wire
Isabeau Vollhardt

*Graphic Design:*
C.S. Rowan, Jesse Gifford, Jolee Moody and Craig Tansley.

*Story Coordinators:*
Devona Brown, Sarah Brown and Tamara Cornett.

*Photo Department:*
Wendy Gay

*Website*:
Jessica Guaderrama and Andrea Hewitt.

*Special Recognition to:*
Molly Bermea, Allan Flint, Anita Fronek and Kimberley Wallan.

THE
**TREASURE**
SERIES

This book is dedicated to the children of Utah.

## Announcing Golden Opportunities to Travel

### Receive Your FREE Gold Treasure Coins

Treasures listed inside this book can also be found on our popular and interactive website: **mcpbooks.com**. For your convenience, this book's treasures are easily located by clicking the corresponding area on the map on our home page. This will lead you to a list of cities covered by this book. Within each city, treasures are listed under headings such as accommodations, attractions, etc.

Look for treasures that have a **Treasure Chest** next to their name. This means they have made a special offer, redeemable by presenting one of our gold treasure coins. **The offer may be substantial; anything from a free night's stay to a free meal or gift. Many offers can be worth $100.00 or more!**

To get your **three free gold treasure coins**, just send the receipt for the purchase of this book to:

Morgan & Chase Publishing
Gold Coin Division
PO Box 1148
Medford, OR 97501-0232

Please include your name and address and we will send the coins to you.

# Table of Contents

# Forward

Welcome to the Treasures of Utah. This book represents the incredible landscape of Utah and its best resource, the people themselves. While the book highlights different people and places, the focus is on why these treasures are so inviting. During the production of this book we met so many friendly, generous people that it seemed as though we'd found ourselves right in the middle of one big, happy family.

Utah is home to the famously breathtaking Brice Canyon, numerous ski destinations and picturesque mountain villages. Wherever you go, Utah is filled with the happy and smiling faces of beautiful children. You will immediately sense their vibrant energy and enthusiasm for life. You can visit the cosmopolitan city of Salt Lake with its bustling and exciting pace or you might prefer to see the famous Salt Lake City Temple and research through its vast genealogical library. Utah's landscape has always attracted many visitors, but it's truly the people who will forge a special place in your memory.

Several places in Utah are well-known to the rest of the world, but we've found there are far more hidden treasures than not. Many people who call Utah home vacation here as well because of the state's outstanding recreational, religious and cultural choices. This book aims to shed light on some of those wonderful attractions, opportunities and people. The treasures in this book were personally selected by secret shoppers, writers and the publisher's representatives. We're certain any place you choose to visit from within these pages will make your visit to Utah, a most memorable one.

Cindy Tilley Faubion

# How to Use This Book

The book is divided by geographic area and type of business.

The primary divisions are Northern Utah, Salt Lake City, Central Utah and Southern Utah. The types of businesses include accommodations, restaurants, wineries, candy and coffees, gift shops, art galleries, health and beauty, flower and produce markets, attractions, museums, personal care, fashion, and lifestyles.

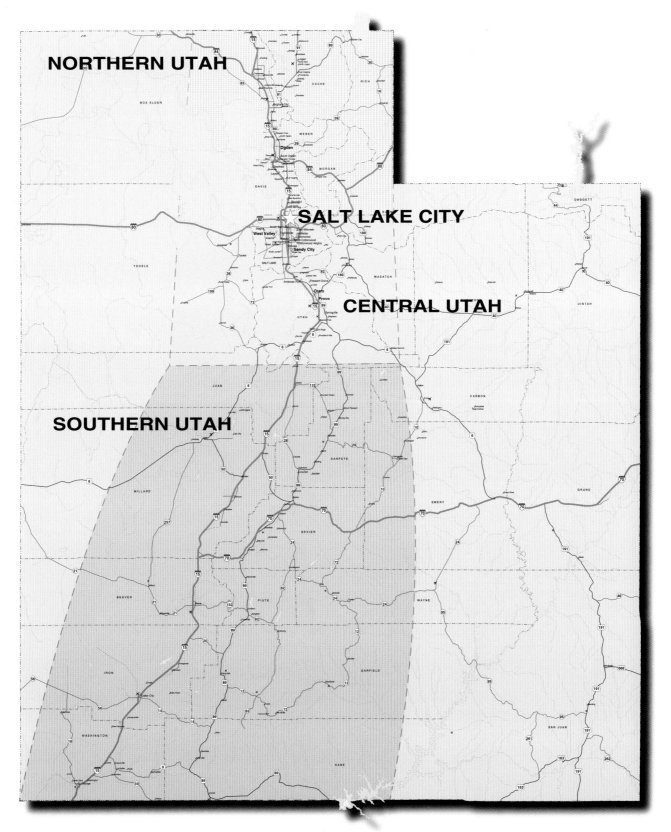

NORTHERN UTAH

SALT LAKE CITY

CENTRAL UTAH

SOUTHERN UTAH

NORTHERN UTAH

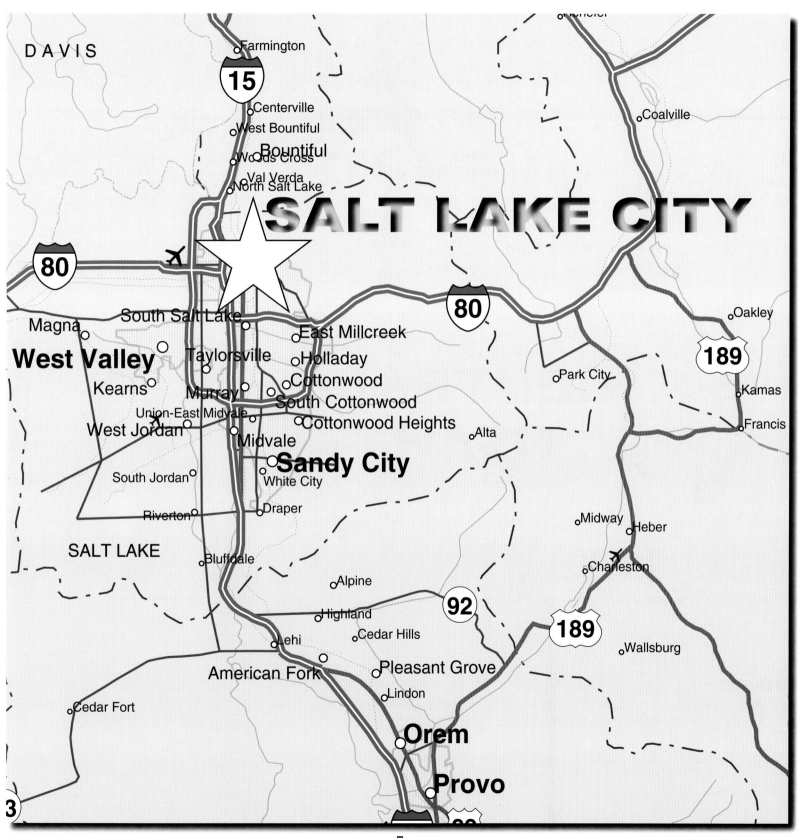

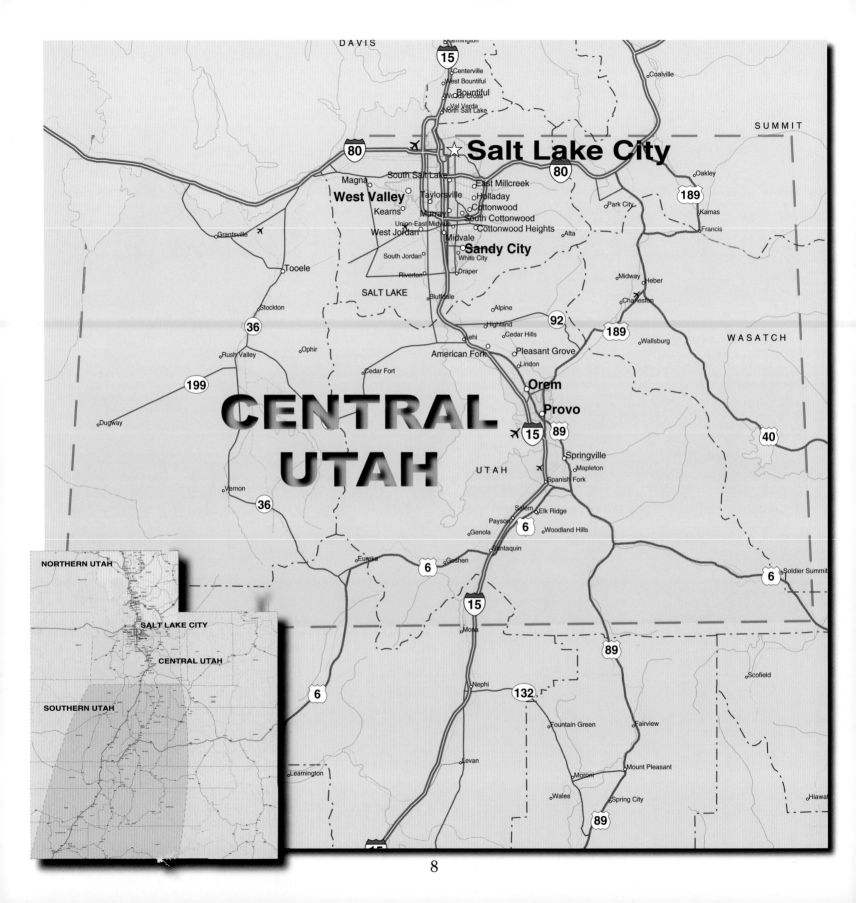

SOUTHERN
UTAH

# Utah State Parks

Explore the history and beauty within Utah's 42 state parks. Venture back in time through discovery of artifacts and remnants of the past. Journey along meandering trails and waterways, or accept the challenge of lush fairways and greens. Marvel at geologic wonders carved and sculpted over time or view the night sky from a secluded campsite. Strikingly diverse destinations are found throughout Utah—State parks of southern Utah provide an escape into the world renowned red rock and desert terrain. Northern Utah parks offer majestic mountain views, endless trails, and clear lakes and reservoirs. Plan your trip to Utah State Parks. (801) 538-7220 or (877) UTPARKS (877-887-2757) www.stateparks.utah.gov

# Northern Utah

## The Barn Golf Club

The Barn Golf Club is a beautiful 18-hole golf course on the foothills of majestic Ben Lomond Peak. The course is rated at par 71, stretching barely over 6,000 yards, but don't let its length deceive you. Between the eight ponds and mature trees, it presents a challenge to golfers of all abilities. The Barn, as it is known by its patrons, was formerly the White Barn. It was purchased in 1986 by Dean and Colleen Randall of Randall Woodland Inc. and has experienced a full, ongoing facelift from that day on. At present it is ranked as one of the valley's most enjoyable and best-conditioned courses.

PGA Professional Kelly Woodland and his staff, including his son Kory, are on hand for all of your golfing needs. Amenities the course offers are a full-service golf shop, lessons, a driving range and practice greens. Dean Randall, Shon Woodland and Shone's nephew Justin are certified members of the GCSAA and are responsible for the changes and grooming that have taken place since the purchase. Notably, this is a family operation, from its staff and employees to its very loyal patrons. Everyone at The Barn would like to extend a welcome to you to come out and join the family.

305 W Pleasant View Drive, Pleasant View UT   (801) 782-7320

# Powder Mountain

Ski and boarding enthusiasts have been known to call Powder Mountain Winter Resort the "most skiable acres of any ski area in the U.S.!" Family owned and operated, the Cobabe Family has designed a resort for those who are passionate about winter with seven lifts serving 2800 acres of groomed and powder terrain. Add in 700 acres of snowcat skiing on Lightning Ridge and the Powder Country shuttle for 5,500 acres of natural snow. Powder Mountain's massive size assures a crowd-free experience on any of the 86 trails. Five hundred inches of snow each year make it easy to find untracked powder. Besides great powder, real snow produces beautifully groomed corduroy runs. For the adventurer, Powder Mountain is home to guided backcountry tours and heli-skiing. Freestylers will love the terrain park at the

Sundown Lift and the park and half-pipe at Hidden Lake. Professional instructors certified in skiing, telemark skiing and boarding offer lessons for the entire family, starting with children as young as three. Specialties include women's clinics, affordable beginner lessons and powder instruction. A complete line of rental equipment and souvenirs is available at either of the two sport shops. Three lodges with a total of four restaurants mean you can satisfy hunger pangs no matter where you are at the resort. Slopeside condominiums and hotel accommodations round out Powder Mountain's services.
Eden UT   (801) 745-3772   www.powdermountain.com

# Mrs. Cavanaugh's Candies, Inc.

Mrs. Cavanaugh's Candies, Inc. was born from a true pioneering spirit a little more than 40 years ago in a small South Dakota farmhouse. Friends and neighbors had long admired Mary B. Cavanaugh for her fantastic pecan rolls and other candies. With a little encouragement and a preliminary order from the banker who gave them the loan, Mary and her husband George began their own candy company. While running the little kitchen and store in town, the Cavanaughs struggled to keep the farm running. In 1972, they moved to Bountiful, Utah to pursue the dream of owning a world-class chocolate business. Today, Mrs. Cavanaugh's Candies, Inc. consists of several retail locations around the Ogden area with hundreds of wholesale accounts including the Utah Governor's Mansion and Weber State University. Mrs. Cavanaugh's boasts a $3 million state-of-the-art candy factory that features daily tours of what they call the top 10 best chocolates made in America. Mrs. Cavanaugh personally mandates the use of only the freshest, high quality ingredients and is adamant about never using chemicals or preservatives in her treats. The Cavanaughs also believe in supporting their community. Mrs. Cavanaugh's Candies, Inc. has made hundreds of charitable contributions to causes such as the Utah Food Bank, local schools and Scout troops. This family-centered company puts their customers and employees first while consistently churning out top of the line chocolates and candies. Experience a taste of Utah at Mrs. Cavanaugh's Candies, Inc.
1993 N Washington Boulevard,
North Ogden UT
(801) 292-2172
www.mrscavanaughs.com

# Hill Aerospace Museum

Offering a hands-on history of the distinguished United States military air services, the Hill Aerospace Museum is a place fanciers of flight will want to wing their way into at the first opportunity. Located on 30 acres on the corner of the Hill Air Force Base, the museum's many exhibits detail the history of military aviation, beginning with the first wooden aircraft and continuing through the 21st century's sleek fighting machines. The museum contains over 80 military aircraft, missiles and aerospace vehicles. You'll find everything from a replica of the plane used in the Wright brothers' first flight to a replica of an atomic bomb. The friendly and knowledgeable staff, many of whom have volunteered at the museum for 10 years or more, can answer all your questions about the many vehicles and exhibits. The Hill Aerospace Museum also offers a variety of educational opportunities with children from all over the region traveling to the museum for field trips. Visit the gift shop to purchase your own flight jacket or other aerospace related items and all proceeds go to the museum. With its wide variety of machines and exhibits, the Hill Aerospace Museum definitely earns its wings as a destination for military and aerospace history buffs.

7961 Wardleigh Rd, Hill Air Force Base UT
(801) 777-6868 or (801) 777-6818
www.hill.af.mil/museum

# Wolf Creek Resort

Wolf Creek Resort is a master-planned community in the beautiful Ogden Valley, just over an hour from Salt Lake International Airport and nestled between three major ski resorts. Away from crowds and noise, away from video games and strip malls, it is so far away from traffic there is not so much as a single stoplight. At Wolf Creek, you don't necessarily step back in time as much as you step away from it. Do they offer the amenities one needs to be comfortable and even pampered? Yes they do. For a wealth of information about the resort and surrounding area, visit Wolf Creek Resort.
3900 N Wolf Creek Drive, Eden UT
(801) 745-3737 or (877) 492-1061
www.wolfcreekresort.com

# Valley Lodging

Staying in the Ogden Valley just may be the experience of a lifetime. With mountains that have often been compared to the European Alps, along with lakes, rivers, and a laid-back attitude, you can experience quality family time, have a screaming ski adventure, or just spend some quiet time discovering the area. Valley Lodging at Wolf Creek has great lodging and vacation packages available to fit a variety of needs from intimate ski condos to large homes with plenty of bedrooms. The staff at Valley Lodging is experienced, extremely enthusiastic, and definitely customer-oriented. They continually go the extra mile to make vacations at Valley Lodging an incredible experience, not just a vacation. Come stay and play at Valley Lodging.

3718 N Wolf Creek Drive, Eden UT
(801) 745-3787 or (800) 301-0817
www.valleylodging.com

# Wolf Mountain

Recently acquired by Wolf Creek Resort and renamed from Nordic Valley, Wolf Mountain Ski Resort is the best skiing value in the West, and quite possibly the entire United States. Wolf Mountain is renowned for its learning programs and family-friendly atmosphere. Improved snowmaking and a new Bombardier groomer will enhance the ski or snowboard experience to a level this mountain has never known.
3567 E Nordic Valley Way, Eden UT
(801) 745-3511
www.wolfmountaineden.com

# Weddings and Banquets

Wolf Creek is the perfect place for a destination wedding, business meeting, reunion or banquet. With full-service catering and planning, there is time to relax or just get down to business, all within the beautiful inspiring scenery of the mountains and valley. What better place to host your wedding or event than in a friendly mountain town that really is called Eden?

3900 N Wolf Creek Drive, Eden UT
(801) 745-3737 or (877) 492-1061
www.wolfcreekresort.com

22

# Golf Course

Golfing at Wolf Creek offers a multitude of pleasures from breakfast in Tracks before warm-up at the range to the incredible views as one maneuvers the 18-hole championship course. This same course was chosen to host the 2005 Utah Men's Amateur and received raving reviews. The front nine is spacious and wide open, with gorgeous views of Pineview Reservoir, Mt. Ogden and Needles Peaks. The back nine becomes more obvious in its intricacy while winding its way tightly through aspen groves and cottonwood trees just below beautiful Ben Lomond Peak. No matter if one is a birdie golfer or a triple bogie is more likely to be scrawled on one's scorecard, golfing at Wolf Creek is ideal.

3900 N Wolf Creek Drive, Eden UT
(801) 745-3365 or (877) 492-1061
www.wolfcreekresort.com

# Connie's Corner

Connie's Corner is the best little gift shop in the valley. There is something for everyone and even great last-minute gifts. From top-of-the-line golf gear to great toys by Melissa & Doug, Connie's Corner features a great variety. Connie also sells native wildflower seeds and items made by local artisans. Her enthusiasm and smiles are contagious in this shop! One simply must stop in and meet Connie Queen of Fun at Connie's Corner.

3900 N Wolf Creek Drive, Eden UT
(801) 745-3365 or (877) 492-1061
www.wolfcreekresort.com

24

# Restaurants

People don't just come to Wolf Creek Resort for the scenery or the golf, they come for the food! One can dine in style in the more formal dining room called The Grille, or experience authentic Mexican cuisine and more in the Rusty Cactus Restaurant. Breakfast and lunch are served downstairs in Tracks, which is known for its house-roasted coffee, freshly baked pastries and burgers. They offer a complete wine and liquor menu as well.

(801) 745-3737  or (877) 492-1061
www.wolfcreekresort.com

25

# Trappers Ridge and The Fairways

Both Trappers Ridge and The Fairways are new single-family communities designed and built by Watts Enterprises, one of Utah's most respected home builders. Trappers Ridge sits high on the eastern bench of Wolf Creek Resort and offers six open floor plans from which to choose, ranging in size from 3 – 6 bedrooms. Each home includes a two or three car garage, perfect for storing all the "toys" we need up in the mountains. Trappers Ridge offers a magnificent clubhouse with an outdoor seasonal pool & sun deck, year-round covered spa and a club room for functions. The views of Pineview and the mountain peaks are fantastic, and the neighborhood is fully landscaped. The Fairways is tucked between holes 14, 15, 16 & 17 on the back nine of the Wolf Creek's golf course. These upscale homes are freestanding with a very high level of finish, including massive copper & glass front doors, copper garage doors and substantial stone pillars. Two different home designs are available, with elegant finishes throughout. The community will feature a pool and clubhouse in the future. Homes can be rented out nightly in both neighborhoods, with a three-night minimum.
3900 N Wolf Creek Drive, Eden UT
(801) 745-2218 or (877) 492-1061
www.wolfcreekresort.com

# Moose Hollow & The Cascades

John Lewis of Destination Eden has been building in the Upper Ogden Valley for over 7 years. Two of his most successful endeavors are the Moose Hollow Condominiums and The Cascades Townhomes. Both are located in the heart of Wolf Creek Resort adjacent to the practice range and Fairway #2. Moose Hollow offers two, three and four bedrooms with log detailing and views all around. Homeowners and lodging guests enjoy amenities such as the pool, oversized spa and sauna. There's also sand volleyball and numerous BBQ areas as well as a cluster of fire pits. The Cascades Townhomes are inspired by Tuscany with rich European finishes. The three and four bedroom homes feature a lock-out suite, allowing maximum usage and rental efficiency. Generously sized, these town homes offer attached garages and large basements, ranging in size from 3,000 to 4,500 square feet.

3900 N Wolf Creek Drive, Eden UT
(801) 745-3737 or (877) 492-1061
www.wolfcreekresort.com

# The Highlands

Wolf Creek Resort's premiere community is high up the hillside with commanding views in all directions, encompassing Snowbasin's peaks, Pineview Reservoir, and 10,000 foot Ben Lomond peak. The neighborhood has been carefully planned with strict design guidelines to protect the architectural integrity of the community. Each homesite includes a Sports Membership to Wolf Creek's amenities. Homesites range from half an acre to slightly over an acre, with all of the improvements already made. The landscaped entryway with cascading waterfall and carved stone monument sets the tone for this sun-drenched community.
3900 N Wolf Creek Drive, Eden UT
(801) 745-3737 or (877) 492-1061
www.wolfcreekresort.com

# Ogden Valley Balloon Festival

There is nothing quite like watching over 40 balloons rise up and drift slowly across the beautiful backdrop of the Wasatch Mountains and the Ogden Valley. At this intimate festival, you can get up close to the action as balloonists perform their magic. Notice the feeling of being an insignificant speck beside the towering gossamer structures of color. Watch as they rise majestically to float across the heavens with views that take your breath away. Enjoy the other festival related activities that take place during the three-day event throughout the Ogden Valley.

(800) 413-8312   www.ogdenvalleyballoonfestival.com

# Snowbasin:
# A Sun Valley Resort

Winter sports enthusiasts can hit the slopes in style at Snowbasin. The majestic mountain resort located in Huntsville offers something for just about everyone. Skiers and riders will delight in the 2,500 acres of terrain with runs for every skill level. If you want to polish your skills or are taking your very first steps on skis or a snowboard there are over 100 instructors available. Snowbasin also offers trails for Nordic skiing and snowshoeing. Snowboarders and skiers can also practice their moves at the resort's two terrain parks. Don't miss the fun at the lift assisted six lane tubing hill with the kids! After working up an appetite, you'll be well served at Snowbasin's three day lodges, which offer sumptuous cuisine and a breathtaking mountain view.

The Grizzly Cub's Den offers day care for little ones so Mom and Dad can hit the slopes and the Grizzly Center offers skis for rent or sale, as well as clothing and supplies. In addition, available ski packages include lodging at the Grand America Hotel, Salt Lake City's only five-diamond hotel. The resort also boasts three restaurants and lounges serviced by a masterful executive chef who creates tasty traditional and contemporary dishes. For all your winter and even summer fun, visit Snowbasin: - A Sun Valley Resort.
3925 E Snowbasin Road, Huntsville UT
(801) 620-1000
www.snowbasin.com

30

# Snowbasin: Delicious Food

Snowbasin's executive chef is at the helm of Snowbasin's many food venues. At the beautifully appointed restaurants and day lounges, Snowbasin's executive chef revisits classic dishes and puts a modern mountain spin on them. For instance, at the elegant Earl's Lounge, a posh bar and dining room at the resort's base, the standard caprese salad is reinterpreted as liquid caprese, a roasted whole tomato filled with a tangy mozzarella and Swiss cheese fondue accompanied by focaccia chips, extra virgin olive oil, and aged balsamic vinegar. Wine-braised homemade sausages of pork, boar, and elk are served over creamy polenta with portobello mushroom chips and black corn tamales are stuffed with lobster and topped with a chipotle pepper cream sauce. Each of Snowbasin's lodges, Earl's Lodge, the John Paul Lodge and the Needles Lodge feature some of the freshest most innovative food found at any ski resort, so even non-skiers will have a great time.
3925 E Snowbasin Road, Huntsville UT
(801) 620-10 00
www.snowbasin.com

# Snowbasin:
# Flying Kangaroos

Snowbasin is the North American home to the Australian women's aerial ski team, also known as the Flying Kangaroos. These awesome women come to Snowbasin from the Olympic Winter Institute of Australia, located in Melbourne. The team consists of the 2006 and 2010 Olympic squads. Members include 2002 Gold Medalist Alisa Camplin, three-time World Champion Jacqui Cooper and current World Champion Lydia Lerodiaconou. This winter, the Kangaroos will be honing their technical skiing skills on the resort's challenging terrain. When the team is at Snowbasin they are easy to spot in their Australian ski team uniforms. Guests are invited to watch the women perfect their

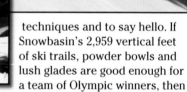

techniques and to say hello. If Snowbasin's 2,959 vertical feet of ski trails, powder bowls and lush glades are good enough for a team of Olympic winners, then certainly everyone under the sun will be able to find something to suit their tastes. In fact, the 64 designated runs consist of 11 percent novice terrain, 45 percent intermediate, and 44 percent expert. Nordic tracks are available for Nordic-style skiers. At Snowbasin, you'll have the opportunity to meet famous skiers from the other side of the world, to learn from the best while you make your way through any number of their well-maintained slopes, and to refuel with delicious food. Come to Snowbasin, one of the world's lushest ski resorts.
3925 E Snowbasin Road, Huntsville UT
(801) 620-1000
www.snowbasin.com

# Snowbasin: Summer at Snowbasin

Whether the snow is melted or not, Snowbasin Resort opens in late June and it remains open Fridays, Saturdays, and Sundays. On Sunday afternoons, Snowbasin hosts free music on the plaza featuring reggae, Celtic, renaissance, and mariachi styles of music. Special barbeque menus are paired with the music for guests' enjoyment. During the full moon of each month, Snowbasin offers a full moon gondola ride and Bavarian accordion music at Needles Lodge where you can indulge in the great food prepared by the in-house executive chef. Snowbasin also hosts stellar mountaintop Star Parties. Summer also brings mountain biking and hiking with mountain bike rentals and guided naturalist hikes readily available. Join us at Snowbasin Resort for the fun atmosphere that provides all the members of your family with activities, entertainment, good food, and music. Staff members are all equally enthusiastic and helpful, geared to providing you with the best time of your life. Visit the Snowbasin, no matter the season, and you're guaranteed to have a great time.

3925 E Snowbasin Road, Huntsville UT
(801) 620-1000
www.snowbasin.com

**Ogden Nature Center**

# Ogden City

In 1826, Trapper Peter Skene Ogden came to northern Utah as brigade leader for the Hudson Bay Company. He traded for many years near what is now North Ogden. However, before too many more years passed, the beaver pelt industry declined and the mountain men moved out. John C. Fremont, known as The Great Pathfinder, scientifically examined and mapped Weber County. It was his reports that led to Capitan James Brown's decision to settle the Mormons in the West. In 1848, Brown and his followers moved into Fort Buenaventura, renamed the location Fort Brown and called the settlement Brownsville. In 1850, Brownsville changed its name to Ogden in honor of the trapper. The railroad came in 1869, quickly changing the landscape from frontier town to rail terminus. Within one year, the population of the city had doubled. Ogden retains a proud military history, including serving as a center for defense installments during World War II. Today, this adaptable and historically rich city has changed its colors once again. With a focus on family, education and the ski industry, Ogden is a place "where it's all within reach," as its motto states. Members of the ski industry have dubbed downtown Ogden The Hub. The old Union Station now holds four museums, meeting and public rooms, a restaurant, visitor's center and theater. While in Ogden, explore the area's extensive history at the many museums, stroll the art galleries or attend lectures and seminars. Outdoor enthusiasts can relax at one of more than 40 city parks, hike area trails or hit the slopes for some skiing. From fine dining to fabulous shops, as a destination to live or visit, Ogden has what you're looking for.
2549 Washington Boulevard, Ste 910,
Ogden UT   (801) 629-8111
www.ogdencity.com

# Ogden City

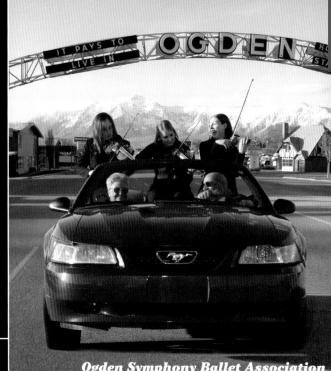

*Ogden Symphony Ballet Association*

Saloon

Gaiety

*Ogden City Amphitheater*

## Ogden/Weber Chamber of Commerce

The Ogden/Weber Chamber of Commerce has deep roots in Utah, as it was created in 1887. Under its original articles of incorporation, the Chamber was organized for the purpose of advancing the general prosperity of the city of Ogden. Even now in the 21st century, the Chamber's official mission statement is nearly the same. The Chamber is committed to supporting businesses to build a stronger community. There are numerous programs, events and services the Chamber offers to make this happen. The Chamber represents businesses in Ogden and Weber County at the State Legislature. It also provides networking opportunities at least once a month to encourage relationships between area businesses. With over ten committees available, from Partners in Education to Military Affairs, there are numerous ways for Chamber members to be involved in community matters. The Chamber offers workshops and seminars based on the needs of the business community. There are also exclusive advertising opportunities within the Chamber to provide businesses with the opportunity for greater exposure in the local market. Through these and others, the Chamber is working to advance the prosperity of Weber County. Visit the website or stop by the offices for more information about the Ogden/Weber Chamber of Commerce. 2484 Washington Boulevard, Suite 400, Ogden UT (801) 621-8300 or (866) 990-1299 www.echamber.cc

# Hampton Inn & Suites

The eight-story David Eccles building was constructed in 1910. By 1913, it was affectionately hailed as the Eccles Skyscraper and was originally used as an office building that housed dentists, architects, jewelers, notaries and a safety razor company. Now this stately historical building is the home of the Hampton Inn and Suites, one of Ogden's premier boutique hotels. Located in the heart of the historic 25th Street neighborhood, this exceptional hotel offers 124 beautifully appointed rooms and suites. The unobtrusively friendly staff excels at taking care of every detail to make your stay relaxing and pleasurable. The hotel has a fitness center, same day valet and guest laundry services. The Hampton Inn and Suites further provides valet parking, boardrooms and hospitality and meeting room facilities that are ideal for private or corporate events. For those who just have to stay connected, the hotel's 24 hour business center and every guest room has complementary high-speed Internet access. In the morning, guests can choose from the Hampton Inn & Suites On the House Breakfast™ for dining in or grab a quick On the Run™ breakfast bag. The hotel is located near many area attractions such as Lindquist Field, Golden Spike Arena and the Ogden Eccles Convention Center and Peery Theater, which are interconnected with the hotel. Experience the quiet luxury of a private European inn combined with all the convenience of an executive business hotel during your next stay at the Hampton Inn and Suites of Ogden.

2401 Washington Boulevard, Ogden UT
(800) 394-9400   http://hamptoninn.hilton.com

# Alaskan Inn Bed and Breakfast

Old West comfort in a modern world is what the Alaskan Inn provides. Deep in the Ogden Canyon, nature's abundance spills out in a glorious feast for the soul. Lose yourself in the unspoiled wonder of towering pines, snow-capped mountains, bountiful wildlife and rolling alpine tundra. Owner Dan Phelps invites you to explore this magical area and relax at his stunning Alaskan Inn, nestled four miles inside the canyon. Here you can choose to stay in one of 23 Alaskan-themed suites or cabins. Each individually and artfully designed accommodation includes many amenities such as a Jacuzzi or whirlpool tub, king or queen size bed, big screen television and delicious, warm breakfasts delivered right to your room. For those guests who would like to rendezvous outside of the lodge, a picnic by the river package is available to make your adventure special, complete with a wicker basket filled with treats and a blanket. Several biking trails also criss-cross the area and bike rentals are available locally. Those who are drawn to water sports will be delighted with Pineview Reservoir where you can boat, swim or fish. Impatient anglers can choose instead to just walk out the back door of the inn and toss a line right into the Ogden River. Horseback riding, golf and fine dining are just a few more of the delightful recreations awaiting you during your stay at the lovely and rugged Alaskan Inn. 435 Ogden Canyon Road, Ogden UT   (801) 621-8600   www.alaskaninn.com

# Emeritus Estates

Ogden, home of Emeritus Estates, is nestled against the Wasatch Front on the west flank of the Rocky Mountains. Two rivers run through town and wildlife and fishing opportunities abound. The region has everything from mountain trails, pine-forested mountain lakes and desert sunsets to snow skiing. Ogden has many museums as well as theatre, symphony, ballet and opera. Ogden also boasts a thriving nightlife. Ogden was a major player in the development of the Transcontinental Railroad and its Golden Spike monument commemorates the connection of the Central Pacific and Union Pacific Railroads. The friendly atmosphere of Ogden is exemplified in Emeritus Estates Assisted Living Community, where relationships are as important as the high standard of care. The Estates' Join Their Journey program is based on Maslow's Hierarchy of Needs and recognizes the universality of all human needs. The entire staff works to lift residents up the triangle, leading to self-actualization through meaningful interactions and activities. The staff uses a distinctive research process involving collaboration with residents' friends and family to design an individualized service plan for each resident and customizes activities and daily routines for individual residents. Residents are in control, with staff members acting as respectful passengers on their journey. Living quarters include various types of apartments as well as companion or private suites in the Pioneer Wing which features all-inclusive special care. Emeritus Estates invites you to visit with a free luncheon for you and a companion. The staff promises you'll love it here! 1340 N Washington Boulevard, Ogden UT (801) 737-1230  www.emeritus.com

# El Monte Golf Course

Avid and casual golfers alike will delight in a round of golf at historic El Monte Golf Course at the mouth of scenic Ogden Canyon. Owned and operated by the city of Ogden, it is the oldest public golf course in Northern Utah. For over 75 years, it has continued to evolve from its simple beginnings. The clubhouse is on the National Historic Registry and if the walls could talk, they would tell stories of years of notoriety. The Great Depression hit Utah very hard and federal programs were extensive in the state. Built with federal funding between 1934 and 1935, the clubhouse documents the impact the New Deal had in this area. Several golf pros have played El Monte Golf Course on a regular basis since the late 1930s. In 1944 Byron Nelson, the greatest golfer of his time, played in the first annual El Monte Pro Amateur. Locals, visitors and beginners have also enjoyed top-notch golf at a competitive price and many people have learned to play on this course. Known by the community as everyone's golf course, El Monte remains a very important part of Ogden. After your game, dine at the Timbermine Restaurant and visit the Blue Ribbon Stables for family-friendly outdoor recreation at its finest. Thousands of golf enthusiasts visit here every year. Make plans today to visit the beautiful El Monte Golf Course.
1300 Valley Drive, Ogden UT    (801) 629-0694

*Photos by Brian Oar*

# The Golden Spike Event Center

Located in Ogden, The Golden Spike Event Center's name comes from a major historical event. In 1869, the nation's eastern states were finally connected to the western states with the completion of the transcontinental railroad in the northern Utah wilderness. The focal point of this highly anticipated event was the driving of a final golden spike. Today, The Golden Spike Event Center is the final spike for many successful national and local events. The center features a state

of the art horse facility as well as a competitive convention and exhibit facility. For more information call or browse the website for The Golden Spike Event Center. For an exciting event from rodeos to professional theatre and concerts, visit The Golden Spike Event Center in person. 1000 N 1200 West, Ogden UT
(801) 399-8798 or (800) 44-ARENA (442-7362)
http://www.ogdencvb.org/gsec.html

# KW Aviation

KW Aviation in Ogden can teach you to fly. T. Wayne Law and partner B. Kim Matthews provide a service that literally puts your head in the clouds. Students trained by KW flight training are qualified to be airline pilots through programs tailored to fit the client's schedule and needs. You can obtain your pilot's license at an affordable price in a safe and fun training program operated by experts. In addition, charter and scenic flights within 350 miles of Ogden provide an intimate airborne sightseeing experience, complete with no waiting in line. They can be ready to go on your agenda, and are able to serve smaller airports. Flying above beautiful Northern Utah is spectacular in any season. See the changing of the leaves in fall; view the Wasatch mountain valley cities, and the Great Salt Lake. Bring your camera, or use a camera provided by KW. They have special planes rigged for aerial photographs, and also offer their own aerial photography service. In addition, they perform capable restoration and aircraft maintenance, with over 45 years of exemplary repair service experience to round out their full catalog of accommodations. They have a comprehensive fleet of small planes, including several different Cessnas, Piper Ragwings, Cherokee and Mooneys Woodies. For a truly uplifting adventure, let an experienced pilot show you the scenic view of Ogden, unencumbered by obstacles on the ground.
4221 Airport Road, Ogden UT   (800) 399-9723   www.kwaviation.com

# Silver State Helicopters

Silver State Helicopters is a golden resource for those who want to take to the skies. With locations in Ogden and Provo, the firm offers a wide variety of airborne services with pilots flying both day and night. Those needing still or motion picture photography will find all the aircraft they need to complete their project. If you're just interested in getting a topside view of the surrounding area, Silver State offers aerial tours. The company also assists in aerial law enforcement operations. Winter thrill seekers will want to check out Silver State's helicopter skiing and snowboarding adventure packages. Silver State Helicopters also offers a variety of agricultural and charter services. If you want to learn to take to the skies yourself, Silver State offers a competitively priced full-service flight academy, where you can achieve both a private and commercial helicopter pilot's license. The sky has no limit for the aerial services Silver State Helicopters can provide.

3811 S Airport Road, Building #850, Ogden UT   (801) 393-8687
800 S 3110 W, Provo UT   (801) 373-8687
www.silverstatehelicopters.com

# The Ogden Amphitheater

The Ogden Amphitheater is a beautiful outdoor venue that hosts a variety of events, festivals, concerts and musicals during the good weather months. It also hosts live entertainment nightly during the holiday season in conjunction with Christmas Village. The Ogden Amphitheater is owned and maintained by Ogden City Corporation. Management of the facility is through the Arts, Culture and Events Division. For event information visit the Ogden Amphitheater website.

343 25th Street, Ogden UT
(801) 629-8311
www.ogdencity.com
www.ocae.org

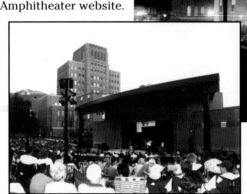

# Ogden Symphony Ballet Association

For more than 50 years, the Ogden Symphony Ballet Association has been bringing the arts within reach of Utah residents. In 1949, two Ogden women brought the Utah Symphony to town for a single performance. Six years later, the Junior League helped form the Ogden Symphony Guild which would later become the Ogden Symphony Association. Ballet West performances were added to the season in 1982 and the association changed its name to the

Ogden Symphony Ballet Association. The annual budget has reached nearly $1 million, supporting over 20 performances each year. The OSBA Educational Outreach program provides the opportunity for more than 4,000 students to attend performances of live music and dance each season. The Youth Guild for the Performing Arts is an exciting experience that enhances appreciation and promotes future audiences for classical music and dance. Membership is open to all students in grades nine through 12. OSBA also provides informative discussions for theatergoers prior to the Utah Symphony Classical concerts and Ballet West performances. The organization contracts with Weber County to provide a ride for any senior living in Weber County. The service is available free to patrons, picking them up and delivering them back home after concerts. The future looks promising for the Ogden Symphony Ballet Association, which is building a legacy of fine dance and music while enriching the lives of friends and neighbors and adding to the economic development of the area. Here's to the next 50 years of dance in Northern Utah!

638 E 26th Street, Ogden UT
(801) 399-9214
www.symphonyballet.org

# Christmas Village and Holiday Parade

The Ogden Christmas Village and Holiday Parade story is worthy of turning into one of those feel-good, holiday made-for-tv movies. On a crisp December day in 1961, Jerry and Maxine Green, and their five-year-old son, Tommy, were standing in the most perfect spot of all for the big Christmas parade. Warmed by their growing anticipation, they eagerly looked for the parade to come. It began suddenly with the screaming sirens of the police cars. A big, flatbed truck rushed by with Santa Claus waving to the hundreds of children who came to see him, and that was it. That was the end to the Christmas Parade. Tommy's disappointment was overwhelming, and Jerry Green knew that something had to be done. But what? After many sleepless hours that cold winter night, Jerry Green came up with an idea, an incredible vision! It was that of a Christmas Village with all the toy and candy shops you would find at Santa's North Pole home as well as a really big and wonderful Santa Claus Parade. Jerry Green knew the idea was good, but he was worried about how to make it happen. The original cost estimate for this venture was a whopping $25,000. It was with great trepidation that he approached the town merchants. The response was immediate and enthusiastic. In a matter of weeks, the merchants were out seeking pledges for the village idea. Utah Power and Light agreed to donate the electricity for the lights. Several merchants donated materials and it seemed that everyone in the city was pitching in with the construction of the village. On November 23, 1962, the very first Christmas Village and Holiday Parade opened Ogden's holiday season. Those involved with the first Christmas Village hoped that it would continue on through the generations, bringing joy to all those who come to visit. This hope is alive and well today, and carried on by a dedicated Christmas Village Committee. It is their goal to continue this wonderful tradition by expanding, improving and refurbishing the winter fantasyland displays. You and your family are invited to make the Christmas Village and Holiday Parade a wonderful part of your Christmas traditions.
Municipal Park Grounds, Washington Boulevard and 25th Street

# Ogden Nature Center

If you want to get in touch with nature, then Ogden Nature Center is the place for you. The Center's 152-acre wildlife sanctuary is home to many different species of birds. Look for songbirds and birds of prey such as eagles, falcons, hawks and owls. You can take an afternoon hike down one of the center's many trails and find yourself at the spotting tower overlooking Avocet Pond or at the tree house at Dumke Picnic Grove. A visitors' center features educational exhibits, programs, special events and an extraordinary gift shop. The Ogden Nature Center is a perfect getaway in winter, with opportunities for cross-country skiing and snowshoeing. So gather up your friends and family and make a stop at Ogden Nature Center.

966 W 12th Street, Ogden UT
(801) 621-7595
www.ogdennaturecenter.org

# Eccles Community Art Center

Located in the historic David Eccles mansion, the Eccles Community Art Center provides a wide variety of services to residents and visitors. The 112-year-old Victorian mansion is listed on the National Registry of Historic Sites and is the only non-profit art center in the greater Ogden area. The main house and carriage house galleries display temporary shows of local and national artists who work in a variety of media. Works from the art center's permanent collection are on display in the offices and hall on the third floor. Classes in visual arts and dance are offered throughout the year. Gallery talks and tours of current exhibits and the center's historic building are available to school groups and interested individuals. Please contact the staff or view the website for more information or visit the center itself for a trip through the arts.

2580 Jefferson Avenue, Ogden UT
(801) 392-6935
www.ogden4arts.org

# Eccles Dinosaur Park

What do you get when you cross six acres of parkland with a Parasaurolophus? A really great time, and it's all happening in Ogden at the George S. Eccles Dinosaur Park. This family oriented theme park offers an exciting and engaging array of educational programs designed to teach visitors of all ages about fossils, paleontology and geology. The park features numerous exhibits and several different facilities to explore. At the Elizabeth Dee Shaw Stewart Museum, you can experience dramatic and hands-on exhibits that feature the latest dinosaur finds from around Utah and the world. Tour the beautiful grounds, and see these amazing creatures in their natural habitat. With the tiniest effort of imagination, you will feel as though you were transported back in time, to the Permian through the Cretaceous period, to find yourself walking amongst the dinosaurs. Eternal residents of the park are Utah Natives such as the Parasaurolophus, Triceratops and the Utahraptor. In the summer, the park offers wonderful day camps for kids ages four through 12. Throughout the year, the park hosts special events for the whole family and can arrange birthday parties for the kids. With so many trails, playgrounds, exhibits and wonders available at the George S. Eccles Dinosaur Park, the family will want to come back again and again.
1544 Park Boulevard, Ogden UT   (801) 393-DINO   www.dinosaurpark.org

# Fort Buenaventura

Fort Buenaventura was built in 1846 by Miles Goodyear. Miles established the fort as a supply station for westward-bound emigrants. In 1847, however, the fort was sold to Mormon settlers. The Mormon presence lasted just three years before spring flooding from the Weber river drove them to higher ground. Today, the fort has been reconstructed on its original site. Cabins, heirloom gardens and livestock demonstrate the interaction with Utah's first citizens. With more than 100 acres of river bottom and uplands, Fort Buenaventura offers facilities for camping, hiking, canoeing and family reunions. On several weekends every year, the fort features living history events. For more information, call or visit the website.
(801) 399-8099
http://www1.co.weber.ut.us/parks/fortb/

*Ogden, circa 1883*

# Ogden Eccles Conference Center

Ogden was once called Junction City, and because it continues to be a gathering place, the David Eccles Conference Center was built to provide a place to spark the imagination in glorious comfort. The two-level conference center was designed in conjunction with the restoration of Perry's Egyptian Theatre, located right next-door. The Center offers 60,000 square feet of attractive, flexible and practical space for meetings, exhibits and banquets. Large windows and daylight-filled hallways offer tantalizing views of the changing mountain scenery. The grand ballroom can be partitioned into a variety of configurations and is equipped with lighting trusses for special effects. This room's 19-foot ceiling covers a total of 13,860 square feet, with enough space to seat 1,500 or hold 1,000 people for a banquet. In the smaller ballroom, the elegant staircase can be seen through a glass wall. The Executive Room, is a technical jewel, featuring state-of-the-art technical accommodations. Each of the six meeting rooms features individual lighting systems with dimming capabilities. The center is customized with limestone and subtly-hued brick, with desert landscape colors and bird's eye maple. Catering is available, offering anything from snacks to the incomparable Pharaoh's Dinner. Parking is abundant. An extensive audiovisual service is provided. An event coordinator stands ready to greet you and carry out your plans for an unforgettable conference.
2415 Washington Boulevard, Ogden UT
(801) 395-3200 or (800) 337-2690
www.oecenter.com

# Ogden Pioneer Days

For more than 70 years, Ogden Pioneer days have drawn locals and curious travelers to participate in a variety of captivating entertainment. Most events are located in downtown Ogden and highlights include five nights of rodeo under the stars in a beautiful world-class arena. From little cowboys on sheep to the world's most skilled cowboys, clowns, and performers, the fun never ends. Three of Utah's biggest parades take place during Pioneer Days. These include the Children's Parade, the Horse and Hitch Parade with over 500 horses, and the Ogden Pioneer Days Parade on July 24th, a family tradition for many. The Pioneer Days parade features over 100 entries of covered wagons, horses, handcarts, vintage vehicles, floats, and marching bands. The culmination is the Miss Rodeo Utah Competition, with the winner being crowned by the state Governor. Fashion shows, horsemanship exhibitions, and a variety of public events provide a chance for appreciative audience members to meet and greet the contestants. The Festival of Western Arts and Culture offers a spectacular art show and the opportunity to purchase some of the West's most accomplished fine artists' paintings, sculpture, and other creations. The annual Cowboy Poetry and Music Gathering provides a forum for the finest cowboy poetry and the lively energy of western music. An Old West Lecture by the foremost authors in the Western genre is always a treat. The festivities also include an antique car show, cowboy breakfast, and a farmers' market. Bring the family for fun nights filled with movies and concerts. Contact the Ogden Pioneer Heritage Foundation for more information, then proceed to Ogden for summer fun and the Ogden Pioneer Days events.

(801) 668-2555   www.ogdenpioneerdays.com

# Peery's Egyptian Theatre

Located in the heart of downtown Ogden, Peery's Egyptian Theater was the dream of brothers Harman W. and Louis H. Peery. On the site of the fire-ravaged Arlington Hotel, which was also the site of the Peery's first Ogden home, the brothers envisioned a movie palace so grand they called it The Showplace of the West. The design was influenced by the recent discovery of King Tut's tomb. Premier local architects Hodgson and McClenahan studied West Coast theaters before drawing the plans. The structure boasted an atmospheric auditorium where the flick of a switch turned the daytime sky into a magically star-strewn dark night. A Wurlitzer pipe organ accompanied the first silent films shown at Peery's Egyptian Theater. The venue went through several refurbishing projects, some that were unkind to the original design, and the Wurlitzer was discarded. The building was nearly destroyed due to health code violations. In the 1990s, the Weber County Heritage Foundation took an interest and purchased the theater for roughly the same price as it cost to build. Through a complex partnership and many donations and grants, the

building was saved and fully rebuilt in a major restoration project. After decades of absence, a magnificent Wurlitzer is back. The theater now provides many outreach programs, including Blues in the Schools workshops for students, films and a full range of performing arts. The staff invites you to view a performance in this one-of-a-kind, historic showplace of the west.
2415 Washington Boulevard, Ogden UT
(801) 395-3222
www.peerysegyptiantheater.com

47

# The Ice Sheet

The Ice Sheet became part of Utah's history when the Salt Lake Organizing Committee for the 2002 Olympics selected it as the Olympic Curling Venue. Even before the games were held, the local community caught curling fever, founding a curling club and hosting the 2001 World Junior Curling Championships at The Ice Sheet. Administered by Weber County, this 40,500 square foot facility opened in April of 1994 and was partly funded through $1 million in local donations. The community takes real pride in their arena, making it the home for all sports that can be played on the ice. Both the Golden Spike Amateur Hockey League and the Rocky Mountain Collegiate Hockey Association play here. Figure skating and speed skating are also perennially popular. You don't have to belong to a club to enjoy any of these activities because you can drop in during numerous public sessions. If you don't know how to skate or would like to hone your skills, the special learn to skate program featuring instructors affiliated with the U.S. Figure Skating Association is open to all. Everyone is warmly invited to The Ice Sheet.
4390 Harrison Boulevard, Ogden UT
(801) 399-8750   http://www1.co.weber.ut.us/icesheet/

# Treehouse Museum

You're invited to dream and enter a magical place where you and your children can step into a story. The award-winning Treehouse Museum has been named one of the Top 50 Children's Museums in the Nation by Child magazine. It has earned numerous local and national distinctions including three federal awards from the Institute of Museum and Library Services. Celebrating over 10 years of family literacy. The Treehouse Museum is a nonprofit, educational organization featuring interactive play exhibits, hands-on programs and imaginative displays based on literacy, literature and the arts. Each display encourages children to develop language and higher level thinking skills. With over 10,500 square feet of exhibit and program space, there is plenty of room for the extensive variety of programs and exhibits for children of all ages. School tours are offered with themes such as Legends & Fairy Tales, World Tales, Utah Tales and American Tales, featuring a replica of the President's own Resolute Desk. The wonderful world of play stimulates children's mental acuity and creates a desire for learning as little minds are strengthened with language and literacy. Come visit the Treehouse Museum on your next trip to Ogden and be prepared to delve into imagination in this whimsical, fantasy storyland.
347 22nd Street, Ogden UT   (801) 394-9663

# Kemp Aviation

The Kemp Ogden Airport Gateway Center is a 47-acre, privately owned, master-planned business airpark, designed for aviation manufacturing, regional commercial and corporate aviation. The developer of the center is Mel Kemp, CEO of Kemp Development and Boman Kemp Steel Company. In the business for 40 years, Mel has been a steel contractor for numerous upper-scale commercial developments, including the Delta Center in Salt Lake City, the San Jose Convention Center in California, the Stratosphere Tower in Las Vegas and the Aerospace center in Ogden. Assisting Mel is Project Manager Bryce Gibby. The Gateway Center is centrally located in the heart of the Western states. Jet operators can depart from Ogden's non-congested airport and be in Denver in less than an hour, in Los Angeles in just over an hour and in Dallas in two hours. The center is the new home of the Adam Aircraft facility, which will be manufacturing aircraft in the center's Kemp Jet Services terminal. Kemp Jet Services offers complete jet flight support operations. Kemp Ogden Airport Gateway Center is a state-of-the-art business park with a highly functional layout, offering both air and ground access.

3909 Airport Road   Ogden Airport, Ogden UT
(801) 732-8600

PHOTO BY BRIAN GRIFF

# Weber State University

Founded in 1889, Weber State University serves the educational needs of nearly 19,000 students today, with more than 200 degree programs and the most comprehensive undergraduate offering in Utah. This mountainside, Ogden campus has abundant classrooms and laboratories, a new computing center, outstanding performing and visual arts facilities, a spacious library and a well-equipped health and fitness complex . The university meets changing community needs with a modern and growing high-tech campus in Layton, courses at schools, health facilities, off-campus centers and work sites throughout the state and the Intermountain West. Independent study, online and evening courses and an early-college program for high school students provide additional learning opportunities. In the community, WSU promotes student participation on projects that benefit local business and industry. The Science and Mathematics Education Center is one of many examples of partnerships that strengthen local businesses while providing hands-on experience for students. WSU is large and complex enough to offer stimulating educational challenges and bachelor's degrees, two-year associate's degrees, professional certificates and Master's in several disciplines, but small enough to care about the welfare of individuals. As the northern Wasatch Front cultural center, WSU showcases a variety of speakers, performers and touring groups in the renovated Val A. Browning Center for the Performing Arts. Local fans cheer on the Wildcats in some of the best sports facilities in the Big Sky Conference. You are invited to visit the Ogden and Layton campuses or click on weber.edu to see what Weber State University can offer you. 3850 University Circle, Ogden UT   (801) 626-6000   www.weber.edu

# SymbolArts

Mike Leatham founded SymbolArts in 1986, when he set out to establish a company that could provide both creative design and high quality finished products in the custom ring market. His efforts grew into a company that now produces jewelry quality products, including badges, medallions, coins, pins, key chains, patches, rings and awards. In 1994, SymbolArts recognized the opportunity to expand into the public safety market by applying its creative design and jewelry quality manufacturing standards to badging. The company entered the public safety market by producing a limited number of badges for a small number of departments that were commemorating the Utah State Centennial. The company's reputation for jewelry quality products soon led to rapid and widespread recognition both inside Utah and on a national level. SymbolArts now sells products in all 50 states and has earned respect from customers and competitors alike for its craftsmanship and creative detail. This reputation has helped SymbolArts develop within two other significant markets: corporate recognition and special event licensing, including the 2002 Olympic Winter Games. From the initial creative process of designing a custom product for a specific need to the actual materials and manufacturing processes and timely delivery, SymbolArts takes great care to meet the highest quality standards. For high quality products that allow your business to visually express your values, interests and events, SymbolArts is unbeatable.

6083 S 1550 E, Ogden UT (801) 475-6000
www.symbolarts.com

# Smith and Edwards

Smith and Edwards has everything you want or they'll help you find it. In 1947, Bert Smith formed Smith and Edwards based on his ability to find a practical use for otherwise useless pieces of government surplus. Bert's ingenuity and vision paid off and as his trade and clientele grew, so did his inventory and his need for more space. In the late 1950s, he bought a 60-acre piece of land north of Ogden and moved his business there, filling the yard with spectacular buys. Smith and Edwards maintained a slow but steady growth. In addition to the on-site saddle maker and manufacturing facility, product lines include hardware, house wares, snacks, government surplus, toys and automotive and marine paraphernalia. Smith and Edwards is an ongoing supporter of the local community with special involvement in various schools, youth rodeos and Scouting activities. Smith and Edwards even offers a joint gift registry for the bride and groom. For a 171,000-square-foot shopping experience like no other, stop in to Smith and Edwards.

3936 N Highway 126, Ogden UT
(801) 731-1120
www.smithandedwards.com

## Pitcher's Sports

Owner Dixon Pitcher and General manager Michael Tobert of Pitcher's Sports believe in jumping! In the late 1950s, Lynn Pitcher brought trampolines to Ogden. Lynn was a gym teacher with an interest in gymnastics and proper trampoline instruction. She also wanted the best equipment for jumping. Dixon started selling trampolines out of this house. Quality equipment, safety and proper instruction are their forte. In 1994, Dixon opened the Pitcher's Sports showroom and retail facility. If you care about quality trampolines and playground sets for your backyard and about safety, then Pitcher's Sports is the place for you. Designed to last a lifetime!

6658 S Highway 89, Ogden UT    (801) 476-8090
10763 S State Street, Sandy UT   (801) 571-8080
www.jumping.com

# Rainbow Gardens

Located just below Rainbow Falls at the mouth of majestic Ogden Canyon is Rainbow Gardens, the largest gift emporium in Utah. For over 65 years, the King family has owned and operated this facility during its many incarnations. The property originally began as a hot springs site and during the early 1900's operated as a Victorian spa. In the 1940's, a ballroom ushered in the big band era and eventually gave way to a swimming and bowling recreation center of the 1950's and 60's. Today the exterior of this white edifice belies its collection of dining and shopping venues inside. Begin your Rainbow adventure by plunging into the old indoor swimming pool, now the "Gift Garden," a sunken garden of exotic plants and unique gift items. Dance through "Ballroom Boutiques," the very room where Glen Miller once played, and shop in a collection of stores featuring the best in home and seasonal décor. Take a stroll along the porch, suspended over the beautiful Ogden River, that in September becomes the "Christmas Porch" while the entire Rainbow Gardens becomes the premier Holiday shopping destination in Utah. Out of town visitors and the younger set will be sure to get a strike in "Planet Rainbow," the old bowling lanes, now a fun store featuring Utah books, gifts, and souvenirs. The Utah Book Nooks features nine Utah-oriented books stores. Don't miss the exotic Rainbow Visions New Age venue, as well as the Olympic Museum and Gallery that exhibits an original Olympic torch, pin set collections, and other memorabilia from the 2002 Salt Lake Olympic Games. To complete your stop at one of the most unusual shopping destinations in the west, be sure to enjoy a meal

at "The Greenery," Rainbow Garden's vintage restaurant. This smart bistro café with stunning mountain views offers salads, sandwiches, and superb specialty dishes for both lunch and dinner. Don't forget to try one of the Mormon Muffins that are so famous that they are shipped to admirers across the country. (See The Greenery Restaurant, next page).
1851 Valley Drive, Ogden UT
(801) 621-1606
www.rainbowgardens.com

# The Greenery Restaurant

Situated at the mouth of beautiful Ogden Canyon inside the historic Rainbow Gardens complex, the Greenery Restaurant waits for your visit. This vintage café offers the casual ambiance of a Victorian greenhouse with its wrought iron and lattice detailing, lush plants and airy skylights. The adjacent Greenery porch offers spectacular mountain and river views. For over 30 years, this elegant but comfortable restaurant has been pleasing patrons with its friendly staff and delicious menu. Owned and operated by Russ and Peery King, The Greenery whisks you into a European setting without breaking the bank. Combine that with remarkable specialty dishes and traditional fare like you might find in your own kitchen, and you have what has made The Greenery such a perennial success. Designed to compliment and enhance the Rainbow Gardens' gift shops, The Greenery has a light and airy feel that brings patrons back time and time again. This destination eatery offers soups, salads, sandwiches and superb specialty dishes for both lunch and dinner. With notable items like the Gabby Crabby, turkey enchilada, and chicken fettuccine Alfredo, plus entrées like New York steak or grilled halibut, everyone is bound to find something to suit their tastes. The Greenery also offers wine and beer selections and a tempting array of desserts. The caramel apple pie is sure to fill that last space in your tummy. Or try a slice of Chocolate Decadence, the Greenery's deep, layered chocolate cake. Grab a box of our famous Mormon Muffins, bran muffins made from a treasured pioneer recipe and served with Utah honey butter. Look for the Mormon Muffin in Planet Rainbow's Olympic Museum and Gallery, where it has been immortalized as an Olympic pin.
1875 Valley Drive, Ogden UT (801) 392-1777   www.rainbowgardens.

# The Oaks Eatery

With a rugged Western feeling appropriate to the surrounding scenery along the gorge of the Ogden River and with displays of historical photographs, maps and postcards, The Oaks Eatery is a feast for the eyes as well as the appetite. The menu offers hearty fare that the whole family can enjoy, with specialties that include The Oaks' world famous egg burrito and the pasta of the day. Outdoor dining is available, enabling you to get the maximum enjoyment out of both your meal and your location. Settling back in the evening on the deck with a cold Utah microbrew and watching the sun set from The Oaks Eatery is an unforgettable experience. The Oaks is such a perfect match for its site that it's hard to imagine it could be anywhere else, but when it opened about a century ago, it stood a mile away from its present location and was a resort, not a restaurant. The food came after it was moved a mile up Ogden Canyon in 1933 and was converted to a snack bar. In 1981, Keith and Belinda Rounkles acquired the property. After extensive renovation, they reopened it as a full service eatery serving breakfast, lunch and dinner. In 1994, they purchased 160 acres surrounding their restaurant to preserve its wonderful setting. For a fabulous casual dining experience surrounded by Ogden's natural beauty, eat at The Oaks.

750 Ogden Canyon, Ogden UT
(801) 394-2421
www.theoakseatery.com

# Bavarian Chalet

With the snow-capped Wasatch Mountains providing a backdrop reminiscent of the Bavarian Alps, stopping at the Bavarian Chalet may make you think you've been magically transported from Utah to Europe. When Owner-manager David Browne and his wife Pong Gale took over the restaurant, some were concerned that the place would lose its traditional feel. David and Pong quickly allayed those fears. Since its opening in 1983, the Chalet has retained the feeling of warmth and good cheer the Germans call gemutlichkeit. As David puts it, "it's like sharing a meal in a German home."  Many of the longstanding repeat customers at the Chalet are military personnel from nearby Hill Air Force Base who acquired a taste for the local cooking when they were stationed in Germany. They praise the authenticity of the food and come back again and again for the spätzle and knödel (German dumplings), knockwursts and wiener schnitzel. Naturally, there are also imported beers and wines and a hearty selection of vegetarian offerings. Leave room for dessert! The motto at the Bavarian Chalet is Good Food to Good People.
4387 Harrison Boulevard, Ogden UT   (801) 479-7561

# The Prairie Schooner Restaurant and Steakhouse

Circle the wagons and move the horses because we're dining at The Prairie Schooner Restaurant tonight. Pulling into The Prairie Schooner parking lot takes you back to about 150 years ago. You can swagger up to the hitching post and stand a moment under the shade of the 100-year-old cottonwoods that remind you of yesteryear, when it was not unusual to hear a lone wolf howl or the wagon master's dinner call. The restaurant sits on one of the spots where the Mormon pioneers came down along the Ogden River when settling this area. Jim Koertge, proprietor of this landmark, takes pride in uncompromising dedication to personal service and serving delicious food. House specialties include aged, hand cut and trimmed steaks, mouthwatering prime rib, fresh halibut and walleye fillet. Be sure to try the famous au gratin potatoes, similar to the Dutch oven style dish of the pioneers. Wagon master Jim can dish out an inexhaustible collection of tales about the wild west and the historical Ogden River area. Patrons will be delighted by the ambiance inside. On entering the dining area, guests are welcomed by the sound of old time western music and then seated in a private covered wagon. Move back in time again as you dine beside the warm campfire surrounded by a prairie setting under the stars. For a truly notable dining experience you will always remember, visit The Prairie Schooner Restaurant.

445 Park Boulevard, Ogden UT
(801) 621-5511 or (801) 392-2712
www.prairieschoonerrestaurant.com

# Sandy's Fine Food

Ogden is close enough to the city to allow for cultural experiences galore, but far enough away for living a country life. Sandy's Fine Food restaurant accompanies that life, or the desire for it, with down-home comfort food. Founded by Lyle and Sandy Evertsen in 1976, the establishment is family owned and currently operated by their son Brook Evertsen. Some of the servers, like Pat Eucetsen, have been at Sandy's for over 20 years, long enough to know what their customers want before they sit down. The catering service, created a year after the business opened to fulfill the high demand, has a full service menu with an extensive variety of choices, just like the restaurant experience. The salad bar is to-die-for, one of the largest in northern Utah and fresh every day. The award-winning pies bring customers from near and far. People have been known to fly in from New York just to eat one of Sandy's peach tarts. Sandy's serves wholesome homemade soups, meat loaf, pot roast and fried chicken, as well as foods from other countries, including Mexican, Swiss, Greek and Italian fare. Sandy's uses all local growers and makes everything from scratch. Some people say their chicken noodle soup will cure any illness. Eating at Sandy's feels like home; it is so familiar and comfortable. Come in and join the family for a heart-warming meal.

3233 S Washington Boulevard, Ogden UT

(801) 399-0032

# The Timbermine Restaurant

The Timbermine Restaurant is rustic, authentic and a trip back in time. For the last 20 years, Dean and Karen Hill have been serving up great steaks, excellent service and an old Wild West ambience. They started in the restaurant business in 1972, and with their partners, Carl and Pat Jorgensen, bought the present day Timbermine in 1984. After extensive remodeling, they opened the restaurant in 1985 with only 35 employees. Located at the mouth of Ogden Canyon, by the Ogden River and surrounded by cottonwood trees, it looks like you've stepped onto an old John Wayne movie set. When you first walk through the doors, you are greeted by a beautiful display of rocks and gold mining memorabilia. Nostaligiac items throughout the restaurant will take you back 140 years to a time most people have only read about in history books. Check out the museum of antiques and liquor bottles, boasting the largest collection of liquor bottles and mini liquor bottles known of in Utah. There is plenty of room for special events such as wedding receptions and high school or family reunions, and facilities for banquets. Come to the Timbermine for nostalgia, authenticity and a one-of-a-kind experience.

1701 Park Boulevard, Ogden UT    (801) 393-2155   www.timbermine.com

61

# Ligori's Pizza and Pasta

Ogden has long been a popular destination and home for outdoor enthusiasts. Whether you come to view wildlife, hike rugged trails, fish abundant streams or browse the plethora of shops and galleries, Ogden has something for everyone. When it's time to take a break from all the adventure, follow the locals to Ligori's Pizza and Pasta on Harrison Boulevard. Owners Diodori Ligori and Michael and Lucy Anne Morelli have been emphasizing great food and family for so long that they've seen customers' children grow up and bring in their own families. The staff here knows many of their customers by name, catering primarily to students, folks on lunch break and visitors to the Ogden area. The restaurant's most popular lunch is the chef salad, which includes pizza toppings and a small amount of sauce. Ligori's also serves fantastic pizzas with a vast array of ingredients. If you're in the mood for pasta, they have several varieties, all served with freshly made sauces using traditional Ligori family recipes. Sandwiches, soups and salads are also on the menu. Kids will be delighted with the children's menu items such as hot diggity dog twisters. When you're ready for something sweet, try the cheesecake or the cake du jour. This family-oriented restaurant is the perfect place to grab a bite after a busy day. Ligori's Pizza and Pasta is on a simple mission to offer good food, good service and good prices. 4421 Harrison Boulevard, Ogden UT  (801) 476-0476

# Studio North
# Mac Stevenson

Vibrant landscapes, luxurious still life and impressionistic scenes full of colors so intense they take on a life of their own are just a few of the amazing gifts that artist Mac Stevenson gives us through his work. Mac and his wife Ann invite you to visit Studio North Mac Stevenson, a charmingly furnished gallery in North Ogden where Mac paints and displays his finished products. Mac's artistic career spans several decades during which he has played the roles of both student and master. While attending Ben Lomond High School in North Ogden, Mac was awarded an art scholarship to Weber State University where he earned a bachelors degree in art education in 1968. He later studied at Brigham Young University and earned a master of fine arts degree for painting, drawing and sculpture. Mac went on to pursue a 26-year career with the Ogden City School District. In 1994, while teaching at his old high school, Stevenson was chosen by Utah State University as the Utah High School Art Teacher of the Year. With seven years of University training and 29 years of teaching behind him, Mac is now a practicing artist with works that range from traditional to abstract. Each piece is a magnificent expression from an artist who understands the shifting beauty of the world, enriching us all by placing what he sees on canvas. Experience the magic at Studio North Mac Stevenson.
1175 E 1925 North, North Ogden UT
(801) 391-853
www.macstevenson.com

63

# Picture This Gallery and Gifts

Sometimes a career change can be an enlightening experience. It certainly was for Mark D. Hansen of Picture This Gallery and Gifts. Inspired by his brother Scott who loved art and galleries, Mark traded a career in hazardous waste removal and bomb diffusion for a more artistic balance in his life. Picture This Gallery and Gifts was owned by Scott since its inception in 1981. Two years ago, Mark bought the business, continuing the store's tradition of helping people select quality custom frames as well as fine art limited edition prints, original canvases and giclee prints. Known primarily for carrying artwork from local and regional artists, Picture This Gallery and Gifts provides the best overall selection for its valued customers. The gallery features American and international art from such well-known artists as Thomas Kincaid, Armini, Millcreek and Summerset Artists. Foundation art and religious art are also available as is an eclectic collection of affordable gifts. Whether you're searching for a piece for your home or office or want a custom shadowbox for your memory project, the friendly and capable staff at Picture This Gallery and Gifts will help you with your every artwork need. Mark invites you to stop in and say hello today.

3651 Wall Avenue, Suite 1002, Ogden UT
(801) 621-1011
www.picturethisetcgallery.com

64

# Bartholomew Gallery & Frame Co.

Located in the historic restoration district of beautiful downtown Ogden, Bartholomew Gallery and Frame Company has established itself as an anchor of the local arts community. Owners John, Debra and Lee Bartholomew each contribute to the success of this family business. John, a former cabinetmaker and hobby entrepreneur, started the business with his son Lee in 1999. Lee had developed an incredible eye for design and a way of expressing his ideas that helped customers design framing in a way they had never before experienced. Because of the knowledge and design skills of the staff, most framing customers are repeat long-term customers with strong loyalties. Seven years later, business is booming with high-end framing jobs from all over the country. John's wife Debra, after seeing a need for local painting restoration services, became trained as a restoration technician. This has enabled the business to offer even more unique services to clients across the Western states. Bartholomew's has become well known as an exceptional starter gallery (a gallery for both starting artists and beginning collectors). Prices of pieces are reasonable, and the quality of artwork is extremely high. Bartholomew Gallery is the place to shop for the well known artists before they become well known. Some Bartholomew Gallery collectors have seen appreciation rates (the rate that a painting gains retail value) in excess of 80 percent in one year. Simply put, Bartholomew's offers the best in art and framing value and quality. Make sure you shop Bartholomew Gallery and Frame Company, and help them support the local art community. 520 26th Street, Ogden UT (801) 334-7911 www.bartholomewgallery.com

# Historic 25th Street Business Association

Historic 25th Street in Ogden has been at the heart of change, growth and commercial enterprise since the town's earliest days. Today's Historic 25th Street Business Association seeks to maintain that vitality. Early 25th Street was dotted with blacksmith shops, livery stables and hardware stores. Wooden sidewalks kept pedestrians above the street's mud in spring and frozen ruts in winter. Later, the street added bars and brothels to serve railroad workers. Its proximity to Union Station kept 25th Street vigorous during the roaring 1920s when over 100 passenger trains a day discharged travelers into this bustling, rowdy center of gambling joints and dance halls. The famous and infamous all found their way to 25th Street. Butch Cassidy lodged there; Jack Dempsey trained for his boxing matches there; and such notables as Zane Gray, Buffalo "Bill" Cody and William Randolph Hearst visited the area. The Historic 25th Street Business Association is bringing shoppers back to this historical landmark to experience modern entertainment in the original buildings on this fascinating corridor. Tourists enjoy breweries, restaurants, galleries and extraordinary shops. Weekend farmers markets and nightclubs add modern vitality to this 130-year-old street that has witnessed the ebb and flow of lively human interaction while retaining its funky mountain charm. Each historic building has a story to tell, and many carry commemorative plaques describing their lively pasts. The Historic 25th Street Business Association invites you to come feel the pulse of Ogden on Historic 25th Street.

258 25th Street, Ogden UT
(801) 394-1595

# First Friday Art Stroll

Nestled between snow-covered peaks at the confluence of two rivers, Ogden City is home to many artists drawn to the natural beauty and simplicity of this gateway to the Rockies. On the first Friday of each month, the First Friday Art Stroll showcases local and regional painters, ceramists, printmakers, photographers and a variety of mixed media artists in more than a dozen musuems, galleries, cooperatives and studios that form the core of FFAS. Whether you start your evening at Union Station's Gallery At the Station and stroll the legendary architecture of Historic 25th Street or visit Weber State University's state-of-the-art Dee Shaw Gallery, the stroll always has a new story to share and unique artists waiting to be discovered. (801) 393-3866  www.artsogden.org

Arts Ogden

# The Farmer's Market

The Farmer's Market starts off bright and early, in the cool hours of summer Saturday mornings, so shoppers can rise with the sun, select the freshest produce, grab a bite to eat from one of their tempting breakfast vendors and still be home before the day gets cooking.  Look for locally grown varieties of your favorite produce such as berries, peaches, plums, apples and pears; heirloom tomatoes, peppers, cukes, corn, squash, pumpkins and a variety of specialty flowers, herbs and potted plants from summer through fall. The market boasts a mini-arts festival each week, with more than 80 local artisans selling handmade herbal soaps, ceramics, watercolors, bird houses, natural wreaths, paintings, pottery and silks, everything under the sun that's for and from the garden! The market is ready anytime you rise, tempting sleepy-heads downtown with the promise of a mild summer morning and the soothing sounds of local musicians, unique artwork and a cup of your favorite morning brew or an early lunch downtown. 2006 marks the seventh annual market produced by Downtown Ogden, Inc.  Come experience some real local flavor at this quaint open-air market. (801) 393-3866

# Union Station Foundation

Following the completion of the transcontinental railroad in 1869, Ogden became the Junction City of the West, with rail lines converging from the four cardinal points of the compass. The last and most impressive of the city's three depots, Union Station, was threatened with destruction when rail passenger service declined in the early 70s. The State Legislature and the City of Ogden stepped in to fund new public uses for this monument to Ogden's rich history. Now under the management of the Ogden Union Station Foundation, the building houses four outstanding museums, a theater, conference rooms, a restaurant and a model train shop. The museums include the Utah State Railroad Museum, a must-see for train buffs; the John M. Browning Firearms Museum, featuring prototypes from the famous local gun inventor; a Natural History Museum with displays of local gemstones and other wonders of the Golden Spike country; and the Browning-Kimball Museum of vintage automobiles. Two fine art galleries display the works of locally and nationally acclaimed artists. The Foundation is a non-profit organization devoted to raising funds for preserving Union Station, its grounds, and enhancing the museums and displays. For information on how you can contribute and help assure that Union Station continues to serve and educate the communities of northern Utah, visit the website. For an entertaining and diverse encounter with history and art, come in for a visit. 2501 Wall Avenue, Ogden UT (801) 393-9886 www.theunionstation.org

# Artisan Grille

Stroll along historic 25th Street in Ogden, you will enjoy the strains of live jazz as the delicious harmonies waft through the air from a nearby club. Take in the kaleidoscope of inspiring art galleries and original shops that line this 100-year-old way. This famous district is well-known for its culinary delights where a terrific sampling of delicious cuisine can be found at Artisan Grille. Located next to the popular Umé Boutique, this stylish and delightful eatery offers a diverse fare that is well suited to all tastes. Artisan Grille is open for lunch and dinner and is just the right place to take a relaxing break from your explorations and to enjoy a terrific meal. In conjunction with their artful and delicious entrées, Artisan Grille offers an outstanding selection of wines and beers, each specifically chosen to complement each dish. Artisan Grille can also cater to private parties with prior notice. Enjoy an original and inspiring dining experience specially created by those who still revere the art of food at Artisan Grille. 172 Historic 25th Street, Ogden UT (801) 395-0166

## The City Club

The City Club is located in downtown Ogden. Settling on the second floor of the heritage landmark Porter Block Building, The City Club began operations on September 27, 1991. 40,000 members and 15 years later, The City Club is still setting the standards for Ogden club dining and entertainment nightlife. Set in a motif unlike any other in the world, The City Club is a $1,000,000.00 Beatles museum and club where John, Paul, George and Ringo can be heard "eight days a week." The City Club defines "come together" hospitality: exotic, pricey ingredients and starched collars aren't as important to customers at The City Club as great flavors, great presentations, and right now service.
264 Historic 25th Street, Ogden, UT 84401
(801) 392-4447
www.thecityclubonline.net

## Brewskis

Located on notorious 25th Street in downtown Ogden's historic district, Brewskis Historic 25th was founded in 1994. Twenty-four beer tap handles, combined with what everyone agrees is the best damn pizza in town, unique appetizers, humongous sandwiches and killer salads make Brewskis a local favorite amongst those 21 to 90-something. Brewskis is illuminated by the warm glow of neon beer signs. Old neon, new neon, more neon signs than any club you've ever been in. It's really remarkable. A superb sound system, a huge 15-foot sports theatre screen in the game room, live bands every weekend and an energy unsurpassed by any other club in the area make for a rousing good time. You can have that good time seven days a week at Brewskis.
244 Historic 25th Street, Ogden, UT
(801) 394-1713
www.brewskisonline.net

# Tona

Delicate, edible art. That's how people describe sushi, the featured food at Tona Sushi Bar and Grill in Ogden. The entire restaurant, including its design and menu, reflects this perception of the fare. The restaurant offers a modern, elevated dining area for comfortable table seating and a full sushi bar, where guests can watch their meals being prepared. For a more intimate and romantic experience, guests can choose to sit on a carpeted floor with traditional low-rise tables in a semiprivate dining area. The food at Tona is meticulously prepared and attractively arranged. The menu offers a good variety of Japanese dishes, such as teriyaki, tempura and combination plates. For sushi lovers, Tona has a wide selection of sushi rolls, from the simple and delicious California roll to numerous special rolls. Guests can also indulge themselves in delightful sweets, like Tona's homemade cheesecake, killer white and dark chocolate mousse and tasty green tea tempura ice cream. Whether you are an adventurer or a connoisseur of this cuisine, head to Tona Sushi Bar and Grill for an exquisite experience that is sure to please both the eyes and the palate.

210 Historic 25th Street, Ogden UT
(801) 622-TONA (8662)

# Two-Bit Street Café

If you're hungry for great food and wonderful antiques, the Two-Bit Street Café has got everything you need. This Ogden café is located in the same building as Two-Bit Street Antiques, which also belongs to owners Penny Allred and James Dayley. Penny keeps the menu fresh by offering a variety of delicious daily specials in addition to the mainstays. For breakfast, try the potato pancakes, served with the traditional sour cream and spiced apple or chili sauce. You'll also find a variety of omelets and muffins. For lunch, the café offers scrumptious soups, salads and sandwiches. For dinner, you can enjoy such dishes as herb roasted chicken and roast pork tenderloin. The café also offers several low-carb and vegetarian dishes. Make sure to save room for caramelized bananas or cheesecake for dessert. Diners can enjoy a glass of beer or wine with their meal. The café offers free delivery and catering. For great food and good, old-fashioned service among the antiques, the Two-Bit Street Café is a real find.

126 Historic 25th Street, Ogden, UT
(801) 393-1225

# The Timeless Attic

Though Lee Ann and Raymond Premo have been in the antique business for close to eight years, they're new to this lovely location in the heart of historic 25th Street in Ogden. The fine and diverse mix of wonderful shops in the area are the ideal backdrop for this elegant shop. The Timeless Attic continues the reputation they've been building all these years. It is a place where the discriminating collector can find truly one-of-a-kind pieces. Whether you are searching for that perfect antique, collectible or gift, you'll find an astonishing selection of Cambridge, depression, Fenton, Heisey and carnival glassware, Irish Belleek, Royal Doulton, Roseville and Hull pottery, fine collectible porcelain, antique furniture and art, Victorian pieces, home décor, gift items and jewelry. Take a nostalgic step back in time as you walk through the door of the Timeless Attic. You never know what you'll find, but you're sure to have fun looking.

167 25th Street, Ogden UT
(801) 39-ATTIC (801-392-8842)

# The White Fig

The White Fig is a most unusual gift basket company. It is here that the perfect gift basket for anyone or any occasion can be found. It is here that a gift basket in any style, for any circumstance, at any price can be created. It is here where the most appropriate and creative of gift baskets, corporate appreciation gifts and personalized mementos can be purchased. It is here where you can find the most thoughtful and imaginative of gift baskets to celebrate the moment, begin a tradition, bring back a memory, make an impression or say thank you. The White Fig staff takes the time so that you do not have to pay attention to the details. They create gift baskets that make gift giving an art and make the gift, the occasion and the giver worth remembering. The White Fig has gifts that are not only perfect in themselves but in their presentation.

206 Historic 25th Street, Ogden UT
(801) 334-8283
www.thewhitefig.com

# InStile & Rail

Historic 25th Street in Ogden denotes nostalgia and beauty. InStile & Rail, one of 25th Street's businesses, is also committed to the preservation of those qualities. As a Wood-Mode Dealer, InStile & Rail understands the importance of leaving a legacy that expresses the best one can offer at any time. In 1945, Wood-Mode began building high quality metal and wood kitchen cabinets. After the war, new homes were built all over the country. The kitchens were certainly at the very heart of those homes. The kitchen continues to be at the heart of the home, and InStile & Rail is honored to have had the opportunity to restore many of Ogden's finest historical homes to their original grandeur and beyond. Wood-Mode takes pride in handmade craftsmanship. Its craftsmen ensure the product leaving the factory is of the highest quality, giving a lifetime warranty as their seal of approval. InStile & Rail uses Wood Mode as the core for its kitchen designs, which are further enhanced with appliances by Asko, Wolf and Subzero. Hardwood, stone and tile, in addition to other quality, trendsetting flooring products, set the stage for splendor in the kitchen and bath, as do gorgeous solid surface counter tops of granite, Zodiac and Corian. InStile & Rail shares the Wood-Mode commitment to excellence and proudly installs its cabinets and other fine quality products. Wood-Mode approached Don Thomas about becoming a Wood-Mode dealer. They were attracted to him because of his meticulous work and superior cabinet installation, in addition to his 25 years of experience with Wood-Mode products. Don, in turn, approached Brent and Rolene Grimm to make the venture a reality. Mike Mahaffey, who is an expert in home restorations, quickly joined the team. Award winning interior designers Shiree Nixon and Shauna Morris teamed up to created the elegant InStile & Rail showroom. Collaboratively, this team created what has become InStile & Rail. InStile & Rail is committed to the preservation and beauty of Historic 25th Street and expects to be a permanent fixture in this memorable district of Ogden. 110 Historic 25th Street, Ogden UT (801) 399-0313 or (877) 384-6440 www.instileandrail.com

# Trends & Traditions

While strolling down the streets of Ogden's historic district, you'll want to stop by a favorite local shop called Trends & Traditions. For over twenty years, owner Mary Gaskill has endeavored to enhance the public knowledge of design while providing fine gifts and home décor to suit any individual taste. Along with being well known among locals for its decorative offerings, Trends & Traditions recently received a special distinction when the city's Mayor honored Mary's shop with a Design Award, further highlighting her 20 years of exceptional design and service to the city of Ogden. Customers enjoy perusing fine gifts such as collectibles of all types and one-of-a-kind baskets. You can find something for anyone here, even for that person who is difficult to buy for. Handcrafted floral arrangements of extraordinary beauty are designed and made to custom order. Future brides are invited to express their heartfelt gift choices by signing up for the bridal registry enabling their guests to purchase the couple's wedding gifts with true confidence. The next time you're in Ogden, make sure to stop by and shop Trends & Traditions to experience a truly design-centered gift shop.

201 25th Street, Ogden UT

(801) 394-4157

# Olive & Dahlia

Garden beyond the essential. Beauty beyond reason. Olive & Dahlia is a retail establishment that is a utopia of the chic; where cut flowers and garden décor range from the essential to the fabulously extravagant. In this store, it is evidenced how easily the mundane becomes magnificent. Olive & Dahlia is a place that is everything you want it to be. It is a fantasy inspired by the seasons, where the beauty of a single bloom of a cut flower can render you speechless, elicit a smile and break your heart. From the seductive vulnerability of a dahlia to the reliable majesty of a rose, one bloom is all it takes. It is also a

garden adventure where one can discover an object of beauty that conveys pure joy or a functional object that provides a simple satisfaction. Fountains, statuaries, outdoor furnishings and garden art are just a sampling of what you will discover. Olive & Dahlia features unique décor whether it is an essential garden piece, an indulgence for yourself or a gift selected for its personal significance in honor of a passion shared or a time remembered. You are invited to come by often and share a moment surrounded by a garden of unlimited imagination at Olive & Dahlia.
215 Historic 25th Street, Ogden, UT
(801) 627-0340
www.oliveanddahlia.com

# Ruby & Begonia

Ruby & Begonia is not just another gift and decorative lifestyle store – it is the best of everything for you and your home. It is a destination for you to come and wrap yourself in a small but necessary luxury, surrender to a guilty pleasure and discover your creative soul. In unique surroundings that change with each new month, Ruby & Begonia offers distinctive and one-of-a-kind items. Recipient of back-to-back Retailer of the Year awards, Ruby & Begonia is committed to an unequaled level of excellence in customer service, including personal shopping assistance, extraordinary gift wrapping and convenient gift delivery.
204 Historic 25th Street, Ogden, UT
(801) 334-7829
www.rubyandbegonia.com

# Li'l Red's Sweet Shoppe and Catering

Li'l Red's Sweet Shoppe and Catering began as a family tradition, focusing on providing delicious and savory foods using the freshest ingredients. They recognize that everyone has different tastes and for this reason their slogan has always been "Your Imagination Is Our Creation." Located on Ogden's historic 25th Street, their shop takes you back to a time when life was much simpler. Specializing in traditional and gourmet cookies, bars and other tantalizing treats, Li'l Red's is sure to satisfy your sweet tooth. For that special someone who may be a little hard to shop for, they offer a wide variety of gift baskets made to order. Li'l Red's designs baskets for all occasions, including honeymoons, house warmings and holidays. They also provide a full-service menu for those with catering needs. From weddings to lunches, office parties to reunions, they can assist you with any function or event. Deli sandwiches, soups and salads are prepared fresh daily making any lunch a picnic. After a hard day's work they know how stressful it can be fixing a meal that everyone will enjoy. Why not let Li'l Red's prepare a home cooked quality meal for you without fries for a change? Li'l Red's Cottage Cuisine menu offers a wide array of food items sure to fit into even the tightest of budgets. Complete meals can be ordered hot and ready, refrigerated or frozen for your convenience. Stop by Li'l Red's Sweet Shoppe and Catering today. You owe yourself a treat.

135 E Historic 25th Street, Ogden UT   (801) 393-6500
www.lilredssweetshoppecatering.com

# Artists & Heirlooms

Why travel out of Ogden in search of fine art, collectibles or antiques? Artists & Heirlooms, on Historic 25th Street, is fast becoming a premier destination for collectors throughout the area. Owners Tom and Tami Crowley opened shop in August 2004 and have enjoyed a warm reception from area residents, business owners and tourists. Artists & Heirlooms makes its home in a beautiful five-story historic brick building with incredible hardwood floors. It features original work from area artists in addition to stunning handcrafted and estate jewelry, wood carvings and pottery. The main floor offers antique furniture, unique home décor and an assortment of items from Utah's finest collectors. The second floor Loft Gallery showcases a different artist each month. Visitors have the opportunity to meet featured artists at an open reception, complete with live music and great food, on the first Friday of every month.

The work of award winning painter and resident artist Stephen Hedgepeth appears with that of several other local artists in the upper floor gallery. Stephen also serves as an appraiser and instructor for Artists & Heirlooms. Tom and Tami invite you to stop by Artists & Heirlooms and delight in their fine collection of artwork, antiques and jewelry.

115 Historic 25th Street Ogden UT
(801) 399-0606 or (888) 699-0606
www.artistsandheirlooms.com

# Grounds for Coffee

In the tradition of the old coffeehouses of Europe, Grounds for Coffee is Ogden's meeting place. Walk through the door and the aroma of freshly brewed coffee and fresh baked pastries will greet you, while the quiet hum of friendly chatter meets your ears. A gallery of work from local artists graces the walls. Whether it's your first cup of the day or a much-needed boost in the afternoon, Grounds for Coffee is just the right place for sipping cappuccino, enjoying the daily paper or discussing local politics. Tucked away in an Italianate structure built circa 1889, the exterior harkens back to the romance and energy of Ogden's gaslight era. At Grounds for Coffee, you will always get the freshest coffee possible and a great choice of delightful beverages. Beyond fresh-brewed coffee, look for lattes, mochas, iced coffees and coffee shakes plus non-coffee delights. A friendly staff and extensive menu will make your visit to Grounds for Coffee a memorable one.
111 25th Street, Ogden UT
(801) 392-7370   www.groundsforcoffee.com

# Gallery 25

Gallery 25 is a cooperative venture among several northern Utah artists. Staffed by the artists themselves, Gallery 25 enables visitors to meet and talk with the people who create the art. The gallery features various mediums, including oil, watercolor, acrylic, pastel, printmaking, collage and mixed media. Look also for sculptures, handmade jewelry, silk scarves, prints and notecards. Other mediums are displayed as space allows. On-site workshops take place throughout the year. Here, members share their expertise, involvement and artistic perceptions. Included in the Gallery 25 mission is a desire to be a positive force in the historic 25th Street area of downtown Ogden and in the community at-large. Come browse, converse and share at Gallery 25!

268 Historic 25th Street, Ogden UT

(801) 334-9881

www.gallery25ogden.com

# Ogden Blue

Ogden Blue is Utah's premier art, reprographic and instruction facility with 14,000 square feet dedicated to all things artistic. This over 50-year-old business was relocated in 2003 for the sixth time. Ogden Blue now sits on Historic 25th Street, where it has expanded to include an art school, three teaching classrooms, meeting space for local art organizations and art studios that are available for rent. Owned by Company President Richard Scott, this incredible business originally sold printing plans for architects and contractors while supplying local artists with basic supplies. However, over the years it has stepped out of that comfort zone, time and time again, to expand and provide its customers with everything they need to let their creativity flow.

Ogden Blue offers a full line of drafting and art supplies along with artistic gifts and children's supplies. Look for a full service copy center and private studio space too. The Ogden Blue Art School, directed by Theresa Miller, encompasses many creative avenues, including the art of making handmade books plus techniques and tools for creating oil paintings, palette knife paintings and pastels. The school is dedicated to providing professional, individualized instruction and attention to each student and maintains flexible scheduling, open enrollment and classes for both children and adults. Classes range from beginning to advanced levels, and Ogden Blue also hosts specialty workshops throughout the year. Arm yourself with everything you need to let your creativity and imagination run wild with Ogden Blue.

175 Historic 25th Street, Ogden UT
(801) 392-7573 or (800) 367-1749
www.ogdenblue.com

79

# Roosters Brewing Company and Restaurant and Union Grill

One visit to Roosters Brewing Company and Restaurant on Ogden's Historic 25th Street will make you realize that you need to plan several more. Their eclectic menu is a direct reflection of the diverse lifestyle of this mountain town, and the passion of its owners, Pete and Kym Buttschardt. Some days it's mountain biking followed by a burger and a handcrafted brew. Others, it's floating through fresh powder followed by rack of lamb and a bottle of great wine. This upbeat brewpub and eatery embraces every style while maintaining an upscale vibe all its own. If Historic 25th Street is the heart of Ogden, then Roosters is the soul. True to Roosters style, it's just off the beaten path of restaurant row. Whether you're into what has happened or what is happening, Roosters' sister restaurant, Union Grill, located inside Ogden's Historic Union Station, has you covered. Enjoy some time in the museums and galleries for what's history, then spend some time at Union Grill for what's hip. No matter what your palette craves, Union Grill will satisfy it, from fish and chips to filet mignon. And don't forget to check out the comprehensive wine list. Moreover, Union Grill understands that a truly memorable eating experience is more than just the consumption of good food and beverage. It's friends and fun. It's sights and sounds. In other words, don't just eat. Energize yourself at Union Grill or Roosters for a more complete Ogden experience.

Roosters
253 Historic 25th Street, Ogden UT    (801) 627-6171
748 W Heritage Park Boulevard, Layton UT    (801) 774-9330

Union Grill
2501 Wall Avenue, Ogden UT    (801) 621-2830

www.roostersbrewingco.com

*Salt Lake City Temple*

# Roy City Recreation Complex

Running, splashing, jumping, oh my! Welcome to Roy Aquatic Center and Recreation Complex. The original Roy Recreation Complex, in operation for 32 years, added on the Aquatic Center in 2003. The Roy Recreation Complex, open year round, offers a wide variety of classes and sports facilities for basketball, weightlifting, track and racquetball. The Complex is focused on offering a safe and exciting fitness and recreation environment for residents and guests of the city of Roy. Besides traditional swim classes, look for preschool swim classes and a workout called Waterobics. Patrons 14 and older can enjoy the sauna. The Aquatic Center, open from Memorial Day through Labor Day, is the perfect place to beat the summer heat. The water park offers three pools to meet a variety of needs. Small children and their parents can enjoy the shallow wading pool. A large leisure pool features a water playground at its center and two 34-foot water slides. A 25-yard lap pool, equipped with high and low diving boards, rounds out the pool choices.  Roy Aquatic Center is available for rent to large parties in the evening with advance reservations.
Roy Recreation Complex 2150 W 4700 S, Roy UT (801) 774-1050
Roy Aquatic Center 2977 W 5200 S, Roy UT (801) 774-8590

# Ben's Burger Bar

Ben Fowler opened a restaurant that has been on the same famous corner in Roy (if you can believe it) for over 50 years! Ben's son Dave now runs what may be Utah's oldest year round drive-in, the Burger Bar.  The Burger Bar was the first drive-in brave enough to stay open year-round, even through Utah's snowy winters. It may have been crazy, but it has certainly been successful. The Burger Bar will take you right back to the great tradition of the grand old 1950s drive-ins with full pound hamburgers, rich ice-cream milkshakes (so thick they stand more than and inch above the rim), homemade sauces, fresh hand-sliced French fries from real potatoes, and hand-breaded onion rings and mushrooms. The most popular sandwiches on the menu are, of course, the Big Ben, the Barbecue Ben, and the Fish Ben.  All named for, who else? Ben! For years, people have been traveling literally miles out of their way to get one of Ben's giant namesake sandwiches.
This is the kind of good, old-fashioned, quality food and service from years gone by that has been bringing people back for well, for 50 years. You can almost hear Danny and The Juniors crooning At the Hop out in the parking lot.  And once you been to the one and only Burger Bar, you'll have to admit it's true, they just don't make 'em like they used to – except at the Burger Bar!
5291 S 1900 W, Roy UT    (801) 825-8961

# Davis Conference Center

Davis Conference Center offers an ideal place to hold both business and social events. Attached to the Hilton Garden Inn Salt Lake City/Layton in Layton, the center offers top-notch food, service and technology. Davis Conference Center offers more than 32,000 square feet of meeting space. Its Meridian Ballroom alone can seat up to 1,000 guests for a banquet. There are also 16 break-out meeting rooms, which feature XM radio selections and LCD projectors. Additionally, the hotel and conference center offer high-speed, wireless Internet service. The center's atrium overlooks a courtyard, providing a memorable spot for wedding reception lines. The courtyard itself is ideal for social events, and is complimented by a fire pit. The center offers a variety of delicious foods, ranging from snacks to gourmet meals at a reasonable rate. If you're looking to meet for business or pleasure, Davis Conference Center has the meeting spaces, menus and services to make your meeting a great one.
800 West Heritage Park Boulevard, Layton UT
(801) 416-8888
www.davisconferencecenter.com

# Ligori's Pizza and Pasta

The family-friendly community of Layton is filled with museums and attractions that focus on the rich history of the area. Here you can spend an entire day touring landmarks, enjoying the theater or participating in the myriad of available outdoor activities. But when it's time to eat, locals know that the best place to go for good food at a good price is Ligori's Pizza and Pasta on Hillfield Road. Owner Michael Morrelli and his staff have seen several generations of the same families come through the door. This popular neighborhood restaurant also caters to a lunchtime crowd of students and businesspeople along with visitors to the Layton area. They are best known for their superior pizzas and terrific pastas that feature fresh sauces made from traditional family recipes. The most requested lunch item is a special chef salad that includes a dab of sauce and all the pizza toppings. Ligori's menu also includes tasty sandwiches, salads and soups. Even your family's littlest diner will be pleased by the children's menu that offers dishes such as the octo-dog, a hot dog ingeniously cut to resemble an octopus, served over pasta. Make sure to leave room for desserts such as Italian ice or the layered friazos. Ligori's Pizza and Pasta is a true family restaurant where you feel like one of the gang. Round up the kids and enjoy a delicious and relaxing meal.

2798 N 400 W Hillfield Road, Layton UT   (801) 776-8400

# The Outwest Lodge

© 2004 Avid Creative, Inc.

Capture the simple pleasures of the Old West at this beautiful bed and breakfast snug in the heart of bustling Layton in Davis County. Relax amid antique saddles and other collectible odes to the wild west at Outwest Lodge. Guests can enjoy one of two master cabins with private decks, sauna, giant log beds and cozy fireplaces or can select from one of seven magnificently-appointed suites, all designed to bring the western feeling alive. Either choice includes a hot and scrumptious breakfast to help you begin your day. All cabins and suites are smoke and pet free. Just across the street from Outwest Lodge is an executive public golf course and guests are only minutes away from great shopping, museums and over 75 restaurants. If you're looking for a quick getaway but don't have time to plan, let Outwest Lodge's cheerful and dedicated staff organize a special excursion or choose from one of several packages designed to make your visit to Layton magical. Thrill seekers will be delighted with the Away From It All package that includes a chartered plane tour of scenic Wasatch Front and a skydiving adventure. Those who are vacationing solely for the purpose of rest and relaxation will revel in the lodge's Relax and Escape package, featuring massage and reflexology, in-room spa gift baskets and healthy snacks. If you're looking for a taste of the West without all the dust, stop by Outwest Lodge. Room tours are available daily by appointment.

1904 W Gordon Ave, Layton UT   (801) 444-0794 or (888) 4OUTWEST (468-8937)   www.outwestlodge.com

# Cherry Hill Resort

In 1924, Charles Alfred Lloyd began buying tracts of land and founded the Lloyd family farm. In 1967, his descendants named the land Cherry Hill and created a camping resort. While it was originally an orchard, today the stunning grounds are dominated by nearly 200 shade trees, making Cherry Hill Resort one of the most popular destination campgrounds in Utah. The 20 acre resort in now owned by brothers Bruce and Keith Lloyd, who have turned the grounds into a fantastic water park while still retaining 180 campsites. Cherry Hill is the perfect weekend getaway for locals and visitors alike because, as Bruce explains, "Our mission is to provide the finest wholesome atmosphere in Utah." Cherry Hill prides itself on being a true family fun center. Since the resort has been owned and operated by the Lloyds since the beginning, it is not surprising that it is the preferred place to hold reunions, family outings, church gatherings and company picnics. Cherry Hill boasts an Olympic sized swimming pool, the Pirates Cove Activity Pool for children, fountains and the Cardiac Canyon River Run water slide. You can also float along while relaxing in the Grants Gulch Lazy River. When it's time to dry off, you can try a round of 18-hole mini golf, check out the six batting cages or climb the 30-foot rock wall. Break for lunch or a snack at a variety of on-site restaurants and snack bars. Grab your family and your gear and head for a fun-filled adventure at Cherry Hill Resort.

1325 S Main, Kaysville UT   (801) 451-5379   www.cherry-hill.com

# Terrace Plaza Playhouse

Turn off the television and come to Terrace Plaza Playhouse! For northern Utah, it is live theatre at its best. Terrace Plaza Playhouse presents professional quality productions utilizing some great local talent. The year-round community theatre offers well loved musicals, drama and comedy for the whole family. Since 1992, the Terrace Playhouse actors have performed many great shows weekly for the local community, including Annie, Guys and Dolls, Sound of Music and Wizard of Oz. The Playhouse stages a new show every six to seven weeks. For 14 Decembers, the Playhouse has made a tradition of presenting Scrooge and A Christmas Carol. For many local families, it is an annual tradition to attend. Live improv is staged each Friday night. Terrace Plaza Playhouse offers year-round theatre training workshops for children who then stage a live production. Season tickets are available at a discount, and gift certificates are good for any show at any time. Terrace Plaza Playhouse is the dream of Beverly Olsen whose live stage experience, leadership and dedication have made this community theatre possible. Support the arts and live theatre by being entertained at Terrace Plaza Playhouse!

918 E Raymond Road, Fruit Heights UT (801) 393-0070 www.terraceplayhouse.com

# East Canyon Resort

The town of Henefer is extremely small and a true mountain paradise. The East Canyon Resort makes this pristine oasis accessible. Anyone can find the room to stretch their legs on this 9,600-acre legacy of land crossed with historical trails such as the Mormon Pioneer Trail and the Pony Express, Donner Reed and California trails. There are also 63 miles of ATV, horse and hiking trails. Two hot tubs wait to rejuvenate tired muscles. Game-oriented folks will find mini golf, tennis courts and shuffleboard. There is also a full-service restaurant and on-site catering. Indoor and outdoor facilities can provide a setting for any type of event from weddings to business meetings, conferences and banquets. Memberships are offered for seven or 14 days of floating time in one of 32 roomy condos. With membership in the RCI network, this time can be exchanged into one of over 2,500 other resorts in the United States and around the world. East Canyon Resort also has 84 full hookup RV pads and year-round adventure greets all guests. Hunters appreciate the fall hunting privileges on thousands of private acres. In the winter, there is incomparable ice fishing and several world-class ski resorts are within driving distance. For the golfer, there are many excellent courses nearby. Other popular activities are mountain biking, fishing and boating. Don't miss the swimming facilities and hayrides. This facility is all about fun and is a vacation for the whole family, so come to East Canyon Resort and be a kid again.

12 miles south of Henefer on Highway 65

P.O. Box 228, Henefer UT   (801) 359-9030 ext 5 or (877) 767-8400 ext 5

www.eastcanyon.com

# Hale Centre Theatre

Hale Centre Theatre was born of one family's love of theater, and that family continues to be involved in the day-to-day operation of this world-class non-profit arts organization. The Hale legacy of live theater began over 70 years ago with over 20 years in Utah. The Theatre moved to its present award-winning building in 1998. This one-of-a-kind arena theater houses a state-of-the-art million dollar moving stage, a full catwalk and fly system and lighting and sound systems that are second-to-none. An intimate 530-seat house places the audience no more than 8 rows from the stage action, allowing all patrons close-up vantage points for experiencing the sights and sounds of live theater. Expect talented performers, dazzling costumes and sets plus first-class music and choreography. Playing year-round, the theater company mounts more than half a dozen full productions every season. The plays and musicals are selected with an eye to providing captivating family entertainment at prices families can afford. MSN.com recently voted Hale Centre Theatre number 4 on its top 10 list of things to do to celebrate the Christmas holidays. The Theatre has 18,000 season ticket holders, making Utah's premiere family theatre the highest attended theatre in the Intermountain region. Plan ahead, make reservations, and experience the legacy.
3333 S Decker Lake Drive,
West Valley City UT
(801) 984-9000
www.halecentretheatre.org

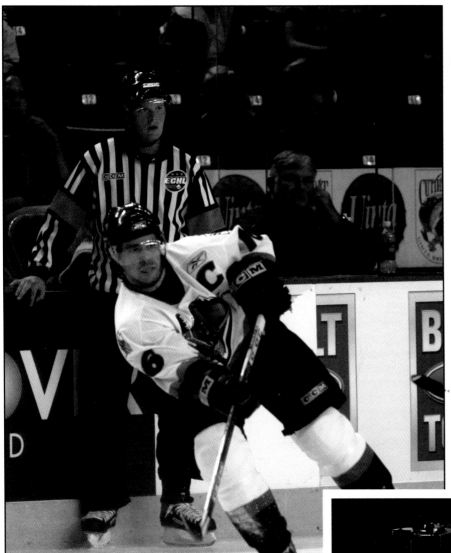

# The E Center

The traditionally successful Utah Grizzlies Hockey Club has made its home in West Valley City at the E-Center, an internationally acclaimed sports and entertainment facility, for nine straight seasons. Perhaps the building's majestic, cutting-edge architecture has something to do with the club's success. The E-Center was built in 1997 and hosted the Ice Hockey Championships at the 2002 Winter Olympic Games. A versatile gem of a building, it is as impressive from the inside as it is from the outside. The center is large enough to host ice hockey games where all 11,200 seats are needed and small enough to house the Ford Theater, which provides a unique and intimate atmosphere, seating as few as 3,700 people. The center also features Harry's, an in-house restaurant with a breathtaking view to satisfy even the most insatiable hockey fan's appetite, and in-house catering by Diamond Creations to compliment any party, banquet, reception or corporate affair. With a state-of-the-art sound system, the center is perfect for concerts and entertainment and has hosted such notables as Neil Diamond, the Mannheim Steamroller Orchestra and Smucker's Stars on Ice, to name a few. The E-Center is sure to offer something for everyone. From holiday ice shows and hockey games to conventions and concerts, it's more than just a building. Stopping by The E-Center will surely make for a memorable visit no matter the occasion.
3200 South Decker Lake Drive, West Valley City UT
(801) 988-8800
www.theecenter.com
www.utahgrizzlies.com

# A. A. Callister Co.

A.A. Callister Corporation has what real cowboys need and what wannabes desire: the tools of the cowboy lifestyle. Established in 1952, A.A. Callister Corporation is a family owned, fourth generation retail establishment that specializes in English and Western-style riding equipment and clothing. The mission of A.A. Callister's is, and always has been, to passionately promote the horse lifestyle with quality horse tack and clothing plus accompanying lifestyle products and services. Art Callister and his father founded the business 50 years ago when it was a 1,000-square-foot wool trading and supply store. As the sheep and cattle ranching industries shrank in Utah and the lifestyle of the urban cowboy caught on, A.A. Callister changed too. Today the store has more than 42,000 square feet and carries a wide variety of equestrian merchandise, including saddles, bridles, farrier supplies, riding equipment, books, clothing, hats, boots, belt buckles, lariats, walking canes, horseshoes and even beef jerky. Mary Ann Callister now runs the family store with her brother Ned. "We carry the real thing here," she says. "The store's devotion to the ranchers and the cowboy lifestyle has never waned." You'll find a complete line of veterinary supplies, feed for horses, cattle, dogs, cats and even pigeons. The Callisters know what to stock, because they have lived the life. If you have a horse, like the life or the look, you must visit A.A. Callister Corporation. The staff is known for its personal, down-home service, and many customers come to feel like family.

3615 S Redwood Road, West Valley City UT
(801) 973-7058 or (877) 78HORSE (784-6773)
www.callisters.com

# Utah Cultural Celebration Center

The Utah Cultural Celebration Center in West Valley City is a joyful, vibrant place. It is dedicated to preserving cultural traditions, promoting cultural exchange and strengthening a sense of unity among the diverse residents of the Wasatch Front. So what better place to celebrate holidays like Vietnamese New Year and the Dia de Los Niños, or to take workshops in subjects like Brazilian Guitar, Pacific Island Dance and Calligraphy? You can also enjoy exhibits of local artists and art from around the world. Covering 60 acres, the Center includes meeting rooms, a great hall with over 10,000 square feet of exhibition and community space, an amphitheater for up to 1,100 people, a festival theater that will accommodate up to 8,000 people on the festival grounds or a special meeting in the boardroom. Among the permanent exhibits is a magnificent, full-sized reproduction of a classic piece of Mesoamerican art, the colossal Olmec Head No. 8 from San Lorenzo, one of only three such replicas presented by the Mexican state of Veracruz to the United States (the other two are in Chicago and Washington DC). Another real treasure is The Spirit of Diversity mural that stands over two stories high and was painted in 24 days by one artist, Mr. Leon Burrows. The Mural includes 24 characters from many lands, all in the spirit of celebration. There is so much more to experience and celebrate at the Utah Cultural Celebration Center, so be sure to visit the website and take a virtual tour. 1355 W 3100 S, West Valley City UT (801) 965-5070 www.culturalcelebrationcenter.org

# Lagoon Amusement Park

Since 1886, Lagoon Amusement Park in Farmington has been one of America's truly great family fun parks. Crowds first came from Salt Lake City via the scenic Bamberger Railway to enjoy row boating, swimming and dancing at the park's pavilion. In 1906, the park installed a beautiful carousel with 45 hand-carved horses, and it's still there. The year 1921 saw the installation of Lagoon's first roller coaster. Since then, the park has exploded into one of America's premiere recreational resorts. Located midway between Salt Lake City and Ogden, Lagoon covers the bases and hits a home run in family entertainment. Experience thrilling rides, like The Bat or the Catapult, and try your hand at go-kart racing at the Double Thunder Raceway. Play arcade games, enjoy live music performances, then go back to Utah's wild west in a 15-acre restoration of a pioneer village. Lagoon-A-Beach has six acres and 550,000 gallons of twisting-turning-splashing water park fun. You'll find food stands scattered throughout the grounds or bring your own family feast to enjoy at the picnic parks. Stay within driving distance of the park at one of 16 inns, hotels and motels or do-it-yourself at Lagoon's RV Park or full-service campground. Bring your family to Lagoon Amusement Park, a theme park designed for wholesome and joyous celebrations.
375 N Lagoon Drive, Farmington UT
(801) 451-8000 or (800) 748-5246
www.lagoonpark.com

89

# Antelope Island

The thought of being stranded on an island has been food for thought for years. But if one were to be stranded on Antelope Island in the Great Salt Lake, they'd have plenty to do, see and eat. For history buffs, there's the Historic Fielding Garr Ranch, named for the settler who built it in 1848. Originally, the home of Mr. Garr, it was operated by the Mormon Church for several years until John Dooly, Sr. took it over for ranching purposes. The changes and eras the ranch went through are evident in the well-preserved buildings that are worth the short drive to the eastern shore of the

island. For outdoorsy types, there are more than 25 miles of backcountry trails to explore or head to the beach and float in a rented kayak in the Great Salt Lake. The flora and fauna as well as the incredible scenery make Antelope Island popular for its unlimited photo opportunities. While venturing throughout the island, be sure to look for the descendents of the 12 original bison Mr. Dooly brought to the island. They share space with hundreds of mule deer, big-horned sheep and plenty of the island's namesake, pronghorn antelope. Birdwatchers can spend hours observing the millions of feathered friends that nest here.  If you want to stay the night, pitch your tent and enjoy the incredible stargazing afforded by the island's lack of streetlights. When you work up an appetite, you can head over to Buffalo Point Restaurant or Bridger Bay Ice Cream. Let your worries get stranded on the mainland and let adventure take over with a trip to Antelope Island.
Seven miles west of I-15 exit #335   (801) 773-2941

# Mandarin Restaurant

Look no further than the Mandarin Restaurant for award winning Chinese cuisine. Renowned both locally and nationally, the Mandarin Restaurant was recently named Best Chinese by Salt Lake City Weekly's Reader's Choice and was profiled in USA Today's September 2005 article, "10 Great Places to Dine on Chinese Food." What began as a 60-seat restaurant in 1978 grew to over 200 seats as the restaurant's popularity

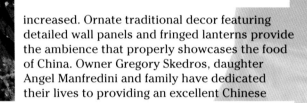

increased. Ornate traditional decor featuring detailed wall panels and fringed lanterns provide the ambience that properly showcases the food of China. Owner Gregory Skedros, daughter Angel Manfredini and family have dedicated their lives to providing an excellent Chinese

dining experience in Bountiful. Their extensive menu of innovative specials and classic entrées, served in Mandarin, Szechuan and Hunan styles, are complemented with a variety of flavorful sauces and prepared with locally grown produce. A staff of well-trained servers provides warm and cordial service. Some customers drive over 50 miles for dinner at the Mandarin Restaurant because the menu and atmosphere is unsurpassed. Make your reservation early, as lines are not uncommon at this dining place on any night of the week. Delicious flavors await you at the Mandarin Restaurant.

348 E 900 N, Bountiful UT
(801) 298-2406
www.mandarinutah.com

*Salt Lake City*

# Temple Square

In the heart of downtown, Temple Square is the number one tourist attraction in Salt Lake City. The magnificent six-spired Salt Lake Temple is the centerpiece of the square and was completed in 1892. It took early pioneers 40 years to complete this remarkable granite edifice. Adjacent to the Temple is the domed Mormon Tabernacle, home of the world famous Mormon Tabernacle Choir and Tabernacle organ. Weekly rehearsals and broadcasts of the choir are free and open to the public as are daily organ recitals. Two visitors' centers feature art galleries, interactive exhibits and an imposing 11-foot replica of Thorvaldsen's Christus. Complementary daily tours of the square are available in 30 languages. Christmas in the 35-acre Temple Square finds the buildings, trees and shrubbery aglow with somewhere around a million lights.
50 W North Temple Street, Salt Lake City UT
(801) 240-4872  www.ldschurch.org

# The Church of Jesus Christ of Latter-day Saints

This 28-story building serves as the worldwide headquarters of the Church of Jesus Christ of Latter-day Saints. Free guided visits to the observation decks on the 26th floor provide the visitor with a wonderful panoramic view of the city and surrounding mountain ranges.
50 E North Temple, Salt Lake City UT
(801) 240-2452  www.lds.org

# Mormon Pioneer Memorial Park

A grassy plot near downtown Salt Lake City is the grave site of Mormon leader Brigham Young and other pioneers like Eliza R. Snow Smith, who was an early women's leader in the Church of Jesus Christ of Latter-Day Saints. The centerpiece of the Mormon Pioneer Memorial Park is a monument honoring the pioneers who lost their lives crossing the plains between 1847 and the advent of the railroad in 1869. For a taste of the history of the Church of Latter-Day Saints, visit Mormon Pioneer Memorial Park.
North of Temple Square, Salt Lake City UT

# Museum of Church History and Art

Visitors to Salt Lake City's Museum of Church History and Art receive an introduction to Mormon history and culture along with an opportunity to view other magnificent and varied forms. Free audio tours, multimedia programs, a puppet show, films, a children's exhibit and activities are also featured. This museum's collection is among the oldest and largest in the Intermountain West.
45 N W Temple Street, Salt Lake City UT
(801)240-3310   www.lds.org/churchhistory/museum

# Joseph Smith Memorial Building

Formerly the Hotel Utah, built in 1911 and completely renovated in 1993, the beautiful Joseph Smith Memorial Building now houses offices, a chapel, meeting and reception rooms as well as two restaurants on the 10th floor with breathtaking views overlooking Temple Square. A large-screen 500-seat theater currently features a free film about the life of Jesus Christ.
15 E South Temple, Salt Lake City UT
Tours of the building: (801) 240-1266 or (866) 537-8457
Restaurants: (801) 539-1911

# Beehive House

Built in 1854, the Beehive House served as the official residence of Brigham Young, the first governor of the Utah Territory and president of the Church of Jesus Christ of the Latter-day Saints. This National Historic Landmark in Salt Lake City is open for free guided tours. Next door, west of the Beehive House, is the Lion House, built in 1856 to house Brigham Young's family. Private luncheons and receptions are held on the upper levels of the Lion House, but the Pantry, a cafeteria on the lower level, is open to the public. The Pantry food can be enjoyed inside or taken to the shaded garden in the summer. East of the Beehive House, spanning State Street is the Eagle Gate, topped by a 4,000-pound eagle with a 20-foot wingspan. For a taste of Utah history, visit the Beehive House and its surrounding attractions.

67 E South Temple, Salt Lake City UT

Tours: (801) 240-2672

The Pantry: (801) 363-5466

# Family History Library and Family Search

The Family History Library in Salt Lake City houses one of the world's largest collections of genealogical records. The facility's four floors are open to the public with books, microfilm and records from around the world. Knowledgeable people provide free assistance. With computers and attendants to help visitors, FamilySearch®, located in the Joseph Smith Memorial building, is a good place to begin searching for information on interesting people or your ancestors.

35 N W Temple Street, Salt Lake City UT

(801) 240-4085 or (866) 406-1830

www.familysearch.org

# THE DAYS OF '47 CELEBRATION

**DAYS OF '47**

July in Utah

In 1847, Brigham Young and a determined company of Mormon pioneers began one of the greatest treks in American history. Pioneers with wagons, handcarts, oxen and a commitment to America's belief in freedom of religion worked their way to the Great Salt Lake Valley. Coming together from many nations of the world, they sought to create a new life. Culminating on July 24, 1847, this trek of the early Utah pioneers exemplified the courage, foresight, and faith that continue to inspire modern-day pioneers. Clearly, the examples set by numerous pioneers have become a living legacy to Utah's bright future.

The Days of '47, Inc. is a private, nonprofit, all-volunteer, charitable corporation to honor Utah's early pioneers and to keep their pioneering spirit alive. Nearly 20 events, most in July, celebrate Utah's unique heritage and current cultural diversity. Most are free to the public thanks to hundreds of sponsors and generous contributors. All events, some attracting as many as 250,000 spectators, are staffed with over 800 volunteers.

# The Days of '47
# KSL 5 Parade

This fun-filled parade is one of the largest and oldest in the United States. Colorful floats, bands, horses, clowns, and other entries thrill thousands of spectators each year. Many camp out on the streets the night before just to ensure a great seat to catch it all. It is televised throughout the intermountain area on KSL-TV Channel 5.

Bleacher seat tickets are available at the Daughters of Utah Pioneers Museum, 801.532.6479 and at Zions Bank branches. Bleachers are located on the south side of South Temple between Main and State Street and on the east side of 200 East between 400 South and 500 South. Route starts at South Temple and Main Street, goes east to 200 East, south to 900 South, then east to Liberty Park at 600 East. For dates, more information and updates, visit www.daysof47.com or call: 801.250.3890

# The Days of '47 Youth Parade

Utah celebrates The Days of '47 with the largest youth parade in the United States. In just four blocks, you can see marching bands, creatively decorated floats, performing groups, and, of course, nearly 5000 children. The performing groups, clothed in traditional dress, delight spectators with instruments, vocal, and dance routines from around the globe. Route begins at 600 East and 500 South, goes west to 200 East and 500 South, and ends at the City/County Building, Salt Lake City. For more information and updates, visit www.daysof47.com or call: 801.250.3890

## The Days of '47 KSL 5 Float Preview Party

Get an up-close view of many of the floats that participate in The Days of '47 KSL 5 Parade. Enjoy bands, clowns, entertainment, and much more. Free admission. For more information and updates, visit www.daysof47.com or call: 801.250.3890

## The Days of '47 Youth Festival

The Youth Festival welcomes all children and families and offers special thanks to those who participate in the Youth Parade. Large and small booths sponsored by local organizations feature games, hands-on learning activities, and crafts. Safety demonstrations, kiddy rides, inflatable slides, and obstacle courses will also be available for hours of fun. Healthy food for purchase is available for the whole family. Snow cones and cotton candy are also available. For more information and updates, visit www.daysof47.com or call: 801.250.3890

# The Days of '47
# World Championship Rodeo

**Delta Center, 301 West South Temple, Salt Lake City**

Approved by the Professional Rodeo Cowboys Association, this is one of the largest rodeos in the world today. It brings together world champion cowboys and cowgirls to compete for an estimated $200,000 in prize money in such events as bull riding, saddle bronc riding, calf roping, bareback riding, steer wrestling, team roping, barrel racing, and wild cow milking. The grand finale is on July 24th. A Family Night allows a family of up to 8 to receive general arena seating for a substantial discount. Watch for Kids Night when half-price tickets are available for kids 14 and under in selected seats. For tickets call 801.325.7328, or visit www.ticketmaster.com. For more information and updates, visit www.daysof47.com or call: 801.250.3890

# The Days of '47 All Horse Parade

The Days of '47 All Horse Parade is an event for people of all ages. Entries in the parade represent the finest horses, carriages, wagons, drill teams, authentic costumes, and other groups—all coming together to celebrate our western heritage. Pre-parade activities and entertainment take place along 500 West. The "Cold Water Gang" disturbs the peace with a Wild West shootout before, during, and after the parade. Join us for an exciting time for the whole family. Free admission. Route begins at 50 North 500 West and goes south to 200 South, then east to Rio Grande Street, the main street through The Gateway, north to 50 North, east to 400 West and north to 200 North (finishing at 200 North 400 West), Salt Lake City. For more information and updates, visit www.daysof47.com or call: 801.250.3890

# The Days of '47 Pioneers of Progress Awards Dinner

This program recognizes six of today's outstanding pioneers whose service and achievements continue the pioneer legacy of industry, integrity, and courage; and whose work benefits present and future generations. The awards are presented in the following categories: Business and Enterprise; Education, Health and Humanitarian Assistance; Historic and Creative Arts; Sportsmanship and Athletics; Scientific and Technology Development; and Posthumous Legacy. For more information and updates, visit www.daysof47.com or call: 801.250.3890

# The Days of '47 Sunrise Service

The Pioneer Chapter of the Sons of Utah Pioneers presents a one-hour program honoring forebears of all faiths who entered the Salt Lake Valley starting in 1847. Members of the Mormon Battalion present the flag followed by music featuring various chorale groups. The Days of '47 Royalty is introduced and the winners of the Days of '47 Essay Contest are announced. Free admission. For more information and updates, visit www.daysof47.com or call: 801.250.3890

# The Days of '47 Celebration of Utah's Cultures

Come celebrate Utah's diverse cultural heritage with lively music, festive dancing, colorful costumes, ethnic foods, cultural art displays, and demonstrations. The grand finale is an electrifying fireworks show beginning at dark! Admission is free and food is available for a small price. Don't worry about parking. It's free on Saturday in downtown Salt Lake, or you can park in nearby parking lots. Better yet, take TRAX! For more information and updates, visit www.daysof47.com or call: 801.250.3890

# The Days of '47 Royalty Pageant

Three young women, chosen from descendants of Utah pioneers, reign over The Days of '47 events. The pageant includes judges' interviews and on-stage questioning in street and formal wear. Scholarships are awarded to the queen and two attendants. The Days of '47 Royalty are available for appearances and speaking engagements from June through August. Free tickets are available by calling the Temple Square Events Office at 801.240.0080 or the Daughters of Utah Pioneers Office at 801.532.6479. For more information and updates, visit www.daysof47.com or call: 801.250.3890.

# The Days of '47 KUTV 2 Pops Concert

**Abravanel Hall, 123 West South Temple, Salt Lake City**

Come experience music from Broadway, patriotic pieces, and other favorites in one of Utah's most beautiful halls. The concert is free to the public, but tickets are required. Doors open at 6:15 p.m. Those without tickets will be seated on a first-come, first-served basis after 7:15 p.m. Tickets are at Abravanel Hall, Capital Theatre, and Daynes Music. For more information and updates, visit www.daysof47.com or call: 801.250.3890

# The Days of '47 Pioneer Kids Service Project

**This Is The Place Heritage Park
2601 East Sunnyside Avenue (800 South),
Salt Lake City**

Elementary school children from all over the Salt Lake Valley join together for a service project that includes such pioneering skills as white washing fences, pulling weeds, and planting flowers. Work becomes fun as today's children emulate what pioneer kids did decades ago. For more information and updates, visit www.daysof47.com or call: 801.250.3890

# Deseret Morning News/KJZZ TV Marathon/10 K/5K Fitness Walk

Come join the fun and exercise. Be a part of The Days of '47 celebration while running to the cheers of thousands of spectators along the parade route. For more information and updates, visit www.daysof47.com or call: 801.250.3890

# The Days of '47 Essay Contest

For years, The Days of '47 Essay Contest has encouraged students to reflect on topics of importance to the creation of strong communities and to recognize the sacrifices made by pioneers in the early days of the State of Utah. Coming from numerous countries, those pioneers had to grasp differences in language, customs, appearance, and many other features. Each year's theme encourages students to reflect on what can be learned from history and how the lessons can apply to the future. First-, second-, and third-place prize money is awarded, as well as a prize to the teacher of the first-place winner. Students must be in 9th through 12th grades during the school year. Students must sign their essays and teachers must certify that students wrote the essays. For more information and updates, visit www.daysof47.com or call: 801.250.3890

# Liberty Days and Pioneer Festival

**This Is The Place Heritage Park**
**2601 East Sunnyside Avenue (800 South), Salt Lake City**

Honor the arrival of the pioneers to the Salt Lake Valley where the trail ended at This Is The Place Heritage Park. Enjoy a parade, take a wagon ride, and see living history portrayed just as it was in the 1860s. Meet a historic character. Hear a brass band. Savor an inexpensive, tasty, Dutch oven meal, or just have a treat and shop for charming arts and crafts. Truly a Utah original! For more information and updates, visit www.daysof47.com or call: 801.250.3890

# THE DAYS OF '47

## The Days of '47 Family Fun Day

A day of family activities that include games, carnival rides, competitions, crafts, mini king and queen contest, and prizes. Farm activities and musical entertainment are provided throughout the day. Hot dogs, chips, watermelon, and drinks are free to the public. Free admission. For more information and updates, visit www.daysof47.com or call: 801.250.3890

# United States Dutch Oven Championship Cook-Off

Smell the aroma of great outdoor cooking and watch world-class Dutch oven cooks prepare mouth-watering meals as teams compete for the first place prize. For more information and updates, visit www.daysof47.com or call: 801.250.3890

# The Days of '47 Finale and Deer Valley Music Festival Opening

**Deer Valley's Snow Park Lodge Outdoor Amphitheater, Park City**

The Days of '47 helps the Utah Symphony & Opera's Deer Valley Music Festival usher in its summer season when the Utah Symphony hosts a wide range of performing artists. Bring a picnic, kick off your boots, and lounge under the stars while you enjoy the Utah Symphony and the harmony of world-famous singers. The mountain nights can get chilly so dress warmly. For more information, and to order tickets contact: Abravanel Hall box office, 801.533.6683, or www.deervalleymusicfestival.org

# The Days of '47 and Deseret Morning News Landscape Art Show

The annual Landscape Art Show celebrates the distinguished tradition of landscape painting in the State of Utah and offers a showcase venue for artists who work in the genre. Free admission. For more information and updates, visit www.daysof47.com or call: 801.250.3890

The Days of '47, Inc.
Executive Committee
P.O. Box 112287
Salt Lake City, UT 84147-2287
Office, 801.250.3890
www.daysof47.com

Scott W. Loveless, President
Bruce Bingham, Executive Vice President
Kent Cannon, Executive Vice President
Kathy Loveless, Vice President, Public Affairs
Brad Harmon, Vice President, Rodeo Chair
Jodene Smith, Vice President, Parade Chair
Holly Clayton, Vice President
Brian G. Lloyd, Vice President
Brent J. Anderson, Treasurer
Kathi H. Izatt, Secretary

*Photos Courtesy of:*
*Marilyn and Andy Shearer,*
*Leslie Davis, Kent Vaughn, Brent Halliday*

The Days of '47 KSL Parade

The Days of '47 KSL 5
Float Preview Party

The Days of '47 Youth Parade

The Days of '47 Youth Festival

The Days of '47
World Championship Rodeo

The Days of '47 All Horse Parade

The Days of '47
Pioneers of Progress
Awards Dinner

The Days of '47 Sunrise Service

The Days of '47
Celebration of Utah's Cultures

The Days of '47 Royalty Pageant

The Days of '47 KUTV 2
Pops Concert

The Days of '47
Pioneer Kids Service Project

Liberty Days and Pioneer Festival

The Days of '47 Family Fun Day

United States Dutch Oven
Championship Cook-Off

The Days of '47 and
Deseret Morning News
Landscape Art Show

The Days of '47 Essay Contest

The Days of '47 Finale and
Deer Valley Music Festival Opening

Deseret Morning News/KJZZ TV
Marathon/10K/5K Fitness Walk

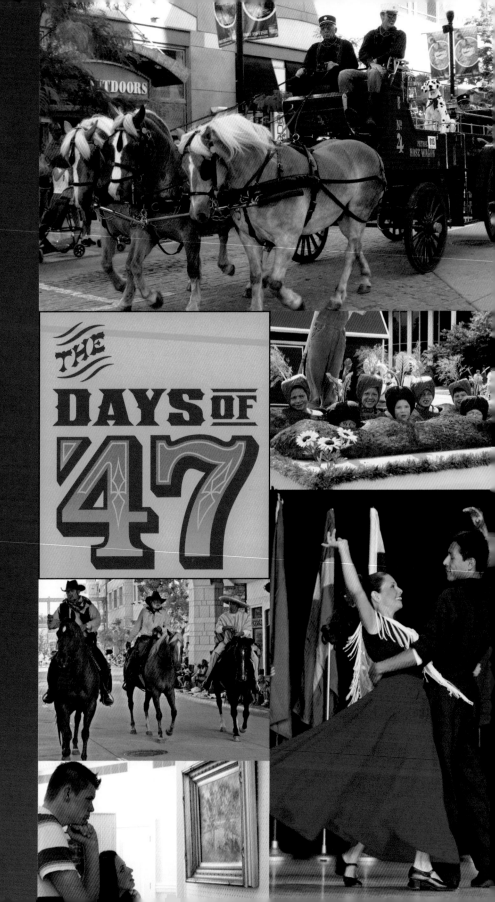

# Salt Lake To Go

The past and present of Salt Lake City and Utah come alive at Salt Lake to Go, the official gift shop of the Salt Lake Convention & Visitors Bureau. You will find it in the heart of the city, just a few blocks from The Gateway and Pioneer Park. Every aspect of the city and state is represented in the store. Natural sandstone sculptures evoke the beauty of Utah's famous red rock arches, and adorable stuffed animals represent Utah's native wildlife. An exclusive selection of gift items created in Utah memorializes the human history of the area, of Indians, Latter-Day Saints, railroad builders (A spike with a pewter cap commemorates the driving of the Golden Spike at Promontory Point in 1869) and even Wild West outlaws. Look for clothing, books, stationery and foodstuffs, like gourmet Utah honey. Salt Lake To Go is a must-see stop for visitors with something for everyone.

90 S West Temple, Salt Lake City UT
(801) 521-2822 or (800) 541-4955
www.saltlaketogo.com

***detail from The Great Salt Lake of Utah, Thomas Moran, 1874***

# Salt Lake City Accommodations

## Marriott Residence Inn, Salt Lake City Airport

When you are away from home, turn to the Marriott Residence Inn for a great place to stay. With 50 percent more space than typical hotel rooms (for about the same price), the Marriott's versatile suites offer plenty of room for working or relaxing with separate living, dining and sleeping areas plus fully equipped kitchens. For exercising, try the Sport Court, the workout room or the pool. Relax in a heated whirlpool. Visit the Marriott's inviting dining area for a complimentary breakfast and newspaper. Each morning features tantalizing breakfast choices. The professionally trained staff will go out of its way to accommodate your special needs and to provide a friendly, comfortable atmosphere. Nearby attractions are the Salt Lake International Center, Temple Square, Delta Center/Salt Palace, the State Capitol Building and the University of Utah. The Salt Lake City Airport Residence Inn is only five minutes from downtown and 45 minutes away from major ski resorts. Its services include round-the-clock complimentary shuttle service to the Airport.
4883 W. Douglas Corrigan Way, Salt Lake City UT  (801) 532-4101

## Highland Cove

Highland Cove is Utah's only retirement center with 14 park-like acres offering complete seclusion from busy streets. Beautiful apartments look out on ponds, trees, lawn and a putting green. South-facing apartments have a full view of the Watsach Range and Oquirrh Mountains. Highland Cove offers a continuum of care, from completely independent living with housekeeping, meals and activities to assisted living with medication, bathing, dressing, grooming and meal escorts. There is also an on-site intermediate care facility that features round-the-clock nursing. Owned by Life Care Centers of America, Highland Cove delivers living accommodations to more than 260 residents. It is one-stop convenience with on-site physical massage and therapy, podiatry, beauty salons, fitness classes and transportation to activities and shopping. The Highland Cove focus on wellness is reflected in their motto, "Keep moving ...just for the health of it." Personal training, walking clubs and water aerobics are among the activities available to maintain an active and healthy lifestyle. Whatever your needs may be, Highland Cove is there to meet them, now or in the future. To best experience the advantages of living at Highland Cove, make an appointment for a guided tour and a complimentary meal prepared by the award-winning staff.
3750 Highland Drive, Salt Lake City UT   (801) 272-8226   www.highlandcove.com

# Radisson Hotel

Conveniently located in the heart of downtown Salt Lake City right next door to the Salt Palace Convention Center and the Delta Center, the 15-story Radisson Hotel offers 381 rooms of full-service luxury. Every room offers high-speed Internet access and the hotel has more than 15,000 square feet of space for meetings and banquets. Fine dining is available on-site at the High Rock Steakhouse, a popular destination for guests and non-guests alike with specialties like buffalo steaks and the signature High Rock Ale. Look for specials every night that the Utah Jazz basketball team plays a home game. If you're a fan, you can watch on one of the nine television screens. Recently renovated, the Radisson is perfect for both business travelers and vacationers. The business center features fax and copy services and the hotel is just minutes away from the Gateway Open-Air Shopping Center, Temple Square, Symphony Hall and Capitol Theater. Work out in the fitness center or relax in the whirlpool or sauna after a busy day. When you're in Salt Lake City, you can make the Radisson your center of operations in downtown.

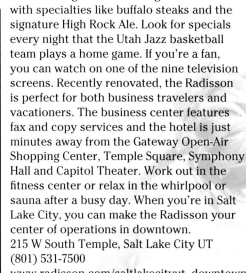

215 W South Temple, Salt Lake City UT
(801) 531-7500
www.radisson.com/saltlakecityut_downtown

## McCune Mansion

Originally built in 1900, the McCune Mansion has been lovingly restored by Salt Lake's Philip McCarthey and family. The family has returned the mansion to its original architectural splendor while also working to restore its historical legacy and community prominence. The mansion is now used as a venue to host special events, corporate retreats, business meetings and weddings. Early American entrepreneur Alfred W. McCune built the mansion for his family in 1900 after amassing his fortune in railroads, timber and mining. Alfred's wife Elizabeth chose the promising architect S.C. Dallas to design a home that would be the best money could buy. Interior details include the finest materials, such as Utah onyx and Nubian marble. Exotic woods, including bird's-eye maple, South American blond mahogany and 300-year-old English oak resonate throughout this Victorian showpiece. Hand gilding adorns many of the canvas-covered walls, along with ethereal murals, imitation marble columns and detailed artwork echoing century-old brushstrokes. Russian impressionist originals accent the décor, while the flicker from the mansion's several fireplaces, along with antique lighting, casts subtle spotlights on the grandeur of this spectacular mansion. The exterior of the mansion was built of native Utah sandstone and topped with tiles made in the Netherlands. Truly a setting unlike any other in the Western United States, the McCune Mansion is a beacon of historic elegance and grace. Perched on a flower-studded hill, the restored McCune Mansion's ruddy sandstone and red brick radiate opulent warmth and comfort. The lush landscape and fragrant gardens welcome guests outdoors to captivating views of the sunset over Salt Lake. Flanked by the majestic Wasatch Mountains and overlooking a picturesque cityscape, the McCune Mansion is perfectly poised for your next special event.
200 N Main Street, Salt Lake City UT
(801) 531-8866
www.mccunemansion.com

# Inn on the Hill

Designed by Utah State Capitol architects Hedlund & Wood, the Inn on the Hill was built in 1906 for retired physician and surgeon Edward D. Woodruff and his family. The 26-room mansion, built in the architectural style of the Second Renaissance Revival, features an interior fashioned after an English Manor, with extensive hand painting by local artist William Culmer. Leather-covered walls, oriental rugs, Maxfield Parrish Tiffany glass, hand carved hardwoods and a grand staircase are just a few of the features that demonstrate the craftsmanship and beauty of the home. The McCarthey family acquired the property in December 2003; as with all of the McCarthey properties, exquisite design, quality furnishings and an exceptional staff were the first orders of business. The family operates the Inn of the Hill as an upscale bed-and-breakfast, and guests enjoy its quiet elegance. The rooms, designed with a guest's ultimate comfort in mind, include such luxuries as down bedding, jetted tubs, fireplaces and spectacular views. Surprise someone special or relax after a stressful day of business. A stay at the Inn is relaxation defined. Enjoy complimentary snacks and beverages while shooting pool and watching sports on the Plasma television, or retire to your room and find comfortable robes, a flat screen television with a DVD/CD player, wireless Internet, and bath and body products by Aveda. Ask about the romance package and gift baskets. Perched on Capitol Hill, two blocks above downtown, the Inn on the Hill puts you within easy walking distance of museums, historical sites, performing arts centers, restaurants, shopping malls and art galleries. You'll find the State Capitol, the LDS Temple, Living Aquarium and Clark Planetarium in the neighborhood.
225 N State Street, Salt Lake City UT
(801) 328-1466
www.inn-on-the-hill.com

# Armstrong Mansion Bed and Breakfast

Francis Armstrong, a Canadian woodworker, set out to California in 1859 on his way to the gold fields of Australia. When he arrived in Salt Lake Valley, he decided to stay. Francis quickly rose to prominence and served two terms as mayor of Salt Lake City. In 1893, construction was completed on the mansion he had promised as a wedding gift to his wife, Isabel. Originally the scene of a gala social scene, the mansion went downhill after Isabel's death in 1930. In the 1990s, investors restored it to its former glory and now the building enjoys a new life as one of the area's most romantic bed and breakfast hotels. With 12 rooms named for each month of the year, an attic hideaway, a cottage suite and a parlor and dining room available for meetings and receptions, the Armstrong Mansion offers more than most bed and breakfasts, even without its extraordinary history. Modern amenities such as by appointment in room massage, theater ticket delivery and DVD players add convenience to the authentically reproduced Victorian décor. For information about special offers such as Ski Utah packages, a virtual tour of the mansion's sumptuous splendor and a reservation calendar, visit Armstrong Mansion's website.

667 E 100 South, Salt Lake City UT (801) 531-1333 or (800) 708-1333
www.armstrongmansion.com

# Salt Lake City Marriott City Center

For the perfect blend of comfort and convenience, each of Salt Lake City Marriott City Center's 359 luxury guest rooms and suites comes complete with opulent furnishings, fluffy down comforters, breathtaking views and high speed Internet access. Concierge level guests receive upgraded amenities, including a continental breakfast and exclusive use of the library and VIP lounge. Dine at the Marriott's elegant signature restaurant and finish the day by the fire in a contemporary lounge. For the ultimate treat, you can order from the in-room dining menu. Throughout your stay, you'll find that the health club and serene indoor pool are the perfect place to unwind and invigorating spa services provide an array of excellent choices. Nearby, discover the beautiful park-like setting of Gallivan Plaza or take a short drive to one of the seven best ski resorts in the West. The Salt Lake City Marriott City Center is a premier host of celebrations and special events with its majestic venues and sweeping city views. The atmosphere of sheer luxury is enhanced by state-of-the-art technology and innovative culinary creations from an experienced chef. The result is an unforgettable setting for you and your guests at Salt Lake City Marriott City Center.

220 S State Street, Salt Lake City UT
(801) 961-8703
www.marriott.com/slccc

# John W. Gallivan Utah Center

For those interested in concerts, art, conducting business or just plain relaxing, the John W. Gallivan Utah Center is a great gathering place. Located in the heart of Salt Lake City, the center includes an ice rink and pond for skaters to show their talents during the winter. A huge outdoor chess board will keep strategists plotting their next moves for some time, while bird-lovers can enjoy the center's aviary. The John W. Gallivan Utah Center hosts musical acts, ranging from local favorites to internationally known entertainers. The park's waterfall is the perfect locale for weddings. The center offers a full kitchen for your party's catering needs with plenty of accommodations for guests nearby. The center's meeting room seats up to 150 people, and is an ideal location for business meetings and company parties. Offering both beauty and a wide variety of services, the John W. Gallivan Utah Center is the ultimate location to congregate for both business and personal enjoyment.

239 S Main Street, Salt Lake City, UT   (801) 535-6110   www.thegallivancenter.com

# Red Lion Hotel
# Salt Lake Downtown

The Red Lion Hotel Salt Lake Downtown offers travelers comfortable rooms, a great view and affordable prices. Guests staying in any of the hotel's 392 guest rooms and suites will enjoy the private balcony views of Salt Lake City and the nearby Wasatch mountains. Each room features high-speed Internet access and large, comfortable workstations. Relax in your newly renovated room and treat yourself to room service and an in-room movie. You can work out in the hotel's state-of-the-art fitness center and then refresh yourself in the heated outdoor pool or oversized whirlpool. Enjoy a family-style meal any time of day at the Café Olympus. For upscale dining, you are sure to relish the choices at the Charcoal Room restaurant and the Sky Bar nightclub. Businesses appreciate the Red Lion's flexible meeting space with room to seat up to 1,000 people. The Red Lion Hotel Salt Lake Downtown is the ideal destination for business and vacation travelers looking for an upscale experience at an affordable price.

161 W 600 S, Salt Lake City, UT
(801) 521-7373
www.redlion.com/saltlake

116

# Little America Hotel

Centrally located in Salt Lake City's business, historic, cultural and entertainment center, Little America Hotel is just 10 minutes from the international airport and a short drive from Utah's famous outdoor attractions. The hotel's superior service, accommodations and meeting space make it an ideal location for any meeting. Centralized booking, billing and support staff coordinate all functions seamlessly.
Little America Hotel   500 S Main Street, Salt Lake City UT
(801) 596-5700 or (800) 453-9450   www.littleamerica.com

# Accommodations/Dining and Recreation, Little America Hotel

Little America Hotel offers 850 luxurious, oversized guestrooms and 23 suites, each with 31-inch televisions, down pillows and other luxury amenities. The grounds are beautifully landscaped with fountains and flower gardens. Attended to by an eager and friendly staff, your group will be impressed by the quality of service and commitment to excellence. A superb steakhouse, coffee shop and award-winning Sunday brunch make dining at Little America a distinct pleasure. Indoor and outdoor pools and a fabulous health facility complete with hot tub and sauna complement the hotel's amenities. Nearby attractions include the Utah Jazz Basketball, the Utah Symphony Opera, Ballet West and historic Temple Square, home to the world-renowned Mormon Tabernacle Choir.

500 S Main Street, Salt Lake City UT
(801) 596-5700 or (800) 453-9450
www.littleamerica.com

# Meeting Facilities, Little America Hotel

Little America Hotel offers more than 22,000 square feet of meeting space, with 18 conference rooms. Delectable menus catering to your group's specific tastes and needs will satisfy even the most discriminating palates.
500 S Main Street, Salt Lake City UT
(801) 596-5700 or (800) 453-9450
www.littleamerica.com

# The Grand America Hotel

From the genuine smiles that greet you as you walk through the lobby doors to the overstuffed down pillows that bid you good night, there's little wonder why this hotel is grand in every sense of the word. Inspired by the charm and craftsmanship of Europe's classic hotels, the Grand America offers 775 luxurious rooms, including 395 exquisite suites. The 24-story Grand America Hotel overlooks a beautifully landscaped 10-acre footprint in the heart of downtown Salt Lake City.

555 S Main Street, Salt Lake City UT　(801) 258-6000 or (800) 621-4505　www.grandamerica.com

# Accommodations, Grand America Hotel

Murano crystal chandeliers, handcrafted Richelieu furniture, English wool carpets, Carrara Italian marble and the finest fabrics are featured in all suites and rooms. Elegant French doors separate the bedroom from the living area in the astonishingly spacious 880 square foot suites. All rooms offer marble bathrooms, high-speed Internet connections, 32-inch television sets and dual-line telephones.

555 S Main Street, Salt Lake City UT
(801) 258-6000 or (800) 621-4505
www.grandamerica.com

# Meeting Facilities, Grand America Hotel

The Grand America Hotel offers 75,000 square feet of meeting space with three ornate ballrooms, each with private pre-function space and 21 exquisite meeting rooms and boardrooms. All meeting rooms have extensive telecommunication and audio visual backbone cabling systems, which allow for numerous telephone, data, video, and audio distribution via fiber optics, data-rated twisted pair and coax.   555 S Main Street, Salt Lake City UT
(801) 258-6000 or (800) 621-4505   www.grandamerica.com

# Salt Lake City Attractions

## Clark Planetarium

Visitors to the Clark Planetarium are in for an out-of-this-world experience. The facility, located in Salt Lake City, will leave you literally seeing stars. The planetarium features a 55-foot dome ceiling theater where visitors receive a three-dimensional tour of the cosmos and journey across planetary landscapes. The planetarium also features Utah's first three dimensional IMAX theater, complete with a 12,000-watt digital surround sound system. Among the free space exhibits is a giant model of the solar system. You'll also be moved by Newton's Daydream, an audio-kinetic rolling ball sculpture. Space history buffs will be thrilled to get a look at a real rock from the moon carried home by the astronauts of the Apollo 15 space mission. The Wonders of the Universe science store offers a variety of science toys, binoculars and telescopes for those looking to bring home some wonders of their own. If you want an up-close view of the final frontier, you would do well to trek to the Clark Planetarium.
110 S 400 W Salt Lake City, UT   (801) 456-4966   www.clarkplanetarium.org

## Salt Lake County Equestrian Park and Events Center

For over thirty years, Salt Lake County Equestrian Park has been known as a premier racing, training and show facility.  In the face of continuing urbanization, Salt Lake County residents and visitors alike can appreciate the Park for its location amid the mountain landscapes of South Jordan.  Managing Director, Corey Bullock says, "We help Salt Lake County citizens live a little bit of the country life in the big city." The new Events Center, among the largest in the western states raises this facility to world-class level.  The Laurel Brown Racetrack, well known for its Quarter Horse racing, is the finest in the state and attracts the industry's top horses, trainers and jockeys.  When the snow flies and the temperatures drop racing fans can also enjoy the uniquely Western sport of chariot racing. The events Center is located just minutes from Interstate 15.  See you at the races at Salt Lake County Equestrian Park.
10800 S 2200 W, South Jordan   (301) 254-0106

# Cathedral of the Madeleine

The Cathedral of the Madeleine is the Catholic cathedral of the diocese of Salt Lake City and the parish church for a small but diverse community of about 500 families. The Right Reverend Lawrence Scanlan, Salt Lake City's first bishop, led construction on the South Temple cathedral which began in 1899 and was completed in 1909. The cathedral, designed by Architects Carl Neuhausen and Bernard Mecklenburg, features a primarily Romanesque exterior with a Gothic interior. Reverend Scanlan purchased the site of the cathedral for $300,000 in 1899. In 1991, a $9.7 million renovation began and the renewed building was rededicated in February of 1993. The cathedral serves as the mother church of the diocese and hosts the local church's important religious events and celebrations. Cathedral of the Madeleine provides valuable social outreach to those in need in downtown Salt Lake City. In keeping with the ancient traditions of cathedrals, the Cathedral of the Madeleine also supports arts events, concerts and conferences. People of all faiths and denominations are invited to make a place for themselves within the walls of the Cathedral. The Cathedral of the Madeleine Choir Concert series, the Eccles Organ Festival and the Madeleine Festival of the Arts and Humanities are all sponsored by the cathedral and free to the public. Visit the website and see why you might want to visit The Cathedral of the Madeleine, an extraordinarily beautiful and inspirational spiritual site.

331 E South Temple, Salt Lake City UT
(801) 328-8941
www.saltlakecathedral.org

# The Madeleine Choir School

Listed on the National Register of Historic Places and the Utah State Register of Historic Sites, the Cathedral of the Madeleine is the mother church for the diocese of Salt Lake City. This welcoming cathedral is the site of art events, the Eccles Organ Festival, The Cathedral of Madeleine Choir Concert Series and the Madeleine Festival of the Arts and Humanities, all free and open to the public. This is also the church that founded The Madeleine Choir School, an after-school program that became a full-time academic institution in 1996. This is the only co-educational choir school in the United States and its rigorous curricula and masses, concerts, performance tours and CDs have an established reputation for excellence. The school's mission is to encourage students to grow intellectually, physically, spiritually and emotionally. The choir sings mass five days of the week and on holy days. The students also provide free public concerts, providing community spirit and sharing a beautifully inspirational form of uplifting entertainment. Mr. William Hambleton serves as principal of the school, Mr. Gregory Glenn is the director and The Very Reverend Joseph M. Mayo is rector of the cathedral. The sweet voices of the choir are true auditory treasures. Join in the celebration and enjoy a celestial sound at the next Madeleine Choir School's enchanting performance.

205 First Avenue, Salt Lake City UT
(801) 323-9850
www.madeleinechoirschool.org

# Rose Wagner Performing Arts Center

The Rose Wagner Performing Arts Center is a hub for emerging and established arts organizations in Salt Lake City. The center grew out of a need for additional rehearsal space for tenants of the Capitol Theatre and affordable performing space for the myriad arts companies that have developed over the past 25 years. It houses three performing spaces: the Jeanné Wagner Theatre, the Leona Wagner Black Box Theatre and the Studio Theatre. The Center was built with both public and private funding and is named after its major donor, Izzi Wagner's mother Rose, and opened on Izzi's 86th birthday in March of 2001. Izzi's family owned the Wagner Bag Company on this site, and Izzi was born on a kitchen table in the living quarters behind the store. One theatre is named after Izzi's wife Jeanné and another after his sister Leona. The Rose Wagner Performing Arts Center has been well-received by the community and by performing and cultural organizations. The Ririe-Woodbury Dance Company, Repertory Dance Company and the Gina Bachauer International Piano Foundation and Competition call the Rose their home and have offices at the facility. The Rose has been used by dozens of companies, including SB Dance, Dance Theatre Coalition, Plan-B Theatre Company and Pygmalion Theatre. 138 W 300 S, Salt Lake City UT   (801) 355-2787

# Utah Museum of Fine Arts

As the only museum in the state to house a collection of world art works, the Utah Museum of Fine Arts has a mission to engage and educate the public about the artistic expressions of the world's cultures. They do so by offering patrons a wide range of experiences designed to explore the many ways that art can inform and enhance the human experience. This exciting and innovative museum is housed on the University of Utah campus and offers an oft-changing venue of traveling exhibitions, films, lectures and family art activities that encourage a better understanding of the role of visual arts in our society. The museum strives for excellence in every aspect of serving the university and the diverse communities of Utah and is accredited by the American Association of Museums. The architectural award-winning Marcia and John Price Museum Building, plays host to more than 20 galleries displaying original world art that ranges from 5,000-years-old to present day. These facilities are available to rent and are ideal for business retreats, special performances, fundraisers or weddings and receptions. While the Utah Museum of Fine Arts is enjoyable for those of all ages, they have also created a special program for youngsters called Kidsmuse with interactive art activities for kids and families. Explore the wonders of our world's cultures, all in an afternoon, with a visit to the Utah Museum of Fine Arts. 410 Campus Center Drive, University of Utah Campus, Salt Lake City UT   (801) 581-7332   www.umfa.utah.edu

# The Utah State Fairpark

The Utah State Fairpark hosts many events during the year, including the annual Utah State Fair held each September. The Utah State Fair is the largest single annual event in the state, attended by over 310,000 people at the 150th anniversary celebration in 2005. The state fair holds true to its agricultural roots while offering entertainment, education and a quality family experience. The Utah State Fairpark has been the home of the State Fair since 1902. Prior to the acquisition of the 65 acres as a permanent venue, various locations in Salt Lake City played host to the State Fair. The beautiful grounds and historical buildings lend ambience to weddings, quinceañeras, reunions and concerts in addition to many trade shows and conventions throughout the year.
155 N 1000 W, Salt Lake City UT
(801) 538-8400
www.utahstatefair.com

# Utah Museum of Natural History

The Utah Museum of Natural History is located on the University of Utah campus in Salt Lake City. The museum showcases inspiring permanent collections in anthropology, biology, paleontology and a variety of other disciplines. Paleontologists work on real dinosaur bones in the on-site paleontology laboratory. The facility also houses a model silver mine along with incredible rock and mineral specimens. The museum represents the native people of Utah through old and new art and artifacts, reflecting an intriguing diversity of history and cultures. Traveling exhibitions go forth throughout the year while fascinating classes, workshops and programs help participants develop an informed passion for the natural world. A gift shop makes it easy to find a keepsake of your experiences. In addition, gift and basic memberships to Utah Museum of Natural History provide lasting interactions that benefit both the museum and the members. A few of the many perks of membership include free admission for a year, two free guest passes and discounts on field trips, education events, birthday parties and purchases made in the Museum Store. The free admission benefit extends to over 280 participating museums and science centers around the world. Take the time to visit the Utah Museum of Natural History and it will take your breath away.
1390 E Presidents Circle (200 S), Salt Lake City UT
(801) 581-6927  www.umnh.utah.edu

# The City Library

The City Library in Salt Lake City is the largest library in the state, serving over three million visitors annually. The library provides free Internet access, materials in 90 different languages and programs for kids and teens designed to encourage reading and learning. It also hosts events such as the Dewey Lecture Series, The Human Rights Video Project, and Authors On Stage. The City Library is home to the Utah Center for the Book, an affiliate of the Center for the Book in the Library of Congress. The Library is a true gathering place for the community's use and advancement. Housed in a magnificent building that is an awe-inspiring work of art, the Library reflects the city's imagination and future aspirations. Visitors have plenty of space to explore in this huge facility, with its 300 seat auditorium, reading galleries, spiraling fireplaces, and a stunning rooftop garden. The City Library also features the Shops at Library Square where you can find unique gifts, and provides community services at the English Garden, The Library Store, The SLC Film Center and KCPW radio are also located here. The City Library is leading the way toward the library of tomorrow, so come in and explore everything that this inspiring institution has to offer.
210 E 400 S, Salt Lake City UT   (801) 524-8200   www.slcpl.org

# Downtown Farmers' Market

The Downtown Farmers' Market is a natural gathering place to meet friends and neighbors, socialize and shop the more than 100 vendors that each year provide the freshest seasonal produce, flowers, baked goods, farm-style preserves and garden-related crafts. It's held Saturday mornings from 8 a.m. to 1 p.m. June through October.
Pioneer Park (300 S. & 300 W.), Downtown Salt Lake City, UT
(801) 359-5118
www.downtownslc.org

# First Night Salt Lake City

First Night is Salt Lake City's New Year's Eve celebration of the arts held in downtown Salt Lake City. First Night celebrates the diversity of downtown through the visual, cultural and performing arts with six hours of entertainment. Over 100 different performances make up the fabric of First Night entertainment including music, theatre, art, kids activities, projection installation, games, and much more! First Night is built around the concept that the entire community can share in an evening of fun and excitement safely and inexpensively. The activities start around 6 p.m. and last through midnight, cumulating in a Midnight Finale Extravaganza that counts down the seconds to the New Year.
Downtown Salt Lake City, UT   www.firstnightslc.org   (801) 359-5118

# Live Green:
# Sustainable Living Downtown

Held in May, Live Green is a sustainability festival that teaches and promotes basic principles of how to be more environmentally and ecologically conscientious while promoting downtown as a sustainable community. Companies involved in environmental preservation and conservation, renewable energy, health and wellness, sustainable agriculture, green design and eco-tourism are available for discussion and education.
Pierpont Avenue between West Temple & 200 West, Downtown Salt Lake City, UT
(801) 359-5118 www.downtownslc.org

# Holiday Lights On!

Downtown Salt Lake City lights up for the holidays during Lights On!, the official kickoff for holiday lights and shopping held annually on the day after Thanksgiving.  Visit the Downtown Malls on Main Street and South Temple for a traditional lighting ceremony, complete with a visit from Santa Claus and festive performances. Go ice-skating at the Gallivan Center, and hear the Light Up the Night Concert at The Gateway.
Various locations in downtown Salt Lake City, UT   (801) 359-5118   www.downtownslc.org

# Capitol Theatre

Capitol Theatre in Salt Lake City has known its share of crowded galas since it first opened its doors as the Orpheum Theatre in 1913. This architectural jewel hosted the great stars of vaudeville, welcomed the age of motion pictures and ushered in a revival in performing arts. The original Orpheum was a sumptuous building, costing $250,000 and designed with tapestry brick and polychrome terracotta, a technique employed by only one other major building in Salt Lake City. The theatre was a miracle of innovation with more modern mechanical contrivances than any other theater in the Intermountain West. In 1923, the Ackerman Harris vaudeville chain purchased the theater and vaudeville continued to reign supreme with movies as a sideline. A few years later in 1927, the theatre sold again to Louis Marcus, the much-respected mayor of Salt Lake City and a Utah movie pioneer. Marcus enlarged the seating to 2,260 and installed a Wurlitzer with the organist for the Salt Lake Tabernacle as spotlighted musician. A sunburst in the ceiling mimicked a cathedral in Lyon, France. The Orpheum became the Capitol Theatre and introduced the first all-talking movie picture in 1929. By its next facelift in 1947, movies had become the main attraction at the theatre. In December 1975, Salt Lake County residents passed an $8.6 million bond which provided for renovation of the old Orpheum into a performing arts center. Since reopening in 1978, it has been home to exceptional theatre, dance, opera and music. For a taste of the performance arts in a decadent theatre with history, head to Capitol Theatre in Salt Lake City.
50 W 200 S, Salt Lake City UT   (801) 355-2787

*Orpheum Theatre, 1913*

# Abravanel Hall

Abravanel Hall in Salt Lake City was named for beloved Maestro Maurice Abravanel, founder and conductor of the Utah Symphony. The hall is an acoustical masterpiece created by Dr. Cyril M. Harris, the acoustical consultant for such renowned performing spaces as the Kennedy Center in Washington, D.C. and the remodeled Avery Fisher Hall in New York City. Abravanel Hall is a concrete building inside a brick building with a beautiful concert hall inside these outer shells. To reach the concert hall, the visitor passes through sound lock corridors designed to prevent lobby noise from spilling into the hall. The hall's convex curved surfaces and six giant brass chandeliers with 18,000 hand-cut beads and Bohemian crystals were all carefully chosen for their acoustical properties. Elaborate details abound with a four-story lobby crowned with a ceiling of white oak and solid brass and the concert hall adorned with more than 12,000 square feet of 24-karat gold leaf brushed on by hand. The lobby orients itself toward the east and the former home of the Utah Symphony, the Salt Lake Tabernacle, with 5,400 square feet of tempered glass made in England. Experience the sights and sounds in Abravanel Hall, home to the Utah Symphony and the site of numerous concerts and special events.
123 W South Temple, Salt Lake City UT
(801) 355-2787

# Skywalker Balloon Company
# & Utah Outventures

Utah is among the greatest concentrations of spectacular geological wonders in the world. The landscape literally reaches out to you, offering twisting canyons, delicate arches, sheer mountains, ridges and colorful shadows, from its desolate, red rock canyons to its soaring, pine-covered peaks. Utah presents spectacular landscapes to explore, each exploding differently as Utah's bold seasons progress. Ballooning in Utah is a breathtaking experience that allows you to seize the beauty, an approach that cannot be achieved any other way. Floating serenely above the landscape sends your soul into the heavens and your mind wondering if you are simply dreaming. With the change of seasons in Utah, each balloon ride becomes equally unique. Ballooning through the desert heat to icy peaks, glittering, white mountain tops, brilliant fall foliage, explosive wild flowers or the intense blue skies of radiant summers can only be summarized by one word, "Wow!" Utah Outventures is an association of professional guides, outfitters, travel experts and vacation planners working together to make visiting Utah absolutely unforgettable. Utah Outventures brings you to the most famous places. They guide safe and exciting tours, including, but not limited to, whitewater river rafting, fly fishing, national parks, ATV and motor-cross, mountain biking and exclusive tours. Wilhelm "Will" Drummer, came to Utah from Austria. He was immediately struck by Utah's beauty. With proper technical training in the old ways of ballooning, Will began his new life's passion of owning and piloting his hot air balloons. Safety is always his first priority. Will is committed to ensuring that all passengers enjoy the experience he can provide; a memorable encounter to last a lifetime. Will prides himself on planning an unforgettable Outventure, custom to your desires. Utah Outventures and Skywalker Balloon Company invite you to dance across the Utah skies, European-style ballooning, 365-days-per-year, or simply let Will organize your vacation to Utah.

Skywalker Balloon Company
(866) HOT-AIR2 (468-2472)
www.utah-travel.net

Utah Outventures
(866) 366-UTAH (8824)
www.utahoutventures.com
or www.utah-travel.net

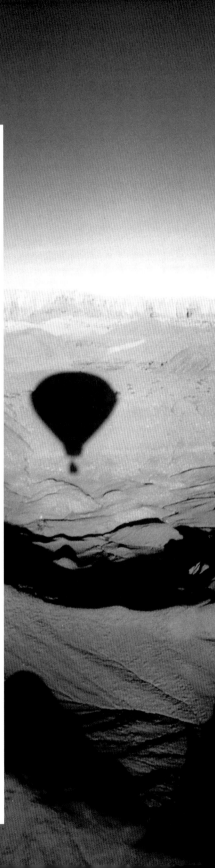

# Cloud 9 Soaring Center

Soar high above beautiful deserts with Cloud 9 Soaring Center, the largest paragliding school in the United States. Located in beautiful Draper, Cloud 9 Soaring Center offers instruction, tandem flights, equipment, repairs and everything else anyone from a beginner to a seasoned pilot could need. If you've never flown before, sign up for a tandem flight with one of Cloud 9's experienced pilots, and, if you like the experience, they'd be glad to help you learn to pilot yourself. No matter your level of athletic ability, you'll be flying with the birds in no time. According to Cloud 9, paragliding is a fun, safe way to experience flight in its simplest form. It works by inflating a wing and using wind currents to stay afloat, sometimes for hours at a time. Landing is equally easy and gentle. Their instructors are experienced, friendly and extremely knowledgeable, and safety is their first concern. Cloud 9 also stocks beautiful kites and supplies for kite boarding, snow kiting and a number of other fun and exciting sports at their supply store in Draper. Open since the early 1990s and owned by Steve Mayer, they now offer a Web store that will ship to anywhere in the world, so no matter your location, you'll always be able to access the fun that Cloud 9 offers. For an exhilarating experience like no other, visit Cloud 9 Soaring Center in Draper.

12665 S Minuteman Drive, Draper UT

(801) 576-6460

www.paragliders.com

133

# The Organ Loft

In the heart of Salt Lake City is one of today's most unusual and fascinating places, The Organ Loft, home to a unique historical treasure. The story of The Organ Loft is the story of the late Lawrence Bray and his dedication to the restoration and preservation of the theatre pipe organ. Lawrence's passion for the instrument began when he was a young man and heard George Wright and Gaylord Carter performing on the Wurlitzer organ at the San Francisco Fox Theatre. Intrigued with the sound, he acquired several old theatre organs before combining two consoles to build today's Colossus five keyboard console with 378 stop tabs, which control the present 2,400 highly unified pipes. The Organ Loft is available for business lunches, parties, wedding receptions and holiday festivities. Private party prices are based on a minimum of 50 people, and include hall rental, dance floor, taxes and gratuities. The atmosphere is exciting and the courteous staff provides the perfect setting for the ultimate entertainment experience. The Organ Loft also features a state-of-the-art sound and music reproducing system. Ask about their schedule for screening classic silent movies accompanied by the power of the pipe organ.
3331 Edison Street, Salt Lake City UT   (801) 485-9265   www.organloftslc.com

# Classic Cars International

Get yourself revved up for a timeless adventure into the history of one of the greatest inventions of all time: the automobile. Known as a premier western museum for restored cars, Classic Cars International promotes the legacy of the creative and pioneering automobile industry. For more than 30 years, Owners Richard Williams and his son Stacey have provided a glimpse into the past by offering to its visitors over 300 one-of-a-kind, fully restored classic and special interest cars from 1906 to the 1970s. These beautiful and rare luxury cars have been carefully rebuilt and are fully operational. The displays are rotated regularly to ensure guests get the chance to see something different on each visit. The museum operates as a nonprofit, with the entire price of admission donated to the Utah Boys Ranch in West Valley City. For the extreme auto enthusiast, limited duplicates of classic cars are offered for sale by request. Next time you're in Salt Lake City, plan to spend the day perusing the showroom and prepare to be impressed by this impeccable collection of classic vehicles restored to the finest integrity. Special memories are yours to experience with a day at Classic Cars International.

355 W 700 South, Salt Lake City UT
(801) 322-5509
www.classiccarmuseumsales.com

# Salt Lake Community College

Salt Lake Community College takes the "community" in its name to heart. Under President Cynthia A. Bioteau's direction, this accredited, multi-campus college is thriving while serving the diverse needs of the Salt Lake City community. The college's open-door enrollment policy allows it to serve more than sixty thousand students annually. Its offerings of credit and non-credit courses as well as varied workshops make SLCC the largest institution of higher education in the state. Despite the dramatically increasing student enrollment, the college manages to preserve its personalized feel with a

student-to-faculty ratio of 20 to 1. To accommodate the needs of students, SLCC has three full-service campuses: South City, Redwood, and Jordan. It also offers eleven teaching centers around the Salt Lake Valley and features an e-Campus for distance learning. Courses are offered in both traditional and accelerated semesters and are available during the days, evenings, and weekends. SLCC prides itself on long-term success that has been built on a philosophy that integrates six important educational components called "The Six Pillars of a Community College." Individually, each pillar plays a critical role in educating students. Working together, the pillars provide an educational powerhouse to ensure economic growth and the success of students and the Salt Lake community. SLCC offers courses in general education, transfer programs, career and technical education, apprenticeships, continuing education as well as many others. "We're building tomorrow's workforce and strengthening Utah's economy every day." Visit a campus to see what Salt Lake Community College can do for you.
4600 South Redwood Road, Salt Lake City UT
(801) 957-4111
www.slcc.edu

# Wheeler Historic Farm

The Wheeler Farm story began on June 17, 1886, when Sariah Hankinson Pixton married Henry Joseph Wheeler and they made their home together on a 75-acre farm near Salt Lake City. In 1969, Salt Lake County purchased all 75 acres, and turned it into Wheeler Historic Farm, a restoration of the turn-of-the-century dairy farm. In 1976, it was placed on both the Utah State and National Register of Historic Places. Today, it is a demonstration farm of the rural lifestyle in Salt Lake County from 1890 to 1920, and represents the best farming methods of the Progressive Era. Visitors are encouraged to observe the animals and stroll along Little Cottonwood Creek. The adjoining Wheeler Woods offers several trails to walk, jog, bike or hike. Back at the farm, there

are art and photo galleries to explore and an old-style country store to browse through. For a more authentic experience take a tractor-drawn wagon rides; help gather chicken eggs or try milking a cow. Make reservations for your birthday party or celebrate the holidays with their seasonal special events. The activity barn, ice house, stage, south lawn or the entire farm can also be rented out. See what the real simple life was about with a visit to Wheeler Historic Farm.
6351 S 900 E, Salt Lake City UT
(801) 264-2241
www.wheelerfarm.com

# Trolley Square

Trolley Square is a shopping plaza with a difference. It's a living museum of Salt Lake City's trolleys and streetcars, built not only on the site of the original trolley depot but in the actual car barns. Past and present come together here in buildings that once housed smithies and carpenter shops. Now they house popular stores like the Pottery Barn and restaurants like the Hard Rock Café. Salt Lake City's trolley car system was created by railroad magnate E. H. Harriman, and at its height there were more than 144 trolleys running on a system that encompassed the entire valley. Recognized as a site of historic significance by both the state of Utah and the National Register of Historic Places, Trolley Square houses important artifacts from around the state, some of them re-purposed, like the mining trestle from the Anaconda Mines near Tooele, which now serves as a sky bridge connecting the shops and the parking lot. The original 97-foot-high water tower now doubles as a neon sign welcoming visitors. With over 90 specialty shops, restaurants and a movie theater surrounded by fascinating glimpses of Salt Lake City's rich history, Trolley Square has more than earned the right to be called one of Utah's treasures.

367 Trolley Square (600 S 700 E),
Salt Lake City UT
(801) 521-9878 www.simon.com

# Red Butte Garden

When it opened to the public in 1985, Red Butte Garden featured 13 acres of display gardens, now expanded to 18. Among the newest features are the Children's Garden, opened in 1999, and the Orangerie, an enclosed space designed for citrus trees and unusual flowering plants that require a warm, humid environment. Outside the display gardens, nearly three miles of hiking trails allow visitors to experience the still-wild ecology surrounding the garden. Red Butte Garden traces its origins back to 1961, when Utah's State Arboretum was established at the University of Utah in Salt Lake City. In 1983, the University dedicated 100 acres at the mouth of nearby Red Butte Canyon for the purpose of creating a regional public botanical garden. The choice of Red Butte Canyon was influenced by two remarkable individuals. Ezekiel R. Dumke Jr., known to all and sundry as Zeke, spent countless hours exploring the site and inviting visitors to come and see for themselves how perfect it would be for a botanical garden. W. Richard Hildreth executive director of the Arboretum, put together the board of scientists and community leaders that made the practical decisions leading to the creation of Red Butte Garden. Red Butte Garden is an authentic Utah treasure.

300 Wakara Way, Salt Lake City UT
(801) 581-IRIS
www.redbuttegarden.org

# The 23rd Floor Event Center

In the heart of Salt Lake City, there's an extraordinary concept in event planning just minutes from the Salt Lake International Airport, the University of Utah, Temple Square and many major attractions and hotels. The 23rd Floor Event Center is a luxurious facility that will provide the perfect setting for your major event, whether it's a corporate function, conference or that main event – your wedding. A full service design team includes your own personal event hostess and event coordinator to help design the perfect backdrop, custom décor and theme for your celebration or business gathering. This prestigious 23,000 square foot facility is Utah's most exclusive and spacious location for any multi-faceted affair. The fully equipped boardrooms can be configured to fit any number of people or type of presentation, with state-of-the-art audio conferencing rooms that will enhance your company's polished and professional image. With a two-story gallery, a sweeping staircase and spectacular views from every room, your wedding will be an affair to remember and cherish. The on-site chef can customize and cater a sit-down dinner for up to 500, a buffet, or a whimsically themed affair. Whatever the occasion, The 23rd Floor's design team will see to every detail, including limousines, photographers, musicians and floral arrangements. With resources, expertise, and caring personalized service, The 23rd Floor Event Center team will create an outstanding occasion worthy not just of your needs – but of your dreams and expectations.
299 S Main Street, Ste 2300, Salt Lake City Utah
(801) 961-4050   www.23rdfloor.net

# Bonneville Salt Lake

When it comes to having a hand on the pulse of the community, no one does it better than Bonneville Salt Lake. Bonneville Salt Lake is made up of the top radio and television stations in the Salt Lake City market. Owner and operator Bonneville International Corporation is headquartered in Salt Lake City and owns additional radio stations in Chicago, Washington D.C., St. Louis, Phoenix and San Francisco. The broadcast group started in the early 1920s with station KZN, Utah's first commercial radio station and later changed its call letters to KSL. KSL Television hit the airwaves in 1949. Today, KSL is synonymous with quality news and entertainment. Keeping Utah listeners and viewers informed every day of the year is top priority for the award-winning KSL Radio and Television news departments. KSL Newsradio, an ABC affiliate, broadcasts on 102.7-FM and 1160-AM and continues to be the dominant ratings leader in the market. KSL-5 Television, an NBC affiliate, is the television news leader in Utah. Log on to KSL.com from anywhere in the world and you can be up to date with the KSL newsroom in seconds. KUTR, 820-AM, Utah's first news-talk station with a focus on women, was launched in May 2005. This innovative new talk station gives the women of Utah an exclusive voice on the radio, addressing everyday issues, topics and ideas. Discussion is lively and sharing is from the heart on KUTR. KSFI, 100-FM, is the top-performing adult contemporary station in Utah, known for playing soft hits with less talk. Providing news, weather, and great music, 100-FM has been Utah's number one listen at home and listen at work music station for 25 years and counting. The classic 103.5, the Arrow, is Utah's leading heritage rock station, known for playing the music you grew up with. From the Eagles to the Beatles, the music creates a memorable experience that keeps listeners coming back for more. Their talented on-air staff combined with a commitment to less clutter and a family-friendly presentation create the ideal radio companion at work or at home. Bonneville Salt Lake stations make a difference in Utah every day.
55 N 300 W, Salt Lake City UT   (801) 575-5555   www.bonnint.com

# FatCats

How much fun can you handle? There's one way to find out: experience FatCats in Salt Lake City, Ogden, or Provo, where the motto is "All Out Fun!" David Rutter and Sean Collins wondered what would happen if they put state-of-the-art bowling, great food and all manner of family entertainment under one roof. They did just that, and now it's up to you to consider a menu of delights that begins with ninety lanes of the country's most sophisticated bowling

technology, from interactive automatic scoring to automated retractable gutter bumpers. After 9:30 p.m., the lights go down, the fog machines start, and everyone glows under the black lights. When you're through with strikes and spares, the Pizza Factory, Costa Vida and Strikers Grill stand by to fill your tummy with Champzz Lounge ready to provide beverages. The FatCats arcade features over 200 games, including the latest video games and traditional favorites. With a sports shop, kid's play land, billiards and banquet facilities, the fun's only beginning at FatCats.

Salt Lake City
3739 S 900 E, Salt Lake City UT
(801) 262-9890

Provo
1200 N University Avenue, Provo UT
(801) 373-1863

Ogden
2261 Kiesel Avenue, Ogden UT
www.fatcatsfun.com

# Raging Waters Water Park

Over a million gallons of water and extreme outrageousness wait for you at Raging Waters Water Park in Salt Lake City. So pack up the family, the entire neighborhood, your company or church membership, and head for the most fun you can have in the water in the Intermountain states. Start with the Wild Wave, a 500,000-gallon pool where you can body surf on ocean-like waves. Then try the multi-level Adventure Cove Activity Pool. See if you can survive the Gallows drop-rope swing, or lock arms with your best friend on the way down the Gang Slide. Next, you're ready for the Rampage, a 35-foot plummet on a water-skimming sled. Now take a deep breath and head for the Blue Thunder, a double tube ride that sends you and your partner twisting and turning through whitewater. Defy gravity. Yes, you'll ascend hills even as you descend from a 40-foot tower. If you like that and want more, try White Lightning, a faster version of Blue Thunder. When you're ready to slow down a bit, float on the slow-moving waters of the Balboa River Expedition. After all that, perhaps a soak in a 15-foot giant hot tub will do you good and get you ready to come back and do it all again tomorrow. The park is open from Memorial Day Weekend through Labor Day Weekend.
1200 W 1700 S, Salt Lake City UT   (801) 972-3300   www.ragingwatersutah.com

# Impact Guns

Never fired a gun but want to know how to do it safely? Trying to get your concealed-weapons permit? Looking for an appropriate weapon to match your personal protection or home defense needs? At Impact Guns, manager and instructors will always point you in the right direction. Whether you're a first time shooter or expert marksman, they have the gear and gun to match your needs. They also offer a full line of tactical and self-defense courses on-site, as well as gunsmithing to give you the best chance to meet your goals. Impact Guns has a good working relationship within the management of the Bureau of Criminal Identification, Utah Attorney General's office, Salt Lake County Sheriff's office, and the Utah House and Senate leadership. At Impact Guns, in-house experts are often called to consult on matters of training qualification, concealed-weapons statutes, and the implication of proposed changes to statutes. Their views, methods and decorum have earned the respect of lawmakers and law enforcement personnel. You can learn a lot from him in just one sitting. For basic gun-handling training or a great place to practice your skills, give Impact Guns a shot.
4075 W 4715 S, Salt Lake City UT (801) 967-8005
2701 S 1900 W, Ogden UT   www.impactguns.com

# Salt Lake City
# Fashion, Health and Beauty

## The Shirōdhara Day Spa

Eva Mileski, an award-winning European aesthetician, and Husband Walter Mileski founded The Shirōdhara Day Spa together to provide necessary and nourishing therapy for the body and the spirit. The spa takes its name from an ancient healing ritual created in India, shirōdhara, which involves bathing the forehead in a steady, fine stream of warm oil. This elegant and simple treatment brings balance to the body and clarity to the mind. The Shirōdhara Day Spa uses techniques developed throughout the world, including Himalayan aromatherapy, Balinese body treatments and European facials. Book a full-day treatment package that includes a gourmet lunch, or a 3 ½-hour refresher or simply choose your treatments a la carte. The spa also sells treatment products for use in your own home; buy them at the spa or order them by phone or from Shirōdhara's website. Eva believes in making these rejuvenating products and techniques as widely available as possible, and to this end she has also created a series of videos on various aspects of facial therapy and aesthetics.

2122 Fort Union Boulevard, Salt Lake City UT
(801) 943-3840
www.shirodharadayspa.com

## Scentsations

How's your skin today? Could it use some pampering? Find it at Scentsations in Salt Lake City, where Owner Susan Sharp offers the finest in skin care with natural botanical products. You will find everything needed to nourish your skin, including a wide assortment of botanical lotions and custom-scented bubbles for the bath. Start by selecting a body care product that has no scent, and customize your scent by choosing from Scentsations' exceptional selection of over 150 quality fragrances and pure essential oils. You will find many indulgences in this great little boutique, where pampering seems to be the theme! Scentsations offers a tremendous selection of pajamas and loungewear, candles and other delights. See for yourself with a trip to Scentsations, located in Foothill Village Shopping Center.

1316 S Foothill Drive, Salt Lake City UT  (801) 364-0168 or (888) 672-3687
www.scentsationslotionsoils.com

# AquaVie Day Spa

For a remarkable day of relaxation, health and well-being with the finest European products, come to AquaVie Day Spa. AquaVie, meaning water of life, offers a vast array of spa services, all of which are based around the healing powers of mineral-rich seawater. Abounding with vital trace minerals and complex nourishment, the sea is a source of life and equilibrium. AquaVie is a day spa with over 30 years of experience in promoting health and well-being through relaxation and individualized spa treatments, including services such as European facials, lymph drainage massage, hydrotherapy, body treatments, manicures and pedicures. The founder, Anneli Johnson, brought her extensive knowledge of esthetics and massage therapy to the United States in 1963. Anneli searched the globe for the best treatments and products available on the market. To keep up with the growing demand for her services, she founded a full service day spa in 1974.  This is where she taught others to render the caliber of services she had mastered in Finland.  With the help of Anneli's daughter, Lenette Casper, AquaVie is the most established and experienced day spa in the Salt Lake Valley.  Anneli's knowledge and passion for esthetics spread not only to her daughter, but now boasts a third generation of involvement in AquaVie Day Spa.

3350 S Highland Drive, Salt Lake City UT (801) 484-0574 www.aquaviedayspa.com

# Dave's Health and Nutrition

Dave and Teresa Card knew that health matters when they opened the first Dave's Health and Nutrition store in 1995. Their mission was to offer people one-on-one guidance for their nutritional questions and needs. Dave quickly established respect and a growing reputation for his ability to help people with natural and safe health care methods. Within four years, the business grew to three stores (in Salt Lake City, Midvale and West Jordan) and over 20 employees. Dave and Teresa are as loyal and committed to their employees as they are to their customers. When you walk in the door, you can relax with the confidence that the products on Dave's shelves are some of the purest and highest quality available. Dave's is proud to provide quality vitamins, sports nutrition, homeopathic remedies and an impressive selection of bulk herbs that have been evaluated for safety and efficacy. You are welcome to sit down and take your time choosing just the right book from the store's carefully chosen array of high quality books about healing and wellness. Dave's experienced and knowledgeable staff provides one-on-one customer care and is always happy to help you chose products for positive results. At one or more of Dave's stores, you may choose from the services of an iridologist, massage therapist or herbalist. Consultations with Dave can be reserved one day in advance or on the same day, if time becomes available.

1108 E 3300 S, Salt Lake City (801) 483-9024
7777 S State Street, Midvale UT (801) 255-3809
1817 W 9000 S, West Jordan (810) 446-0499
www.daveshealth.com

# C.T. Brock & Company

C.T. Brock and Company understands the business executive's need for quality clothing and seeks to meet that need with higher end designer menswear for all facets of the executive's lifestyle. Salt Lake City manager Todd McCabe joins Owners Brock Bennett and Christian Marcheschi in a strong desire to raise the bar on fine clothing selection in Utah. "The hot new trend for business executives is differentiating themselves through their dress," says McCabe. To help clients keep up with the fashion trends, C. T. Brock & Company offers a customer wardrobe evaluation. They will come to a client's home and analyze the contents of his closet, then help him upgrade his wardrobe. C.T. Brock & Company specializes in serving all the clothing needs of the executive, from tailored clothing made from the finest fabrics to premium denim and a full array of weekend ware, even fine shaving products, that complement an executive's complete lifestyle. C.T. Brock and Company knows that today's executives are looking for both image and quality. They understand that people have different needs and tastes. They believe in a demographic of one—you.

1354 Foothill Drive, Salt Lake City, Utah   (801) 581-0600

# Utah Woolen Mills

Currently celebrating its centennial, Utah Woolen Mills is a business that the Stringham family can be justly proud of. Bart and Briant Stringham, current president and board chairman, are the third and fourth generation of Stringhams to work here, Brandon and B.J. Stringham, fifth-generation members, work in buying and sales. The Stringham family's devotion to their business embodies the industrious family values for which Utah is renowned. Hand-tailoring has been an integral part of the business since the beginning; the Stringham commitment to quality demands it. Even though it requires a higher price, the products sell. For example, Utah Woolen Mills sells a pair of wool-corduroy pants that sell out in larger quantities every year (they recently sold more than 450 pairs in a three-month period, which might seem hard to believe considering the price tag of $325). But customers know that the quality and durability are worth it. Unlike mass-produced clothing, Utah Woolen Mills clothing lasts for decades and always looks great. The commitment to customer service is just as strong as the commitment to quality. No wonder that customers develop a lifelong relationship with the company, remaining loyal even if they move away from Utah. Utah Woolen Mills ships custom shirts and other quality clothing to clientele around the world.
59 W South Temple, Salt Lake City UT
(801) 364-1851 www.utahwoolenmills.com

# String Beads

When you walk into String Beads, you enter a world of glistening jewels, eye-catching pearls and extraordinary baubles and beads. This charming store in picturesque Sugar House was founded by Bob and Dinah Ihle in 1994 and remains a family business. A large, U-shaped, workstation lies in the center of the shop where patrons can work on projects with the support of staff members who can answer any questions. This workstation is also used during classes, which are taught-year round. Classes range from beginning jewelry to special techniques and designs. String Beads has an inventory of

at least 20,000 items at any given time and offers more than 25,000 in its database. Beads are arranged by color and type along the walls making it much easier to browse and select the items necessary for your project. The shop also offers a full line of accessories and jewelry making tools. These extras include books, stones, metals, threading material, wire, tools and adhesives. String Beads also makes and sells quality-made examples of lamp work, fused glass, and wearable beaded art. Some of these pieces are currently being shown and sold nationally. The focus of this inspiring shop continues to be on the customer. Providing excellent service, competitive prices and consistent quality is what they are all about. When you're ready to start your next bead project, or if you are looking for a new hobby, stop in and visit String Beads.

2223 S Highland Drive, Salt Lake City UT

(801) 487-1110   www.stringbeadsutah.com

## Envi Jewelers

In the middle of the Utah desert, two flowers blossomed, Tifini and Rebecca. Their dreams came true, and ENVI Jewelers was born. At Envi in Salt Lake City, you will behold a spectacular array of gemstones in a rainbow of colors from the world's leading designers. Many of the couture lines showcased by Envi Jewelers are exclusive to the store. Envi Jewelers has combined its passion for jewelry with fashion, so you can refresh your pallet, enjoy a new flavor and embrace one of-a-kind pieces. The women of Envi invite you to come in and experience their warm and friendly atmosphere. They will ensure that each visit to Envi will be a new experience.
4699 S Highland Drive, Salt Lake City UT
(801) 272-9189

# Richelle's

Owner Teresa Skaggs has created the ultimate shopping experience at Richelle's in Salt Lake City with cutting-edge fashions, an exceptional selection of designer shoes, and a full-service salon and day spa. "My main goal was to bring our clients more choices for unique styles and services," says Teresa. "Customer service is our number one priority." Since 1994, Richelle's has been helping customers choose from select clothing by such designers as St. John, Elie Tahari, Yansi Fugel and Marc Jacobs. For the fine footwear, look for shoes, boots and sandals by Donald Pliner, Stuart Weitzman, Reed Evins, Bettye Muller and Emilio Pucci, to name just a few. If you want to be treated like a Queen for a Day, take the spiral staircase up to Richelle's Salon and Day Spa, where you can receive full spa and hair artistry services from a staff of professionally trained and licensed therapists, aestheticians and stylists. Facials, pedicures, manicures, massages, body waxing and make-up magic are all yours at Richelle's, the only specialty store of its kind in Salt Lake City. And though the merchandise and services are of the highest quality, the prices are remarkably reasonable. One-stop shopping just doesn't get any better.
4699 S Highland Drive, Salt Lake City, UT
(801) 272-3111
www.richelles.com

# Salt Lake City
# Gifts, Home and Garden

## Western Nut Company

Fresh gourmet nuts from around the world make up the bulk of the Western Nut Company merchandise. The fudge, brittle and candies round it out nicely. In addition, their fresh milled natural peanut butter and homemade fruit spreads give a whole new definition to the PB and J sandwich. Western Nut Company also carries a line of gourmet soup, dip and dressing mixes, a rosemary and garlic bread mix, and a country wassail. Products are bundled in award-winning packaging. Specialized wrapping and corporate labeling make gift giving easy. Gift baskets are shipped throughout the country. Each order is hand packed, using the best available product. Filberts from Oregon may share a tin with cashews from India and pine nuts from Utah and California. All nuts are processed in the factory, and the roasting process is done one batch at a time, using only peanut oil. Because roasting is done one batch at a time instead of on a continuous roaster, you taste the nut, not the roast. Western Nut Company's fudge is recognized as an industry best and the brittle recipe, a treasured secret, was specially developed by master candy maker Paul Cushing for this native Salt Lake City company. Shoppers will enjoy the large gift shop and show room. Gift cards are available for the undecided. The family-owned Western Nut Company has proved itself with over 40 years of exemplary products and service. Come see and taste for yourself.

434 S 300 W, Salt Lake City UT
(801) 363-8869 or (800) 825-9912
www.westernnut.com

## Jolley's Corner

Over 50 years ago, Joel M. Jolley opened the first of Jolley's four pharmacies in the Salt Lake area, heralding in a tradition of offering personalized service with a flare for the unique. Today, the Jolley's Corner flagship store on the corner of 1300 South and 1700 East in Salt Lake City continues that great tradition under the ownership of son Bryce Jolley. Customers receive warm care in the pharmacy and, while browsing the store, they discover a treasure chest right here on the east side of the valley. There are hundreds of gift and home décor items that are a far cry from the typical big box variety. A quaint Top Hat Video department that caters to the neighborhood is tucked in there as well. Jolley's specializes in popular candy as well as some long lost favorites. Their premier line is the Salt City Sweets brand. These delicious chocolates are wrapped around dried fruit and nuts, all with a Salt Lake historic theme. Explore the inside garden at Jolley's Stems floral department. Here, talented floral designers create some of the most eye-catching arrangements around. No wonder they are the preferred florist for large events, weddings, hotels and businesses all around the valley, all the while catering to a loyal local clientele. To enjoy all that Jolley's has to offer, it's definitely worth the short drive to the exclusive Harvard-Yale area of Salt Lake at 1676 East 1300 South. Everything is reasonably priced and it's a real treat to find a business with the rare, old-fashioned charm that's harder and harder to find in today's world.

1676 E 1300 S, Salt Lake City UT
1702 S 1100 E, Salt Lake City UT
9720 S 1300 E, Salt Lake City UT
(801) 582-1625

# Sam Weller's

Sam Weller's is Salt Lake's oldest and finest bookstore. Established in 1929, Sam Weller's is a full service book dealer, selling new, used, out-of-print and rare books. With more than 1.5 million books in stock on 3 floors, they probably have any book you are looking for. If they don't have it in stock, they specialize in searching for hard-to-find titles. They have books on all subjects including extensive collections of Western Americana and LDS books and they will ship worldwide as well. Now in the third generation of family ownership, Sam Weller's is an independent bookstore and a member of ABAA, the Antiquarian Booksellers Association of America.

254 S Main Street, Salt Lake City UT
(801) 328-2586 or (800) 333-SAMW
www.samwellers.com

# Hammond Hobbies and Toys

When Gale Hammond, president of Hammond Hobbies and Toys, started the business in the basement of his home in Holladay fifty years ago, he probably didn't guess that he'd just started a company that would grow into the largest independent toy store in the Intermountain area. Hammond Hobbies and Toys is a true family business; Gale let his children get involved from an early age with the philosophy that when they were tall enough to see over the counter, they were old enough to be part of the business. Now his sons Paul, David and Bruce are co-owners, and their children work at the store. When it comes down to it, what child wouldn't want to work in a toyshop?

It's not just family values and a commitment to customer service that draws people, but Hammond's stunning variety of toys and equipment for every kind of hobby you can imagine. The store stocks such favorites as slot car racers, model trains, telescopes, toy gliders and rockets. Gale's wife, Georgia, is the longtime doll buyer and stocks a collection that includes Barbie and Madame Alexander. Model lovers will find classic cars, ships, planes and helicopters, even a scale model of the Salt Lake Temple! Hammond Hobbies and Toys has everything you or your child could want.

4835 Highland Drive, Salt Lake City UT
(801) 277-7056 www.hammondtoy.com

# The Train Shoppe

Since 1972, the Train Shoppe has been providing model train enthusiasts in the Salt Lake City area with everything they need. As owner Lynn Rasband puts it, "If we don't have it, we'll find it." With not only an impressive and complete selection of train cars and accessories from all the major suppliers, including many antique and discontinued models, they can also supply you with a wealth of knowledge that they're happy to share. The six experienced repairmen here can give you the assistance you need in any aspect of model railroading. Their skill has earned the Train Shoppe the honor of being Utah's only authorized Lionel service station. You can judge the expertise of Lynn's staff by examining the amazing train layouts in operation at the store. There are two, a 6' x 14' HO-scale setup, and a 12' x 16' O-Gauge which is currently under construction. You can see these remarkable creations in photographs with accompanying diagrams on their website. Whether you're just discovering the joys of this hobby or you've been doing it for years, you'll be delighted by what you find at the Train Shoppe. Lynn invites you to stop by and "Let our experts make your train modeling experience successful."

470 S 900 E, Salt Lake City UT   (801) 322-2729
www.trainshoppeslc.com

# Edinburgh Castle

If you've got Scottish roots or simply want a wee bit of Scottish flair, Edinburgh Castle is the place for you. For over 30 years, Edinburgh Castle has offered its famous Scottish imports to residents and visitors in the Salt Lake City area. Owners Eric A. and Audrey Ann Gilzean, both natives of the United Kingdom, take great care in providing the very best in quality Scottish merchandise. Each year Eric and Audrey return to the old country to purchase new and authentic Scottish wares for their store. Edinburgh Castle is perhaps best known for its kilts. Customers can rent them for weddings or other functions and can even order them online. The shop's highland attire is popular as well. You'll find Scottish ties and scarves in over a thousand tartans (Scottish plaids) as well as rugby shirts, Kangol caps and hats and lambs' wool tartan blankets. If you've been searching for your family's coat of arms or crest, look no further. Edinburgh Castle's crests are handmade in Scotland by manufacturers that have been approved by the Standing Council of Scottish Chiefs. Of course, customers love the vast assortment of Scottish memorabilia from DVDs and CDs of pipe bands to fridge magnets, key fobs, jewelry and chanters. If you want to try your hand at playing the bagpipes, you'll find those here, too! Next time you're in Salt Lake City, make plans to drop by Edinburgh Castle. You're certain to unearth a bit of the highlands in this cheery store.

124 S Main Street, Salt Lake City UT
(801) 364-1406
www.edinburghcastle.com

# London Market

The London Market, across from Trolley Square, brings Britain to America. Owners Robin and Elizabeth Grey have spent the last five years importing fine British chocolates, groceries, gifts and clothing. They have created a London specialty shop that is delectably authentic. Shoppers enter the quaintly furnished cottage rooms and feel as if they are instantly transported an ocean away. As the old-fashioned bell rings on the door when you enter, you will feel like you walked into a corner store in an English neighborhood. This welcome sense of connectedness ensures a pleasant encounter. In 2006, the market adds a new bakery, where customers can enjoy some tea and British specialty pastries. Visitors new to London Market can savor a host of delights with curious names. Oat bar cookies are called flapjacks, and mousse is called milk jelly. Look for an expansive candy display featuring a visual feast of playfully wrapped goodies. With so many different taste treats to choose from, you'll scarcely know where to start. The Greys and Manager Loraine White invite you to share a morsel or two in merry old England fashion at London Market.

563 S 700 E, Salt Lake City UT
(801) 531-7074
www.thelondonmarket.net

# Audrie's Design

Audrie Klingler, the namesake of Audrie's Design, is renowned in Salt Lake City for her design skills, which have won her many awards in the Salt Lake Parade of Homes. Audrie's Design features her original furniture creations that are unavailable anywhere else and many other treats for your home. Audrie and her family have built a reputation for providing the finest upholstering, framing and sewing supplies anywhere in the state and their customer service is equally famous. The owners estimate that 98 percent of their business comes from referrals and repeat customers. Among the most popular furniture items are hardwood frame beds, which come with solid steel springs that carry a lifetime guarantee. The success of Audrie's Design may be measured by its continued expansion. When it opened in 1994, it was in a leased 7,000-square-foot showroom and the furniture was built off-site. The present building, owned by the Klinglers, features a 10,000-square-foot showroom and a 10,000-square-foot furniture workshop. In addition to furniture, upholstering and framing, Audrie's Design is also the best place for window treatments, bedding and custom rugs and floral arrangements. You can't go wrong with Audrie's Design.

930 E 6600 South, Salt Lake City UT    (801) 288-9665

# Dancing Cranes Imports

Owners Jim Platt, Matt Platt and Jana Svobodova are the three dancing cranes of Dancing Crane Imports in Salt Lake City. They buy merchandise that they love from around the world, and their store provides public access to the world treasures they find. In January 1994, they opened the first 800 square foot Dancing Cranes Imports, but soon outgrew the space. They moved to 2,000 square feet in 1995, to 7,000 square feet in 1997 and finally, in 2000, to their current 20,000 square foot store. Among the treasures that you will find at Dancing Cranes are clothing, jewelry, pottery, tapestries, fountains, incense, wind chimes, music and body care items. Dancing Crane Imports also offers inspiration in furniture, feng shui, lighting and ethnic art. 673 E. Simpson Avenue (2240 S), Salt Lake City UT (801) 486-1129

# Surroundings

Surroundings is one of Utah's finest treasures. Relaxation reigns the moment you enter the showroom. Creative lighting enhances the mood in the store and gives special effects to original paintings and artful vignettes. A variety of trees, palms, greenery and florals abound in dramatic sizes, shapes, and designs in exotic containers and distinctively unique vases. Plump upholstered pieces, accented with a rich collection of trims, allow you to invest in elegant, yet functional furnishings. A wealth of one-of-a-kind accessories fill the showroom or you might find a hand-painted piece that will set your home apart. David and Lucinda Cordova, Surroundings' owners, search marketplaces nationwide to carefully select the distinctive accessories, furniture and artwork that will please the aesthetic tastes of the discriminating homeowner. Their floral custom creations are unrivaled in Utah, have appeared in Architectural Digest and their custom creations are shipped throughout the country. Surroundings' exquisite gallery will dazzle you and surpass your expectations. The warm, friendly, helpful staff will make you feel right at home too. Come experience a garden of variety and fine taste at Surroundings.

6910 S Highland Drive, Salt Lake City UT

(801) 947-0888

www.surroundingsinc.com

# Adib's Rug Gallery

Adib's Rug Gallery is achieving a reputation among interior designers and Salt Lake City residents for its terrific selection of authentic and hard-to-find Persian and Oriental carpets. Importing directly from India, Pakistan, Turkey, Iran, China, Tibet, Caucusus, and other prime sources, Adib's offers a breathtaking variety of extraordinary designs and colors. The owner, Dr. Hamid Adib, has been selling high quality imported rugs to delighted clients for more than 27 years, with the past 19 years spent in Utah. The showroom in Salt Lake City is one-of-a-kind; it is open to the public, so feel free to stop by and view the displays even if you're not presently thinking of buying. Dr. Adib believes in letting the merchandise speak for itself in a pressure-free environment. The Gallery also offers services, including traditional hand washing and mothproofing, that ensure years of durability and beauty for each rug. If you have a carpet that needs work, the Gallery is one of the few locations where you can find museum-quality rug restorers. In many ways, Adib's is as much a museum as it is a store, a fascinating place not only buy but also to learn about the intricacies of these woven wonders.

3142 S Highland Drive, Salt Lake City UT
(801) 484-6364 or (888) 445-7874
www.adibs.com

# Quilter Candle Company

Soy candles are healthy candles. Leslie and Mike Quilter created the Quilter Candle, an environmentally safe, 100 percent non-toxic soy candle. The candle is a significant departure from paraffin candles. Paraffin is a by-product of petroleum distillation and emits 11 known toxins and carcinogens. Leslie first discovered the advantages of soy candles when she started looking for a candle that wouldn't leave a sooty residue on the walls. Soy wax, as she was delighted to discover, can be easily cleaned off with soap and water. As she looked into the differences between soy and paraffin, she discovered the harmful nature of paraffin versus the benign nature of soy. She also learned soy wax burns longer than paraffin. Plus using soy helps support American farmers. No wonder soy candles are gaining popularity. The Quilter Candle difference extends to fragrances used in the highly scented candles. The Quilters use over 50 different oils, all of the highest quality. Scents range from berries and flowers to pine forests and home-made cookies. Visit the Quilter Candle Company website to see a full range of products or place an online order.

7594 S 2700 W, Salt Lake City UT

(801) 561-1386

www.quiltercandles.com

# The Basket Loft

Trolley Square has been Salt Lake City's favorite shopping destination for decades, and The Basket Loft has been there since the beginning. While other stores have come and gone, Linda Beck's shop has stayed the course, though it has undergone a few changes: Linda originally called it Americana Mercantile. The name Basket Loft came about six years later. But don't let the name fool you into thinking there's nothing but baskets here. The Basket Loft carries housewares and other merchandise from over 1,000 different vendors. Home decorative items, dishes, kitchen linens, rugs, wall art, lamps, candles, bath products, plus collectibles, including Department 56, Jim Shore, and Williraye – if it belongs in a house, chances are Linda stocks it. The Basket Loft is also locally renowned for its diverse selection of holiday and seasonal merchandise, more than virtually any other local store. Its commitment to offering such a wide array of products and providing the best in customer service too has helped the Basket Loft expand from its original 255-square-foot space at Trolley Square to three stores in the Salt Lake area that total over 12,000 square feet. The other stores are located in Holladay Center and Foothill Village; pick any of the three to visit, and you'll see why this is more than just a store —it's a Salt Lake City tradition. The Basket Loft is well worth a visit.
219 Trolley Square, Salt Lake City, UT (801) 355-3343

# Twigs Flower Company

Where do you find The best roses in Utah? According to Salt Lake Magazine, they are at Twigs Flower Company in Salt Lake City. That draws a big smile from Twigs Owner Raymond, who, among other things, hands out 3,000 roses to benefit the Utah AIDS Walk each year. When not working with roses, Raymond and staff spend a lot of time on wedding floral arrangements and design, claiming more weddings than any shop in Utah. From the bridal bouquet to the pew, altar and candelabra decorations, with the table centerpieces and wedding cake decorations in between, Twigs Flower Company has the experience to do it all. Says Raymond, "Without the details, a wedding is just another day." Then of course, the shop has arrangements for everyday occasions, get-wells, plus sympathy, celebration, birthday creations and simply the best for your floral need. If it's floral, it's at Twigs Flower Company, where they will make something special just for you.
888 S 900 E Salt Lake City, UT
(801) 596-2322 or (800) 584-3122
www.twigsflowerco.com

# Home Again

One step into Home Again, and you quickly see why it is a Utah favorite. Home Again sells a wide range of furniture, rugs, dishes and other home furnishings on consignment. Home Again receives items regularly from a variety of sources including designers, design showrooms and local estates. Importers of Chinese, Indian and Thai goods also consign items to the store. Local artists, who create anything from benches to pillows, are a staple at Home Again. Other staple products are the custom Adirondack chairs and benches, available in custom sizes and colors at reasonable prices. Home Again also carries a selection of hand painted one-of-a-kind items made from recycled and found items. Discover sofas built using old doors, benches made from old headboards and bookshelves constructed out of old kitchen cupboards. The creativity will delight you. Home Again carries the national furniture brand Kincaid, a custom furniture line featuring a choice selection of over 100 fabrics. With items coming and going daily, Home Again never gets stale. And no matter the budget or style, Home Again has something for everyone.
1019 E 2100 S, Salt Lake City UT (801) 487-4668

160

# Bloomingsales

You are always welcome at Bloomingsales. For over 20 years, Bloomingsales has been recognized for fine imported and unique gifts, personal accessories, tabletops for home, sumptuous lines for body and bath, leather and silver gifts, selected and significant books, a charming children's collection, as well as fresh cut flower stems and orchid plants. Bloomingsales is synonymous with designer-type handbags, jewelry and personal accessories at attractive prices. Inventory is ever changing, specially selected and high quality, including the latest styles and classic traditional. Shoppers can find a generous selection of items, from delightful hats to stylish shoes plus a wide variety of personal care items, soaps and lotions, room fragrances and candles from some of the most respected manufacturers. Bloomingsales' home accessories include beautiful tabletop gifts, gorgeous vases, high quality and classic picture frames and clocks, table linens and welcoming doormats. Perfect presents for men, brides or new babies range from fine leather journals to sterling silver gifts. Shoppers can also find a delightful children's collection of specialized clothing, snuggly bedding and treasured children's book classics. The location in Foothill Village offers complimentary and convenient parking, unique gift-wrap and personal shopping attention. Near the University of Utah, Bloomingsales is a short distance from downtown Salt Lake City and easily accessible from mountain resorts.
1358 Foothill Drive, Salt Lake City UT   (801) 583-9117

# Elaine's Quilt Block

Walking in the door at Elaine's Quilt Block is just like visiting a trunk in your grandmother's attic. The colors, fabrics and displays in this amazing treasure will send your mind reeling with ideas for projects of your own. There are three incredible levels in this quilter's paradise. The top floor, which has a full display of quilt samples, is reserved for classes and quilting instruction. The middle level is filled with a huge selection of seasonal fabrics and almost anything else your heart desires. There is also a fantastic color wall that shows you the color choices of fabrics carried throughout the store. The basement is where you'll find a tremendous selection of baby, children's and 1920s fabrics. The store also carries the Kaffe Fassett line of fabrics for those with a more discriminating taste. Elaine's Quilt Block has a friendly, knowledgeable team who can answer any question you can dream up. Classes are regularly offered for beginners through advanced instruction, and long-arm quilting is always available. With more than 15 instructors, you are sure to find a class that meets your individual needs. Even if you aren't a quilter, Elaine's has a plethora of visual delights that will inspire you to become one. If you've always wished you could create something beautiful for your family, Elaine's Quilt Block can help you make that dream become a reality.
6970 S 3000 East, Salt Lake City UT   (801) 947-9100
elainesquiltblock.com

# Salt Lake City Restaurants

## Stoneground Restaurant and Pub

As with anything Italian, Stoneground Restaurant and Pub has improved with age. The menu is a collection of secret family recipes, some updated with a modern twist, and new personal favorites that reflect the taste Owner Bob McCarthy. With an attention to detail, he has created simple, yet flavorful meals. You can choose from mouthwatering appetizers, unbelievable salads, like the signature house salad, classic sandwiches, hearty pasta dishes, or thin crust New York style pizza. For dessert, the chef has assembled a distinctive collection of 18 or so specialty pies, or you can build your own from an incredible list of fresh ingredients. Now if that's not enough to make you rush over, then a slice of their award-winning tiramisu definitely will. It is served atop a fresh crème anglaise and raspberry sauce. The dessert alone will keep you coming back for more. Stoneground is decorated in a subtle, yet classic Italian design with soft earth tones. Hints of Italian marble and brushed steel give it a sleek appeal. Stoneground Restaurant and Pub is available for private parties and catering, and sells its tiramisu for take home. Bob McCarthy ends each day as it began with the restaurant's themed tagline, "may the roof above us never fall in and the friends beneath it never fall out." Get your fill of friends and food tonight at Stoneground Restaurant and Pub.
249 E 400 South, 2nd floor, Salt Lake City UT   (801) 364-1368

## Pierre Country Bakery Café

For a soothing, quiet place to catch your breath while enjoying a lemon bar or sandwich with a cup of coffee, head for the Pierre Country Bakery Café in Salt Lake City. Here, Marsha and Brian Smith make all their goodies daily, never freeze their bread, never add sugar or preservatives and use no hydrogenated oils. As a testament to their popularity, their goods are sold throughout the area in restaurants, delis and supermarkets. At the bakery itself, you'll find lunch specials, soups, sandwiches and a full coffee bar. If matrimony is on your calendar, the Smiths can even bake you a wedding cake. For a quick trip in and out, just place your order online. In any case, don't miss the tasty treats at Pierre Country Bakery Café.
3239 E 3300 South, Salt Lake City UT
(801) 486-0900
www.pierrecountrybakery.com

162

# Siegfried's Delicatessen

You know you've got a great job when you love it so much that you buy the business! Daiva Stankyavichuys was the manager of Siegfried's Delicatessen down the block for 16 years before she bought it and moved it to its current location. Today, Daiva continues the tradition of preparing and serving the same authentic German home cooking that made the first Siegfried's legendary. In fact, Daiva has gone even further. She traveled all the way to Germany to refine her cooking techniques, learning first-hand how to make German sausage, chocolates, pickles and sauerkraut from scratch. If genuine German cooking has spoiled you, there's no place in Utah to go but Siegfried's. Everything is made fresh daily with only the finest ingredients. Diners enjoy dishes such as bratwurst, wiener schnitzel and leberkaese with sides of hot potato salad, rotkohl and the not to be missed buttery, handmade spaetzle. There are also shelves packed with imported delicacies you won't find anywhere else in the United States. This place is so steeped in German culture, a Deutschland tour guide recommended Siegfried's to homesick travelers sojourning abroad. If you don't have the time or the resources to travel to Europe, come to Siegfried's Delicatessen for a tantalizing slice of Germany.
20 W 200 South, Salt Lake City UT   (801) 355-3891

# Rodizio Grill

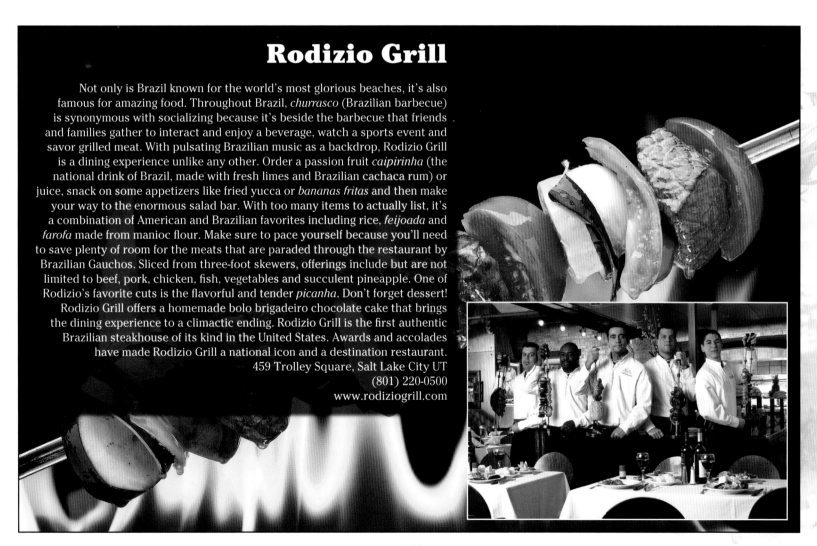

Not only is Brazil known for the world's most glorious beaches, it's also famous for amazing food. Throughout Brazil, *churrasco* (Brazilian barbecue) is synonymous with socializing because it's beside the barbecue that friends and families gather to interact and enjoy a beverage, watch a sports event and savor grilled meat. With pulsating Brazilian music as a backdrop, Rodizio Grill is a dining experience unlike any other. Order a passion fruit *caipirinha* (the national drink of Brazil, made with fresh limes and Brazilian cachaca rum) or juice, snack on some appetizers like fried yucca or *bananas fritas* and then make your way to the enormous salad bar. With too many items to actually list, it's a combination of American and Brazilian favorites including rice, *feijoada* and *farofa* made from manioc flour. Make sure to pace yourself because you'll need to save plenty of room for the meats that are paraded through the restaurant by Brazilian Gauchos. Sliced from three-foot skewers, offerings include but are not limited to beef, pork, chicken, fish, vegetables and succulent pineapple. One of Rodizio's favorite cuts is the flavorful and tender *picanha*. Don't forget dessert! Rodizio Grill offers a homemade bolo brigadeiro chocolate cake that brings the dining experience to a climactic ending. Rodizio Grill is the first authentic Brazilian steakhouse of its kind in the United States. Awards and accolades have made Rodizio Grill a national icon and a destination restaurant.
459 Trolley Square, Salt Lake City UT
(801) 220-0500
www.rodiziogrill.com

# Bohemian Brewery

Bohemian Brewery comes by its name honestly. Its founder Joseph Petras hails from Zlin in the present-day Czech Republic, the historical site of Bohemia. When Joe and his wife Helena settled in Utah in 1980, they couldn't speak a word of English, but they didn't let that stop them. Joe immediately found work, first as a busboy, then as a janitor. The Petras family's dedication paid off when they had enough money to open their first restaurant, Helen's, in 1992. It was Joe who, remembering the rich traditions of Czech beer, never lost sight of the dream to open his own brewery. He worked toward that goal and in April of 2002, Bohemian Brewery began production. Located in a building that once housed a sporting goods store, Bohemian Brewery produces four unique beers including a Pilsener, the beer most closely identified with Czechoslovakia. The brewery grill also offers a complete lunch and dinner menu specializing in Czech-Bavarian pub comfort food. Don't miss the display of vintage Vespa scooters upstairs, courtesy of Joe's son Pete who is Bohemian Brewery's director of marketing. Pete is a multi-talented fellow who also created the brewery's heraldic lion logo which prowls around on much of the Bohemian Brewery gear available on their website. For a true taste of Bohemia, visit the Bohemian Brewery in Salt Lake City.
94 E 7200 South (Fort Union Boulevard), Salt Lake City UT
(801) 566-5474   www.bohemianbrewery.com

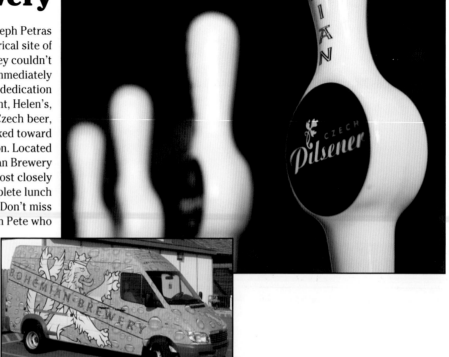

# Tuscany

Travelers looking for Alpine resort ambiance and delicious Italian food will find what they're looking for at Tuscany in Salt Lake City. The restaurant, located at the base of the Wasatch Mountains, specializes in Italian cooking influenced by the ingredients and cooking styles indigenous to the West. Specialties include wood oven roasted mussels in light tomato seafood cream, beef carpaccio with caper vinaigrette topped with shaved parmesan and a host of other mouthwatering delights. You'll find something here for all ages and tastes. Be sure to save room for delicious desserts, such as their tiramisu and old-fashioned chocolate cake served with vanilla bean gelato and chocolate sauce. It's all made in-house. Tuscany offers an award winning list of wines to accompany your dinner. During the summer months, diners can enjoy their feast on the beautiful outdoor patio. Those wanting a more private experience can enjoy drinks and cigars in Tuscany's Private Club. For European elegance and delicious food, take a trip to Tuscany.
2832 E 6200 S, Salt Lake City UT
(801) 277-9919   Group reservations: (801) 274-0448
www.tuscanyslc.com

# Vienna Bistro

Though Frody Volgger has worked around the world for 32 years as an award-winning chef and culinary authority, it's his home, the Austrian Alps, that still lingers in his voice, and now his restaurant. The Vienna Bistro brings that country's finest dishes to downtown Utah's historic business landmark, the Kearns Building. Frody's résumé reads similar to a who's who of the culinary industry: he opened the Lodge at Pebble Beach, The Depot in Park City and managed the opening and closing ceremony receptions for the 2002 Winter Olympics. You don't want to miss this opportunity to experience fine German fare lovingly made by a true native and master. Try some authentic Wienerschnitzel served with homemade tiny noodle Spåetzle, Semmelknödel bread and herb dumplings in mushroom cream sauce, or Jågerschnitzel (veal cutlets in a boar-bacon demi-glacé). This is a gourmet tour of a country's cuisine you're not likely to find anywhere else. The restaurant itself is lovely and the food is almost entirely handmade by Frody himself. The open kitchen creates an aura of soothing warmth between the local art on the walls and the beautiful light hardwood floors with contrasting cherry furniture. It's an effect that's both elegant and casually comfortable at the same time. The food is unbelievably delicious and the staff is delightful reminiscent of Frody. Come in and meet them all at Vienna Bistro.
132 S Main Street, Salt Lake City UT   (801) 322-0334   www.viennabistro.com

# Restaurant Panache/Fresh Air Cafe by Panache

When patrons enter the lobby of the landmark Wells Fargo Center, they are rarely prepared for the beauty and culinary treasures that lie within. Upon reaching the second floor, the Panache logo assures them they have arrived into an area of gastronomic sophistication and delight. To the right of the logo, through a bright red entry, you will find the Fresh Air Cafe by Panache. Lively and exuberant, the cafe is designed for those who insist on high-quality dining, but suffer from time constraints. However, Panache would never mistake informal for ordinary. The Fresh Air Cafe is anything but, using only the highest quality, seasonal and organically raised foodstuffs, to prepare the extensive selection of salads, soups,

sandwiches, specials and bakery items. Take the wood paneled entry to the left, follow the soft music down a well-lit hallway and you will find something quite unexpected. Greeted by soul-warming aromas and even warmer smiles, you'll be instantly aware you've entered a special place, the world of Restaurant Panache. The marble floors, soft woods, original art and ample light, immediately create an Italian garden room. Fresh flowers and greenery abound, while four, floor-to-ceiling, double-glass doors take the eye to the 2000-square-foot deck that gives an impression of spaciousness as it overlooks the beautiful Gallivan Center beyond. Food and service are the first priorities at Panache. Based upon a philosophy grounded in experience, the culinary team shares the belief that gourmet

is when things taste of what they really are. To that end, Chef Maxwell offers an ever-changing, diverse and eclectic menu, where the food elements are clarified, enhanced and thoughtfully combined. The name Panache has become the passionate embodiment of the continual search for the finest of ingredients, prepared with appreciation and artistry, and served with a sense of hospitality and flare. Experience the difference at Restaurant Panache and Fresh Air Cafe by Panache.
299 S Main (2nd Floor), Salt Lake City UT
(801) 254-6322
www.panache.net

# Panache Wine and Tapas Bar

The Panache Wine and Tapas Bar is not just another private club. A true wine bar welcomes food and wine lovers at all experience levels into a comfortable and relaxing atmosphere. It is a place where they might discover something new, or simply enjoy a glass of wine and escape the stress of life. Located on the second floor of the Wells Fargo Center, this stunning space was created with the wine lover in mind. Contemporary in design, softened by warm woods and bathed in atrium light, the environment is ideal for wine appreciation. Even the artwork harkens back to Paris and the Belle Epoque, a golden time of beauty and innovation when the cultural scene thrived. A focal point of the club is the wood-burning oven which sits as a backdrop for the tapas bar. In keeping with Panache's focus on the experience and enjoyment of flavor, food is given equal billing with the wine program. Diverse and ever-changing, the menu features a variety of small-plate offerings, including hot and cold tapas, unique wood fired pizzettis, small batch soups, demi-trios, artisan cheeses and superb deserts. Equally diverse, the wine list is drawn from selections from around the world, based upon flavor profiles rather than expense or point score. Many of the wines are not found elsewhere in the state. You are invited to taste, learn about and experience these discovery wines in their proper context at Panache. Not into wine? The Panache Wine and Tapas Bar also offers a carefully chosen selection of spirits, classic cocktails, beer and non-alcoholic beverages.  While the Panache Wine and Tapas Bar is a non-smoking club, a separate, fully-contained and ventilated Cigar Room is available. It's stocked with some of the world's finest cigars to be enjoyed with their perfect beverage pairing. Should you be seeking a no-pretense atmosphere to indulge your passion for the harmonious interplay of flavors between glass and table, you are invited to come for the wines of the vintage, and stay for the foods of the season, at Panache Wine and Tapas Bar.

299 S Main Street (2nd Floor), Salt Lake City UT
(801) 254-2707
www.panache.net

# Michelangelo Ristorante

Scott Ashley of Michelangelo Ristorante got his start in the restaurant business in the dish room. Soon thereafter, he began working his way up the kitchen ranks in California, Oregon and Utah eateries. More than 15 years later, Scott is now the chef and owner of Michelangelo Ristorante. He took over the restaurant from Poalo Celeste and Marco Gabrielli, who, after nine years of cooking and serving, established a standard of quality and authenticity on the Italian food scene that the people of Salt Lake City had never before tasted. Scott and the staff of Michelangelo Ristorante have continued the concepts and beliefs of true Italian cuisine. Fresh local ingredients served unpretentiously, in season keep the food the main focus of the restaurant. Dishes such as Scott's signature gnocchi, risotto and spaghetti have been hailed as some of the best pasta in the country. A favorite with visitors and locals alike, this neighborhood restaurant in the Sugarhouse district is a Salt Lake City gem.

2156 S Highland Drive, Salt Lake City UT

(801) 466-0961

www.michelangeloristorante.com

# Porcupine Pub & Grille

Start with one-third pound of grilled beef, add bacon, sautéed red onions, barbecue sauce, cheddar and Swiss cheese, lettuce, tomato and herbed aioli. Serve it up on a floured sourdough or spent grain bun. Can you taste it yet? It's called the Big Cottonwood Burger, and it's one of the specialties at the Porcupine Pub and Grille in Salt Lake City. If you're in the mood for a salad, this grille can treat you to baby greens tossed in balsamic vinaigrette with juicy pear slices, blue cheese, fire-dried pecans and mandarin oranges. When you're ready for dessert, try the chocolate porcupine: chocolate cake filled with chocolate mousse, then dipped in milk chocolate and served with almonds for quills and vanilla bean ice cream. This sort of delight has won broad acclaim for the Porcupine from many sources. The *Wasatch Sports Guide* named it Best Apré-Ski restaurant and the *Salt Lake City Weekly* honored it for Best Kid's Dessert. Libations are available and include no fewer than 24 draft beers, many of them from local micros. At Porcupine Pub & Grille, the décor is a cross between urban warehouse and mountain cabin. All sorts of folks from around Salt Lake and the country have enjoyed the atmosphere, including the spectacular mountain and valley views, and now it's your turn.

3698 E. Fort Union Boulevard, Salt Lake City UT

(801) 942-5555

www.porcupinepub.com

# The Dodo Restaurant

Serving Salt Lake City since 1981, The Dodo Restaurant celebrates its 25th anniversary in 2006. This American bistro offers homemade soups, house-smoked turkey and ham, delicious pastas, salads and irresistible appetizers like baked artichoke pie. A key to Dodo's longtime success is Ramon Montelongo, an award-winning pastry chef who has been tempting the sweet tooth of Utah diners for over two decades. Ramon's homemade specialty desserts are baked fresh daily and available by the slice or whole. Choose from key lime pie, Toll House pie, lemon chess tart, chocolate mousse pie and more mouthwatering selections. A *Salt Lake Magazine* writer said, "This Classic American Bistro is a must stop and the best Utah has to offer."
152 S 400 W, Salt Lake City UT
(801) 456-BIRD (2473)
www.thedodo.net

# Red Iguana

For great Mexican food in Salt Lake City, the Red Iguana is the place to be. Ramon Cardenas Sr. and daughter Lucy oversee the preparation of delicious family recipes from all regions of Mexico. Look for specialties from the north and the south, from burritos to mole sauces. The Cardenas family started in the restaurant business in the Salt Lake region over four decades ago. The food has wide-ranging popularity, from the mayor to the governor, from the grandmother to the truck driver.

Ramon, born in San Luis Potosi, and his wife Maria, born in Chihuahua, shared a passion for Mexican cuisine and created recipes that served as rich expressions of their cultural background. Maria passed away in 2002; their son, Ramon Cardenas Jr., executive chef and a beloved and colorful presence in the Salt Lake Valley, passed away in 2004, leaving Lucy, Ramon Sr. and their dedicated staff to carry on the tradition of serving new generations of customers. The restaurant has garnered many honors over the years. The staff of *City Weekly* named The Red Iguana Best Mexican restaurant, noting that "Despite new Mexican eateries proliferating along the Wasatch more rapidly than potholes and Starbucks, North Temple institution Red Iguana remains king. You couldn't go wrong with this menu if you tried."
Convinced? Your table is waiting.
736 W North Temple, Salt Lake City, UT (801) 322-1489
www.rediguana.com

# Log Haven

Today Log Haven thrives, but against the odds. In 1920, a steel baron from Salt Lake City created this palatial residence in Millcreek Canyon as an anniversary gift for his wife. They built it in the log-cabin style, and it came to be known as Log Haven. In 1958, Log Haven was converted into a restaurant, and though it enjoyed many years of success, it was bankrupt by the 1980s. When Margo Provost and her husband Wayne acquired it in 1994, it was in danger of being demolished. With no previous experience as a restaurateur, Margo battled the odds to restore Log Haven to its former glory, and she succeeded, earning awards from *Working Woman* magazine, Merrill Lynch, Avon and many restaurant organizations in the process. Executive Chef David Jones oversees a menu of exotic international delicacies and a wine list that is second to none. General Manager Ian Campbell ensures that the atmosphere at Log Haven is warm and welcoming. Together, Margo, David and Ian work to make your experience at the restaurant as memorable and delightful as the beautiful wilderness setting with its pines, waterfalls and wildflowers. Log Haven is a place to create cherished memories. 6451 E 3800 S, (4 miles up Millcreek Canyon), Salt Lake City UT   (801) 272-8255 www.log-haven.com

# Petrone's Pazzo Vita Deli & Market

Frank and Kamarie Petrone call their Salt Lake City deli and market Petrone's Pazzo Vita, meaning "Petron's crazy life." The name is intended to reflect their particular style and flare in both food and gifts. Petrone's has an industrial look with exposed air vents and high vaulted ceilings. The restored 50-year-old grocery market offers specialty foods and gift items, including a large assortment of oils, spreads, vinegars and deli selections. Frank has been a butcher for 30 years and offers a wide variety of store-made Italian sausage and New York style chicken cutlets. The food is usually prepared from family recipes in the East Coast style, but you can order it any way you choose. When you are satisfied but smacking your lips for more, look into take-home items like the Crazy for Chocolate basket with Belgian chocolate-covered cinnamon biscuits, dark chocolate-covered butter cookies, Italian biscotti and cocoa from Holland. If that's not enough, the basket holds chocolate bars made by Toblerone, Ritter Sport, Perugina and Lindt. Check out the Manga Manga or Office Party baskets as well. One way or another, get crazy; you have Frank and Kamarie's permission.

2005 E 2700 S, #A2, Salt Lake City UT
(801) 485-7299   www.pazzodeli.com

*Salt Lake City Dining*

171

# Salt Lake City Galleries and Art

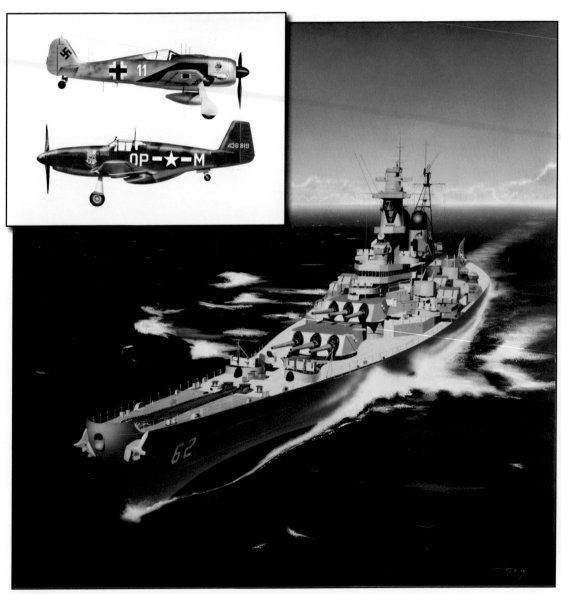

## C.S. Bailey Studios

For aviation and naval art, there is no gallery that compares to C.S. Bailey Studios in Salt Lake City. With prints ranging from modern aircraft to World War II ships, C.S. Bailey Studios is indeed an amazing experience. Owner Chad Bailey, who goes by 'Chuck', paints most of the artwork on display using a technique known as airbrush. "If it flies or floats, I paint it," he says. He's been airbrushing for 25 years, and it shows in the realism, accuracy and precision of his work. A Utah native, Chuck teaches high school in Salt Lake City and also teaches airbrush techniques in his studio. With degrees in both fine arts and education, he is more than happy to share his knowledge with everyone from casual art connoisseurs to hardcore aviation art fanatics. Besides airbrush, he also paints with traditional paintbrushes and acrylics. He can paint just about anything, including Giclee reproductions, original artwork and commissions. In fact, he was commissioned to produce the Great Seal of the Governor of Utah. The United States Air Force also selected him as one of its aviation artists. For a realistic trip through aviation and naval history via art, visit C.S. Bailey Studios. 2066 Greenbriar Circle, Salt Lake City UT (801) 278-3647
www.airartcsbailey.com

# Palmers Gallery

For high-quality photography of the natural splendors of Utah and the West plus finely crafted original artwork by area artists, head for Palmers Gallery with two locations to serve you, in Trolley Square or the contemporary Salt Lake Design Center. Palmers Gallery features the work of photographer Aaron Goldenberg, who is dedicated to preserving the splendor of Western beauty while minimizing any disturbance to it. Aaron, a native of New York, relocated to the West in 1987 to fulfill his dream of landscape photography and the preservation of nature. Discover more about his environmental promise at www.wildearthimages. com. The gallery is owned by Darren Palmer, originally from Boston, and managed by Shawn Stradley, a poet and native of Salt Lake City. Their combined efforts create an extraordinary collection of original photography, artwork, sculpture and glass. Look for the acrylic work of Stephanie St. Thomas, the sculptural and utilitarian forms of Scott Roach, Todd Wesley Greenig and David Lecheminant, and the vibrant glasswork of Ken and Ingrid Hansen, plus many others. The collection includes both traditional and contemporary oil and acrylic paintings by such artists as Pilar Pobil, Shawn Rossiter and Chase Lesley, to name a few. Exhibits are ever-changing and range from oil, acrylic and watercolor paintings to photography, creative home furnishings, silk florals, sculpture and blown glass. Palmers Gallery also specializes in custom framing.

378 W Broadway, Ste 3, Salt Lake City UT
606 Trolley Square, Salt Lake City UT
(801) 532-6952 or (800) 353-9866 www.palmersgallery.com

*Scott Roach*

*Ken and Ingrid Hansen*

# Anthony's Antiques & Fine Arts

Visiting Anthony's Antiques & Fine Arts for the first time, you might suspect that this 24,000-square-foot Georgian revival church built in 1915 houses a good size antique mall or at least a collective of several dealers. There is, in fact, only one dealer here, and this is an antique and art gallery the likes of which are not to be found even in the large metropolitan areas of our country. Owner Anthony Christensen spends several weeks each year traveling in Western Europe to find the best merchandise at the best price. Years of buying this way have built an amazing inventory of high quality French, Italian and other continental European furniture, architectural elements and decorative art. This inventory includes a large selection of French country, Tuscan and Spanish colonial antiques. The gallery also boasts over 400 original works of art from 17th to 20th century Western European artists, Russian artists, American and local pioneer artists, the majority of which are oil paintings. Anthony's Antiques & Fine Arts invites you to come and enjoy a true antique- and art-shopping experience.
401 E 200 S, Salt Lake City UT (801) 328-2231

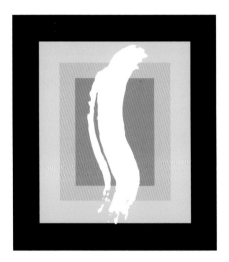

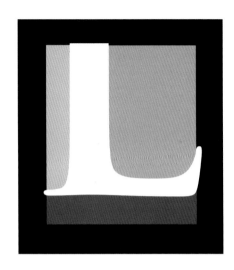

# Salt Lake Gallery Association

*P.O. Box 2812*
*Salt Lake City, Utah 84110*
*801.533.3582*
*www.gallerystroll.org*

The Salt Lake Gallery Association is a partnership of independently owned and operated art galleries, art-related businesses and sponsors, created to provide a unified voice on issues of mutual concern within the local visual arts community.

The Salt Lake Gallery Association hosts a public Gallery Stroll event the third Friday of every month. Gallery Stroll is a fun and informal opportunity for the public to visit galleries after normal business hours and experience the wide variety of fine art represented by our members. There is always something of interest for everyone from traditional, to contemporary and cutting edge.

Gallery Stroll is the 3rd Friday of every month from 6 to 9 pm

Bring Friends.
Meet Artists.
Take Home a Masterpiece.

***BE PART OF ART.***

# A Gallery

*1321 South 2100 East*
*Salt Lake City, UT 84108*
*Monday through Saturday 10 am - 6 pm*
*801.583.4800*
*www.agalleryonline.com*

This well established, full service gallery enters its third decade in a new, larger location. Featuring over 7,000 square feet of exhibition space (including a sculpture garden), "A" Gallery offers a dynamic collection of local, regional and international fine art in a striking setting. Studio "a" features an exceptional collection of fine crafts, including glass, ceramics and sculptural objects.

# Alice Gallery at the Glendinning Home

*617 East South Temple*
*Salt Lake City, UT 84102*
*Monday through Friday 9 am - 5 pm*
*801.236.7555*
*www.arts.utah.gov*

The Utah Arts Council's main offices reside at the Glendinning Home next to the Governor's Mansion on South Temple. The Alice Gallery is named after Alice Merrill Horne, who founded the Utah Arts Council in 1899. The gallery exhibits work from the Utah Arts Council Collection and a variety of group shows featuring artists from Utah.

# Art Access Gallery

*339 West Pierpont Avenue*
*Salt Lake City, UT 84101*
*Monday through Friday 10 am - 5 pm*
*Phone/TTY: 801.328.0703*
*www.accessart.org*

The nonprofit Art Access Gallery, located in the eclectic warehouse district of Salt Lake City, shows the work of established and emerging contemporary artists, both with and without disabilities. In addition to changing exhibitions, the gallery offers workshops for adults and teens, as well as mentoring opportunities.

# Brushworks Gallery

*call for information*
*801.363.0600*

The Brushworks Gallery was founded in 1976 and since has shown a wide variety of contemporary and traditional artists. Featuring oils and watercolors from local artists such as: John and Gary Collins, Richard Murray, Karl Thomas, Graydon Foulger, Kathleen Peterson, Ian Ramsay, Arlo Johnson, Ken Baxter and Linda Budd, Brushworks continues this tradition. Brushworks also offers custom framing, including specialty mat work and moldings.

# Chroma Gallery

*1064 East 2100 South*
*Salt Lake City, UT 84106*
*Wednesday through Saturday 2 - 6 pm*
*801.652.6963*

Located in the heart of Sugarhouse, Chroma Gallery proudly offers a variety of contemporary paintings and sculptures. We are committed to showing and selling high quality artworks throughout the year. We ship and offer all placement services.

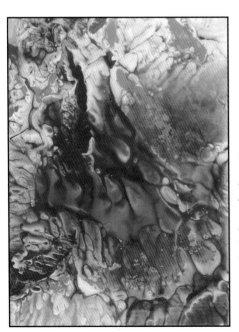

# Contemporary Design and Art Gallery

*30 East Broadway (300 South) #105*
*Salt Lake City, UT 84111*
*Tuesday through Friday 4 - 8 pm, Saturday 11am - 3 pm,*
*Sunday 12 - 5 pm*
*801.364.0200*
*www.newart4utah.com*

Contemporary Design and Art Gallery, located in downtown SLC, represents all contemporary movements in fine arts and interior design. We carry only original art, decorative objects, and designs from local, national, and international artists. Our mission is to bring new artists to SLC and represent emerging local artists. Stop by. There are always new works to see and experience art in a striking setting.

# E Street Gallery

*82 "E" Street*
*Salt Lake City, UT 84103*
*Tuesday through Saturday 10 am - 6 pm*
*801.359.2979*

Located in the Avenues, the E Street Gallery features works of art from oil painting to handcrafted furniture. Ceramics, glass, mosaics, jewelry, turned and carved wood, textiles and rugs as well as collectibles and gift items can be found in the gallery's historic 1909 building. "The art of living, defined."

# Evergreen Framing Co. & Gallery, Inc.

*3295 South 2000 East*
*Salt Lake City, UT 84109*
*Monday through Friday 9:30 am - 6 pm,*
*Saturday 10 - 5 or by appointment*
*801.467.877*

Evergreen Framing Co. & Gallery, Inc., established in 1985, is located in the Millcreek neighborhood. Evergreen exhibits original art with an emphasis on Utah artists and offers a selection of fine art prints, unique gifts and jewelry, as well as full service custom framing with an experienced design staff.

# F.Weixler Gallery

*132 "E" Street*
*Salt Lake City, UT 84103*
*Monday through Friday 9 am - 5 pm,*
*Saturday by appointment*
*801.534.1014*

Located in the historic Avenues area, F. Weixler Co. features a diverse selection of contemporary and early Utah artists as well as custom-made furniture pieces. Featured in the showroom are paintings and sculptures by a variety of artists including Valoy Eaton, Harrison Groutage, Kimbal Warren, Karl Thomas, Richard Murray, Earl Jones, Frank Huff, Clark Bronson and Dennis Smith.

# Finch Lane Gallery at the Art Barn

*54 Finch Lane (1325 East 100 South)*
*Salt Lake City, UT 84102*
*Monday through Friday 8:30 am - 5 pm*
*801.596.5000*
*www.slcgov.com/arts*

The Art Barn, located in Reservoir Park near the University of Utah, is the home of the Finch Lane and Park Galleries. Contemporary work by local artists is exhibited year-round. Built in the early 1930s as a WPA project, the Art Barn is a gathering place for the community as well as headquarters for the Salt Lake City Arts Council.

# HORNE Fine Art

*142 East 800 South*
*Salt Lake City, UT 84111*
*Call for hours or to schedule a visit*
*801.533.4200*
*www.hornefineart.com*

HORNE Fine Art continues a family legacy in the arts started by Alice Merrill Horne in 1899. The gallery offers "depth of talent" from "both emerging painters and arts veterans." Works are presented in "thematic exhibits that fuse the finest in both traditional and modern styles." Come visit this "rich asset for the Salt Lake community."

# Local Colors Artworks

*570 South 700 East*
*Salt Lake City, UT 84102*
*Monday through Saturday 10 am - 6 pm,*
*Sunday 12 - 6 pm*
*801.531.6966*

Visit Utah's largest co-operative gallery featuring the works of 40+ local artists. Located in historic Trolley Square, works include painting, pottery, photography, jewelry, glass, textiles and sculpture. With ever-changing displays, if you haven't seen us this month, you have not seen us.

# Magpies' Nest Gallery

*Corner of I Street & First Avenue*
*Salt Lake City, Utah 84103*
*Tuesday through Friday 12 - 6 pm,*
*Saturday 12 - 5 pm*
*801.363.7764*
*www.magpiegallery.com*

Magpies' Nest Gallery features the work of many outstanding Utah artists. Located in the historic Avenues district (one block north of 700 East and South Temple), Magpies' Nest features traditional and contemporary oils and watercolors, custom framing, antiques, glass and jewelry.

# Main Street Gallery

*299 South Main Street*
*Wells Fargo Building Lobby*
*Salt Lake City, UT 84111*
*By appointment  801.535.4660*
*www.mainstreetgallery.us*

The Main Street Gallery, located downtown in the lobby of the Wells Fargo Building, is the exclusive Salt Lake location for original impressionist art by Kent Wallis, Scott Wallis and Eric Wallis. We also feature original oil paintings by prominent local artists Sandra Rast and Court Naumann. The artwork of Main Street Gallery will enhance any home, office, or private collection.

# Michael Berry Gallery

*754 East South Temple*
*Salt Lake City, UT 84102*
*Monday through Saturday 9 am - 6 pm*
*801.521.0243*

Michael Berry has provided preservation framing for artists and collectors since 1988. Now, at his new gallery on South Temple, watch for monthly shows opening on Gallery Stroll night, featuring some of Utah's best artists including Pilar Pobil, Willamarie Huelskamp, Rebecca Livermore, as well as other contemporary artists and special exhibts.

# Museum of Utah Art & History

*125 South Main Street*
*Salt Lake City, UT 84111*
*Tuesday through Sunday 11 am - 3 pm*
*801.355.5554*
*www.muahnet.com*

The Museum of Utah Art & History (MUAH), draws its exhibitions from the collections of the Utah State Historical Society, the Utah Arts Council, and the Utah State Archives. Exhibitions change every few months, giving visitors a new experience with each visit. MUAH is an exciting venue for corporate dinners, receptions, and weddings because of its beautiful interior and downtown location.

# One Modern Art

*1074 East 2100 South*
*Salt Lake City, UT 84106*
*Wednesday through Saturday 12 - 6 pm*
*801.599.2087*
*www.onemodernart.com*

One Modern Art is Utah's only gallery devoted exclusively to abstract art, established to showcase the work of John Bell who is emerging as one of the area's most prominent abstract artists. Experience a New York style gallery & world-class art. Voted "Best Modern Art Gallery 2005" by *City Weekly*.

# Patrick Moore Gallery

*511 West 200 South*
*Salt Lake City, UT 84101*
*Wednesday through Saturday 12 - 5 pm*
*and by appointment*
*801.521.5999*
*www.patrickmooregallery.com*

Located in the Artspace Bridge Projects, winner of the 2001 American Institute of Architects Utah Merit Award, the Patrick Moore Gallery offers 4,500 square feet of exhibition and event space.

# Phillips Gallery

*444 East 200 South*
*Salt Lake City, UT 84111*
*Tuesday through Friday 10 am - 6 pm, Saturday 10 - 4 pm*
*801.364.8284*
*www.phillips-gallery.com*

Established in 1965, Phillips Gallery represents regional artists working in traditional to contemporary styles in all media. Phillips Gallery participates in monthly strolls and hosts ten exhibits each year with three floors of exhibit space. The gallery provides art services including consulting, installation, art leasing, payment plans and shipping as well as an adjacent artist supply and professional frame shop.

# Red Kiln Gallery

*393 East 1700 South*
*Salt Lake City, UT 84115*
*Tuesday through Saturday 12 - 6 pm*
*801.484.4016*

Established in 1994, the Red Kiln Gallery regularly features 12 Utah artists in sculptural and functional forms. Red Kiln hosts exhibitions of ceramic art in our newly remodeled gallery and we feature work in every price range. Our teaching studio has evening classes for all ability levels. Red Kiln also rents studio space for artists.

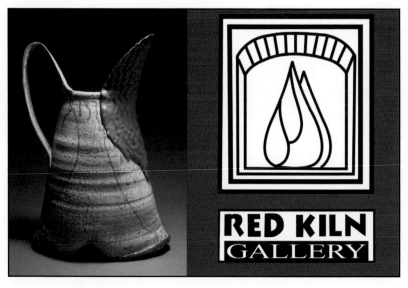

# Rio Gallery

*1300 South Rio Grande Street (455 West)*
*Salt Lake City, UT 84101*
*Monday through Friday 9 am - 5 pm*
*801.533.3582*
*www.arts.utah.gov*

The Utah Arts Council's Rio Gallery is located in the lobby of the Historic Rio Grande Depot. The gallery exhibits group shows including the UAC Fellowship Exhibition, Artist Grantees Showcase, Design Arts Exhibit and Statewide Annual Exhibit. The Rio Gallery is dedicated to promoting emerging contemporary artists as well as established artists by providing a common forum for display.

# Salt Lake Art Center

*20 South West Temple*
*Salt Lake City, UT 84101*
*Tuesday through Thursday 11 am - 6pm*
*Friday 11 am - 9 pm, Saturday 12 am - 6 pm*
*801.328.4201*
*www.slartcenter.org*

The Salt Lake Art Center is dedicated to contemporary art, artists and issues, presenting exhibits which are thought provoking and socially relevant. Art Talks (informal gallery talks by artists, curators and others) are presented year-round. The Orientation Gallery offers Internet research stations, and a book store.

# Southam Gallery

*50 East Broadway (300 South)*
*Salt Lake City, UT 84111*
*Tuesday through Saturday 12 - 5:30 pm*
*or by appointment*
*801.322.0376 or 801.712.5170*

Established in 1982, Southam Gallery represents many renowned Utah artists. We specialize in the American Landscape with styles ranging from realism and impressionism to abstraction. The staff includes an artist and art historian, experts in providing professional advice for private and corporate collections.

# The Unknown Gallery, LLC

*353 West 200 South*
*Salt Lake City, UT 84101*
*Tuesday through Saturday 12 - 7 pm*
*801.521.4721 (toll free) 866.521.4721*
*www.unkgallery.com*

The Unknown Gallery features the artwork of new and emerging artists; including outsider, lowbrow, pop surrealism, and street art from around the world. Join us each month for our live dj spinning records and fantasy fashion models. We offer new, progressive art by changing the gallery's offerings each month with a distinctive, urban feel.

# UTahArtistHands

*61 West 100 South*
*Salt Lake City, UT 84101*
*Monday through Friday 12 - 7 pm,*
*Saturday 12 - 5 pm*
*801.355.0206*
*www.utahands.com*

UTahArtistsHands brings together fine artists and crafters, all exclusively from Utah. You will find oil paintings, acrylics, watercolors and pastels as well as a large selection of fine photography, pottery and sculpture, carved and turned wood, fused and blown glass, leatherwork and jewelry in this most unique gallery.

# Wasatch Frame Shop

*51940 South 1100 East*
*Salt Lake City, UT 84106*
*Tuesday through Saturday 10 am - 5:30 pm*
*801.485.1353*
*www.wasatchframeshop.com*

Art is an expression unique to each person. At Wasatch Frame Shop we strive to celebrate this through artists and exceptional people who are passionate about what they do. Come join the family of friends at Wasatch Frame Shop and see what makes us different. We provide custom framing and the knowledge to choose the appropriate way to preserve your artwork.

# Williams Fine Art

*Eagle Gate Plaza (Lobby)*
*60 East South Temple*
*Salt Lake City, UT 84111*
*Monday through Friday 12 - 5 pm*
*801.534.0331*
*www.williamsfineart.com*

Established in 1988, Williams Fine Art is Utah's premiere art gallery specializing in the sale of the works of early Utah artists, many well-established contemporary painters, and paintings by outstanding Russian artists. Appraisal service is provided for early Utah art. Look to Williams Fine Art, profiled in *Architectural Digest* magazine, for the rare, the historical and the finest. video library for on-site use.

# 3W Gallery at W Communications

*159 West Broadway (300 South) #200*
*Salt Lake City, UT 84101*
*Monday through Friday 9 am - 5 pm and Gallery Stroll*
*801.983.9266*
*www.letter23.com*

3W Gallery at W Communications will curate and host quarterly exhibits in its street-front lobby space as part of the downtown gallery stroll. 3W gallery showcases a variety of mediums from primarily local artists. W is a full-service advertising, public relations and marketing firm that is committed to supporting the arts and the community.

# Ken Sanders Rare Books & Gallery

*268 South 200 East*
*Salt Lake City, UT 84111*
*Monday through Saturday 10 am - 6 pm*
*801.521.3819*
*www.kensandersbooks.com*

Our bookshop maintains a separate gallery space and offers a selection of antique prints, photographs, maps, and artwork in addition to over 100,000 used, rare and antiquarian book volumes in all fields. We have Leatherbound sets, classics of literature, art, photography, architecture, children's and illustrated books, etc. Additionally we produce 6-8 major art shows and exhibitions annually.

OBJECT
247 EAST 900 SOUTH
SALT LAKE CITY, UT. 84111

Rockwell Kent, *Drifter*, 1933
Wood Engraving on Maple

www.object-gallery.com

# Object Gallery

*247 East 900 South*
*Salt Lake City, UT 84111*
*Saturday 10 am - 6 pm and by appointment*
*801.328.2306*
*www.object-gallery.com*

Object presents frequently changing exhibitions that celebrate objects as works of art. We specialize in collections of machine-age industrial design, contemporary art, WPA-era original art, radios, furniture, musical instruments, vintage hi-fi, rare periodicals and illustrated books from the period of 1910 to 1945. We buy, sell, trade and offer services of collection consultation and acquisition.

# Rose Wagner Art Gallery
# Salt Lake County Center for the Arts

*138 West Broadway (300 South)*
*Salt Lake City, UT 84101*
*Monday through Saturday 10 am - 5 pm*
*801.468.3517 or 801.323.4228*
*www.finearts.slco.org*

The Rose Wagner Art Gallery is located in the Rose Wagner Performing Arts Center. The Center features permanent works of public art and provides gallery space for emerging and established artists. Also see the Dale Chihuly Glass Sculpture "Olympic Tower" at Abravanel Hall (123 West South Temple) and Utah Art at the Salt Lake County Government Center (2001 South State Street).

# The Pickle Company

*741 South 400 West*
*Salt Lake City, UT 84101*
*Call for current gallery hours.  801.450.8977*
*www.thepicklecompany.org*

The Pickle Company, facilitated by TRASA urban arts collective, is a multidisciplinary arts center located in the industrial Granary District of downtown Salt Lake City. Built in the late 1800's, the 14,000 square-foot, restored pickle factory provides a dynamic, non-traditional setting for artists to develop, exhibit, and perform contemporary new work. The Pickle Company's studio facilities, combined with our unique exhibition and performance spaces, provide artists of all media the opportunity for in-depth exploration, collaboration, and risk.

# Trolley Square Galleries

*Historic Trolley Square*
*600 South 700 East*
*Salt Lake City, UT 84102*
*Monday through Saturday 10 am - 9 pm,*
*Sunday 12 - 5 pm*

Utah's Premier Festival Marketplace, offers a collection of art galleries, local and national shopkeepers and over a dozen of Salt Lake's favorite restaurants. What better way to spend your day? Fine art, great food and excellent shopping.

BE PART OF ART

# Central Utah

# Make-A-Wish Foundation

Five years after the Make-A-Wish Foundation was created to help children with life threatening illnesses realize their fondest wishes, a small group of volunteers founded the Utah chapter at Hill Air Force Base north of Salt Lake City. The first wish granted that year was to Debbie, who wanted more than anything to go to a private place where she could lie in the sun on a sandy beach and walk along the edge of the ocean. Debbie's wish came true when Delta Airlines contributed plane tickets, and a house was donated on a private beach in Maui. Since then, the Utah chapter has helped grant the wishes of many Utah children as well as children outside the state who have wishes that can be realized in the state. These wishes can be as diverse as meeting Karl Malone, watching the Jazz play at the Delta Center, digging for dinosaur bones, hearing the Mormon Tabernacle Choir or simply seeing snow for the first time. With a new office building dedicated in February 2004, the Utah Make-A-Wish Chapter continues to thrive, thanks to the generosity of businesses, foundations and individuals who have chosen to contribute their money and time. To find out how you can help, visit the website.
771 E Winchester, Murray UT (801) 262-9474 www.makeawishutah.org

# Day Murray Music Education House

Music is a basic law of life; it helps us live, love and learn. If you agree with that sentiment, you must visit Day Murray Music Education House in Murray, Utah. This business has been owned by the same family, dedicated to promoting your quality of life through music, since 1946. Started by John and Arlette Day, it is still in the original location and is now owned by Klint and Rosanne Day, with sons Adam and Jared helping. The Days' inventory of sheet and choral music is the largest in Utah, and they choose employees and instructors based on their interest and ability to provide good customer service. If they don't have what you need in stock, they will get it for you fast. The Days' motto is "Lasting Reputation; Reliable Destination." Within their walls, the Days house a warehouse full of music. The wide selection includes popular sheet music, plus choral, vocal, instrumental, classical, seasonal and educational music. Customers can also find piano benches, statuettes of composers and musical games. "Our vision," says Klint "is that through music we can assist individuals, families and friends to unite in a musical cause while building personal self-confidence and helping to create musical legacies for future generations."
4914 S State Street, Murray UT   (801) 266-3537 or (866) DAY-1946 (866-329-1946)
www.daymurraymusic.com

191

# Braza Grill Brazilian Steakhouse

If you're tired of the same old restaurant, get yourself to Braza Grill Brazilian Steakhouse to sample some of the finest recipes Brazilian cuisine has to offer. This mouthwatering array of food is sure to be a cultural inspiration for your appetite. Here the chefs create delicious meals from fresh ingredients and offer up to 10 kinds of meat. From top sirloin and lamb to pork, chicken and turkey, each one is cut and cooked to your order. You can enjoy frothy Brazilian strawberry limeade and tempting starters as you wait to build your own kabobs at the table. The Brazilian sampler appetizer is a wonderful introduction to this country's food, with chicken coxhinha, cheese risolis and essiha which are bread pockets stuffed with spiced beef. There's also a hot and cold salad bar with tempting selections such as meaty rice and fried bananas as well as traditional favorites. Meat is still the main order of the day, and meat is what one comes to a churrasco (Brazilian barbecue) restaurant for. The meat is sliced from a sizzling, skewered slab right there at your table. Of course, most appetites aren't big enough to try everything in one night, and that alone is sure to keep you coming back for more from the wonderful menu at Braza Grill Brazilian Steakhouse. For a mouth-watering taste of Brazilian barbecue, visit Braza Grill.

5927 S State, Murray UT   (801) 506-7788

http://salt-lake-services.com/Salt_Lake_City_Services/Brazilian_Restaurant_Salt_Lake/Braza_Grill.html

# Murray Arts Centre

Bill and Susan Wright, the couple who created the Murray Arts Centre, have been married for 45 years, and Susan has been teaching ballet for most of that time. Bill and Susan share a passion for ballroom dancing, and when they got the opportunity to convert a former Grand Central department store into a place where people could learn to dance, they couldn't pass it up. With 12,000 square feet of hardwood floor, the department store makes an outstanding ballroom, and it's more than a place where couples learn how to dance in the grand romantic style. Every Tuesday, Wednesday, Friday and Saturday night, live bands provide the music while couples show off the moves they've learned. You might think running the only ballroom dance location in Utah would be a sufficient accomplishment, but Bill and Susan aren't the types to rest on their laurels. Right across the street from the Arts Centre, the Wrights have opened the Dance Centre, where Friday and Saturday nights are set aside for swing dancing and line dancing. The Ballet Centre is right next-door, and if you need proper dancing attire, stop at Wright Costume and Dancewear, located next to the Arts Centre. Check out Bill and Susan's website to see the full range of services they offer—you'll be amazed!

4874 S State, Murray, UT   (801) 269-1400 or (801) 265-0707   www.wrightwayenterprises.com

"Marilyn Rising" (Loose Canvas)
11 ft. X 3 ft. Acrylic/Oil
Custom Made Fine Art
Portrait/Mural Artist:
Cathi Locati
President
Burnt Purple Corporation
Executive Director—Burnt Purple

# Burnt Purple

The artists of Burnt Purple are a dedicated group of people from all ages and walks of life who see the need for higher education in the business of art. Currently, Universities do not provide or require art business-specific classes to attain a Bachelor of Arts degree. In order for artists to become successful small business owners, they must be able to manage their own art business. Burnt Purple (501 (c) 3 non-profit) takes the starving out of artist by providing an avenue for visual artists to display their work in a retail setting and educates artists on art sales, marketing, accounting, advertising and specific knowledge aimed at managing the business of art. Artists of Burnt Purple learn how to sell the art product, how to market and advertise it and build a strong base for future generations to aspire to Artist as a chosen career field with quantifiable, certified base levels of education and quality levels of training. Since the artists of Burnt Purple set the fair market value price of their work instead of for-profit galleries doubling the price, you receive the half-off benefits whenever you purchase original art from Burnt Purple. Burnt Purple has 4,000 square feet of gallery space on the main floor of Cottonwood Mall in Holladay (4780 S Highland Drive, about 10 minutes south of SLC). The cooperative venture exists through membership dues from artists in all media, cash donations and grants, and sales from artwork. Cathi Locati, founder and executive director of Burnt Purple, holds a B.A. degree in Communications with an Art minor and has over 20 years direct sales and marketing director experience in the advertising and art world. She also is an internationally published professional portrait, mural and custom large format fine artist and the official artist of famed aerobatic pilot Julie Clark with two original Locati paintings slated

for future Smithsonian placement. If you value art and the contributions that artists make to the world, Burnt Purple welcomes your tax-deductible contributions (no amount is too large!) Fed. ID# 20-240-1400.
Mail contributions to:
4835 Highland Drive,
Holladay, Utah 84117.
(801) 604-4564
www.burntpurple.com

*Bradford Greene—Late Triassic*

*Jewelry Design by Philippa Graham*

194

***Provo Temple***

# Utah Olympic Park

The Utah Olympic Park was the competition venue for Nordic jumping and the sliding sports of bobsleigh, luge and skeleton during the 2002 Olympic Winter Games. The nearly 400-acre park features a mixture of sporting facilities and visitor areas for an incredible Olympic experience. The state-of-the art park hosted more than 300,000 visitors and 14 Olympic medal events in February 2002. The Utah Olympic Park now serves as a year-round competition and training ground for recreational and high-performance athletes. The Park is one of two Olympic legacy facilities operated by the Utah Athletic Foundation, joining the Utah Olympic Oval. Visitors are treated to a guided tour of the park, athlete training sessions, 80 mile-per-hour bobsled rides, zipline rides and Quicksilver alpine slide rides. Additional attractions are the Olympic museum and an interactive museum, Freestyle aerial and ski jumping shows are on summer weekends and there is a variety of camps for all ages.

**Utah Olympic Park**
3000 Bear Hollow Drive, Park City UT
(435) 658-4200
www.olyparks.com

# Utah Olympic Oval

The Utah Olympic Oval was built to host the speed skating competitions during the 2002 Salt Lake Olympic Winter Games. Now it serves as a legacy to the State of Utah for all members of the community to enjoy. With an incredible 10 Olympic records and eight world records, the Utah Olympic Oval stands uncontested as the "Fastest Ice on Earth" following the 2002 Olympic Winter Games. The Utah Olympic Oval facility consists of five acres under a clear span suspension roof. Housed within it are a 400-meter speed skating oval, two international size ice sheets, indoor soccer field, a four-lane 442-meter state of the art running track, eight 110-meter sprint lanes, high performance weight room, spacious locker facilities and team rooms, World Record Lounge and meeting rooms, concession stands, Oval Gifts and Gear Pro Shop, skate rental and skate sharpening services are also available.

**Utah Olympic Oval**
5662 South 4800 West (Cougar Lane), Kearns UT
(801) 968-OVAL (6825)
www.olyparks.com

# Alf Engen Ski Museum

Thirteen years ago, Alan Engen had an idea for a ski museum. Today, visitors to the Utah Olympic Park can take a year-round, interactive journey through the Alf Engen Ski Museum inside the Joe Quinney Winter Sports Center. A tour through the 4,000-square foot museum includes a 10-minute film that traces Utah's ski history as well as evolutionary displays on cross-country skiing and Nordic jumping. There are games of skill in ski jumping and touch-screen displays. The Alf Engen Ski Museum was built to preserve the rich history of skiing in the Intermountain region by providing a world-class facility to highlight the many contributions made in ski area development, athletic competition, snow safety, ski innovation and ski teaching techniques.

# 2002 Eccles Olympic Winter Museum

The 2002 Eccles Olympic Museum is located on the second floor of the Joe Quinney Winter Sports Center. Detailed displays include the equipment used by athletes such as Joe Pack, Tristan Gale, Derek Parra, Bode Miller, Sarah Hughes during the 2002 Olympics. The public can hold an Olympic torch, watch Olympic highlights and view displays from the Opening and Closing ceremonies. Pin enthusiasts can admire a pin display which includes every officially licensed pin from the 2002 Winter Olympics.

# Summer and Winter Bobsled Rides

The Comet goes up to 80 miles per hour and lets you experience 5 G's of force, the equivalent of a 40-story drop, in just over a minute on this bobsled public passenger ride. An experienced driver takes three passengers on a thrilling ride down the entire length of the Olympic bobsled track. "The Comet" is available in both the summer and winter seasons. Riders must be 14 years old to ride the Comet in the summer and 16 years old to ride in the winter.

# Xtreme & Ultra Ziplines

If you are looking for the world's steepest zipline, you can only find it at the Utah Olympic Park. Go down the Xtreme Zip at 50 miles per hour along the K 120 ski jump hill or try the Ultra Zip along the winter freestyle hill. The zipline lets you experience the sensation of ski jumping while sitting in a harness and zip down a cable to the base of the ski jumps.

# Quicksilver—Alpine Slide

This European-style alpine slide is the first of its kind in North America. It is a state-of-the-art steel track which allows riders to weave down a narrow course that concludes at the base of the K-64 ski jump. See what it feels like to be a luge, skeleton or bobsled athlete!

# Introductory Sport Camps and Programs

The public can enroll in sport camps for all ages and ability levels in freestyle, skeleton, luge and ski jumping. One-day and multiple-day sessions provide hands on experience at Utah's Olympic playground. You can whoosh down the same track as Olympic gold medalists Jimmy Shea and Tristan Gale! In the skeleton camp you launch head first down the Olympic track just three inches above the ice, traveling at nearly 60 mph. Elite athletes and coaches teach you how to enter a banked corner, what the centrifugal force of three G's feels like and how the track is meticulously shaped and maintained.

The Utah Olympic Park also offers Adventure Camps for youth ages 8-14 that provide a once in a lifetime opportunity to try nine Olympic sports. Experienced coaches will provide each camper with expert instruction and proper equipment to try their skill at ice hockey, speed skating, luge, bobsled, ski jumping, biathlon, curling, freestyle and skeleton.

# Athletes In Action

Witness national and international competitions and watch aspiring youth and Olympic athletes in training year-round on the nordic jumps, freestyle hill, terrain park and bobsled, skeleton and luge track. Many high-performance athletes call the Utah Olympic Park their home. The United States Nordic combined team moved from Steamboat Springs, Colorado to Park City in the summer of 2002. Many freestyle aerialists, including Olympic medalists Joe Pack and Eric Bergoust, train throughout the summer in the splash pool, working on their maneuvers for the upcoming season. The sliding athletes in bobsled, luge and skeleton make multiple trips to the Park for training and competition. The United States ski jumpers also training regularly on the Olympic Nordic hills.

In addition to the Olympic-caliber athletes, many recreational, club and developmental athletes train and compete at the Utah Olympic Park in summer and winter. This combination of athletes, from novice to high performance, means that visitors will likely encounter athletes in training year-round when they visit the Park. The chance to watch aspiring youth and Olympic athletes in training is an exciting part of the Utah Olympic Park experience.

# Bobsleigh/Luge/Skeleton Track

The 1,335 meter, 8/10ths of a mile, track is one of the fastest in the world with athletes reaching speeds up to 90 miles per hour. This track is one of the only three competition-certified sliding facilities in North America.

### Bobsled

In the sport of bobsled, athletes use aerodynamic sleds to race against the clock on an ice-covered, serpentine course. Both men's and women's bobsled competitions include a two-person race, consisting of a driver and a brakeman. Men also compete in a four-man race, in which two other crew members, called push athletes, sit between the driver and the brakeman. Once the track is clear and the green start signal is activated, each team has 60 seconds to begin its run. The start push can make or break a race. Team members must be in top physical condition to sprint for about 164 feet, while pushing the sled from the starting clock to gain momentum.

### Luge

Sliders start in a sitting position on the sled, grasping metal handles fixed to the sides of the track rocking back and forth to maximize launching power. For about the first 16 feet, competitors paddle along the track using gloves with small fingertip or knuckle spikes to help grip the ice and increase momentum. As the sled picks up speed, the racers lie back, holding onto handles inside the sled, for maximum aerodynamics and speed. Raising one's head even slightly can greatly increase drag and slow the sled, so athletes must memorize the track. Athletes steer by pressing their calves inward against the front-runners and using the shoulders to press down toward the rear of the sled.

### Skeleton

The goal of skeleton is to race down the course in the fastest time, which means taking the quickest line down the track without hitting a wall. Athletes sprint from the block wearing shoes with spikes that grip the ice. At about the 164-foot mark, the sliders jump onto the sled, stomach down, with hands at their side. To steer the sled, racers shift the weight of their shoulders and knees, and at times drag a toe.

# Freestyle Skiing Hill/ Training Pool

The freestyle aerials training pool opened in July 1993, and is the summer training site for many world-class aerialists, including Olympic medalists Eric Bergoust and Joe Pack. The pool contains 750,000 gallons of water and is bubbled to soften the impact of landing and give athletes a point of reference. Freestyle aerials is a year-round sport at the Park. A winter freestyle hill and terrain park area is used for various competitions and training on snow. When the snow comes, kickers are built on the hillside between the Nordic jumps and splash pool. Freestyle athletes ski down an in-run to a steep ramp called a kicker, launch into the air more than 50 feet and spend three to four seconds performing a series of flips and twists before landing. A smooth landing is also important for a good score. In a single jump, men may execute up to three rotations and four twists and women up to three rotations and three twists. During the summer months, 30-minute freestyle aerial shows take place on Saturdays at noon.

# Nordic Jumps

The Nordic hills are the highest altitude jumps in the world at an elevation of 7,310 feet above sea level. A total of six nordic jumps have been built at the park with a K10, K20, K40, K64, K90, and K120. Plastic runways on the jumps and landing zones allow for summer jumping. Ski jumpers fly up to 55 miles per hour and cover distances as great as one and a half football fields. During the in-run, the athlete bends forward, with the chest over the thighs and arms back at the sides. In flight, the skier leans forward with legs unbent and skis in a V position. Skiers land in the telemark position, one leg in front of the other, with bent knees to absorb the impact. The athlete must maintain control until passing the fall line five meters beyond the point where level ground begins.

# Group and Event Planning

The Utah Olympic Park offers a variety of activities for small or large groups year-round. The park provides a unique experience for group activities, as it was the home of 14 events during the 2002 Olympic Winter Games. The Utah Olympic Park offers group Comet bobsled rides, Quicksilver alpine slide rides, zip line rides, team building activities, athlete appearances and performances, guided tours and introductory sport camps, catered lunches, receptions and dinners can be arranged. The park is available for a wide variety of functions including corporate retreats, wedding parties, banquets and family reunions. Surrounded by 389 acres, the park can accommodate small or large parties. Best of all, you can receive all these services at a special group rate. From business meetings to social gatherings, the Utah Olympic Park has the equipment and seating available to meet most needs. Whether you have a group of 20 or 1000 people, the Utah Olympic Park will provide your group with an Olympic experience they will remember for the rest of their lives!

OLYMPIC PARKS
UTAH

# Utah Olympic Oval

The Utah Olympic Oval is comprised of two international size hockey rinks (30 x 60m) surrounded by a 12m x 400m Olympic oval. All told the Oval houses 90,000 square feet of ice. Each ice sheet is a separate monolithic concrete pad free of joints. All three are individually monitored to provide optimum ice conditions based on use. The arena space is controlled by a network of 16 sensors constantly measuring air temperature, humidity, carbon monoxide and more all to maintain "The Fastest Ice on Earth". The arena is kept at a comfortable 63 to 65 degrees to allow the ultimate training environment for high performance athletes and recreational athletes alike.

As impressive as the record breaking performances were, it was the performance of the United States Olympic Speedskating Team during the Games that has generated a worldwide buzz surrounding the Utah Olympic Oval. The team relocated to Salt Lake City in January of 2001 to begin training in the Olympic venue 12 months before the rest of the world was expected to arrive. At the end of the 2002 Games, the United States Speedskating team had garnered an astonishing eight Olympic medals won by six individual team members. The depth and success of the United States team caused the rest of the world to take notice and attention quickly turned to the concept of home field advantage. The athletes were generous with their praise, identifying the training environment at the Utah Olympic Oval as a huge factor in helping them realize their full potential as Olympic athletes. The United States Speedskating team continues to use the Utah Olympic Oval as its home training base for the men's and ladies' long track team because of the services the Oval provides and its friendly, experienced staff.

# Public Skating

The Utah Olympic Oval offers public skating sessions year-round. We invite the public to have a fun and affordable experience on the ice made famous at the 2002 Olympic Winter Games. Special activities are offered every month such as Cheap Skate and the Scout merit badge program.

# Learn To Skate

All levels of Learn to Skate classes are available with advanced instruction in figure skating and speed skating for the future Olympian in all of us. The Utah Olympic Oval Learn to Skate program follows the United States Figure Skating Association's Skate with US. program for its introductory skating classes. Classes are held either twice a week for three weeks or once a week for six weeks. The classes are progressive in nature, starting with Basic 1 through Basic 8.

# Running Track

Just outside "The Fastest Ice on Earth" sits what we hope will become "The Fastest Indoor Track on Earth." This beautiful 442-meter Mondo Super X track circles the oval with four lanes of the best running surface under your feet possible. The front straightaway features an eight-lane, 110-meter sprint zone. Regardless of the season, runners train in a climate-controlled environment, averaging 63-65 degrees year-round.

# Soccer

The Utah Olympic Oval features the largest indoor soccer field in the state, located within one of the two international-sized hockey rinks at the facility. The indoor field sports turf, which was manufactured by SRI Sports, was installed in July 2003. Adult and youth leagues beginning play in September 2003.

The specifically designed indoor soccer field is a nylon monofilament with a five millimeter foam backing. The turf has painted lines for indoor soccer and lacrosse. The pile height is 7/16 inch thick and the total system measures 3/4 inch thick, guaranteeing rocket fast ball play. The rolls are 12 feet wide and are sandwiched between the dashers while Velcro maintains the joint underneath.

The field is located on the northernmost 100-feet by 200-feet hockey rink inside the Utah Olympic Oval. The rink has regulation pro grade dasher boards with tempered glass. The soccer goals are all aluminum and measure 8 feet tall by 12 feet wide. The rink also has an L.E.D. scoreboard that displays time, penalties and score. There is bleacher seating for up to 600 people. Soccer is the latest sport program at the Utah Olympic Oval with a variety of high school, co-ed and adult leagues.

# Private Events

The Utah Olympic Oval is an ideal venue for a wide variety of functions including meetings, receptions, corporate retreats, banquets and family reunions. The Oval has distinguished itself by establishing a unique atmosphere and high level of service that is the hallmark of any successful venue. Celebrate your next birthday with one of our unique birthday packages.

207

# Marriott's MountainSide at Park City
# A Marriott Vacation Club Resort

The lovely old mining town of Park City is surrounded by breathtaking mountains and fresh air. While its delightful 19th century ambiance and architecture is still charming, Park City has become a 21st century place to be and when it comes to vacation destinations, the Marriott name has always been synonymous with unparalleled excellence. Marriott's MountainSide at Park City is one of the company's premiere lodgings. Luxurious and modern amenities accentuate the resort's two bedroom villas. Here you can enjoy the conveniences of a five-star hotel together with the relaxation and comforts of home. One of 40 Marriott Vacation Club Resorts around the world, Marriott's MountainSide allows you a look into top notch vacation opportunities and benefits that come with joining Marriott Vacation Club International. Revel in world-class skiing or the Sundance Film Festival in Park City and then enjoy a sunny beach getaway in one of the Marriott resorts in Hawaii, Aruba or Spain. Wherever you go, whether you choose timeshare ownership or vacation rental, the Marriott name ensures a level of quality and service that you can absolutely count on. Let Marriott help make magical vacation moments for you and your family.

1305 Lowell Avenue, Park City UT
(435) 647-4000
www.vacationclub.com

# Washington School Inn

Two blocks from the town ski lift, in the midst of historic Park City, sits an exquisite, completely refurbished schoolhouse that has become an elegant bed and breakfast. The Washington School was crafted with pitched rooflines, a bell tower and locally quarried limestone walls. The Washington School Inn has created 12 guestrooms and three suites, each with private baths, plus fireplaces in two of the suites. All of the rooms, named after former teachers, are filled with beautiful period furnishings, and the beds are dressed with Italian linens and down comforters. The crowning jewel of the Inn is the common area living room, with 20-foot high ceilings and a gigantic stone fireplace. Breakfast is served in the dining room or on one of two limestone patios overlooking Old Town. Washington School Inn pampers its guests with a six-person Jacuzzi and sauna, boot dryers and individual ski lockers. In the mezzanine, guests can watch football, hold meetings, read or play games. The Inn staff has anticipated your needs and prepares to meet them. They will provide chairs, wheeled coolers and picnic dinners for the Deer Valley outdoor concerts. They will book tee times at the golf course; arrange for ski lessons and rentals or for backcountry helicopter skiing; get you a table at a restaurant on Main Street; bake you cookies and uncork a bottle of wine at cocktail hour. School was never this good.   Let the friendly staff at Washington School Inn treasure you.
543 Park Avenue, Park City UT   (435) 649-3800   www.washingtonschoolinn.com

# Hotel Park City

Park City has evolved into a destination for pure enjoyment with its multiple golf courses, ski resorts and breathtaking views. One of the town's most pleasurable offerings is the five-diamond, five-star and AAA-rated Hotel Park City. Your vacation starts at the door when the uniformed doorman not only greets you but offers you a choice of coffee, tea or water. Manager Guy T. Morris is the gracious host of this amiably elegant establishment. The hotel is edged by native trees and is in close proximity to no fewer than three ski resorts and five golf courses. In fact, Hotel Park City is situated on the Park City golf course which can be easily seen from the Sleigh Restaurant. The Sleigh offers guests 24-hour room service, a fine dining room and comfortable seating warmed by the fireplace. For private dining, the Wasatch room is ideal for intimate group gatherings. Cocktails are served by the fireplace in the lounge overlooking the ski runs. The suites feature royal touches like king-sized feather beds and marble bathrooms. Breathe easy under the lofty ceilings as you slip your feet into the provided slippers and thick, cozy robes. Each room is fitted with a writing desk, multiple phones, a fireplace and a terrace or balcony with mountain views. A heated outdoor pool and spa beckon after a day filled with exhilarating activity. Take a memory home with you from the gift shop which is full of local art and merchandise from the hotel, spa and restaurant. For a luxurious stay unlike any other, check into Hotel Park City.

2001 Park Avenue, Park City UT   (435) 940-5027   www.hotelparkcity.com

# Park City Mountain Resort

With 3,300 acres of the Greatest Snow on Earth ™, Park City Mountain Resort's nine bowls and 100 trails will challenge you in steep 'n deep powder, through the bumps, between trees, across rails, over jumps and atop manicured corduroy runs. The Resort serves everyone, from first-timers to black diamond experts. Don't miss the Resort's four top-rated terrain parks and on-the-mountain dining. Intermediate skiers can experience more of the mountain with the new Signature Runs program. Ranked by *SKI* magazine as a Top 5 resort destination for 2006 and host to the 2002 Winter Olympic Games, Park City Mountain Resort is the right setting for a dream winter vacation. Park City Mountain Resort provides direct access to historic Main Street via the exclusive Town Lift and Town Bridge. During the summer, the Town Lift lets you leave Park City behind to experience the beauty and serenity of the mountains. In the winter, ski or ride across the bridge to sample the shops, galleries, bars and bistros that make this town so enchanting. Then journey back to the slopes aboard the Town Lift. What do you do with a world-class mountain when the snow melts? Enjoy the perfect temperatures and experience everything from the Alpine Slide, miles of lift-served mountain biking trails, miniature golf, the ZipRider™ and more at Park City Mountain Resort.

1310 Lowell Avenue, Park City UT
Vacation arrangements: (800) 222-PARK
General Information: (435) 649-8111
www.parkcitymountain.com

# Old Town Guest House

In the heart of Park City, visitors will find a bed and breakfast inn that is every outdoor and sport enthusiast's dream. Old Town Guest House, owned and operated by Deb Louci-Engel, provides guests with the perfect starting point for area adventures. Deb is an avid sportswoman and fan of the great outdoors who participates in several annual marathons, adventure races and mega-competitions. As an active member of her community, she also guides for Utah Interconnect and coaches swimming. With her great love of sports, it's no wonder that she can often be found running, biking or hiking with her guests. Deb has operated the bed and breakfast for 12 years and offers four guest rooms and a common room with fireplace and a hot tub on the back porch. Guests can also be treated to in-room massages, facials and body wraps. Deb really goes out of her way to spoil visitors and to deliver whatever they need to make a truly rejuvenating and memorable vacation. It is no surprise that many begin to feel like part of a family, reserving a room at Old Town Guest House year after year. Outdoor Enthusiast named the inn Best Bed and Breakfast five years in a row. Guests who are headed out to participate in something physical are offered a light early morning meal and can then enjoy a full sit-down breakfast at mid-morning and homemade baked goods for snacks. Come and enjoy the gracious hospitality and infectious enthusiasm that Deb provides at Old Town Guest House.
1011 Empire Avenue, Park City UT
(800) 209-6423 ext. 3710
www.oldtownguesthouse.com

# Park City Golf Club

Park City Golf Club is consistently ranked as one of the premier public locations to play golf in the Intermountain Region. Located in beautiful, mountainous terrain at 6,700 feet above sea level, this course offers 18 challenging, well-kept holes. At that altitude, the thinner atmosphere can actually aid your ball in achieving greater distances. Another bonus, especially in the summer months, is that the temperature is generally 10 to 15 degrees cooler than other courses in the area. Originally constructed in 1963 as a nine-hole William Neff signature course, the Park City course was redesigned in 1973 to its current 18 holes. The 18th hole was redesigned by William Neff Jr. and opened for play in 2003. It's an outstanding finishing hole that's a downhill par five. If you're a long hitter, you can reach its large green in two shots, but it takes accuracy. Be careful of the hazards on this hole; it has bunkers, trees, a lake and a creek that come into play, if you miss-hit the ball. Once you're on the green, take the time to enjoy the magnificent scenery and natural beauty of the area. The pro shop, on the first floor of Hotel Park City, features a wide variety of quality golf products. Park City Golf Club is an inviting course. Be sure to stop and experience all the richness and challenges it offers.
Lower Park Avenue, Park City UT   (435) 615-5800 or (801) 521-2135
www.parkcitygolfclub.org

211

# White Pine Touring

If you're tired of crowds, buzzers, commutes and life in general, it may be time for a vacation. White Pine Touring in Park City can make sure your next vacation is the vacation of a lifetime that everyone wants. For 33 years, White Pine Touring has been providing clients with exciting and educational tours of Utah's scenic landscape. As the oldest touring company in the state, they have a long history of excellence and a known reputation for their friendly, highly knowledgeable instructors and staff. In the winter, you can learn the finer points of cross-country or back country skiing from their instructors with NCAA and Olympics credentials. They also provide Nordic skiing lessons and snowshoe tours. During the summer months, experience the beauty of Utah with a mountain-biking, hiking or rock climbing tour. White Pine Touring offers an extensive selection of tours, programs, and camps that will keep you and your entire family fit and having fun. With so many classes and touring options available, there is something for everyone.  You always have a trained and friendly guide along to help you push yourself to the limit and make it safely back again. White Pine Touring takes outdoor sports seriously and is equally passionate about having the right gear. They have a full-service retail store on-site that is open daily so you can purchase everything you need or rent specialized equipment. Take your turn at having a vacation that your friends will envy with White Pines Touring where one-of-a-kind experiences are the norm.

1685 Bonanza Drive, Park City UT
(435) 649-8710
www.whitepinetouring.com

# Color Rush

Long ago, painters worked to develop a style that captured scenes defined by the play of light and shadow. Out of necessity, they worked fast to capture the essence of what they were viewing before the light changed. This style, prevalent during the second half of the 19th century, became most fully expressed and best known by the rest of the world as Impressionism. Plein Air, meaning "outdoors" in French, refers to this method of painting in outdoor light. Sharon Marquez, an experienced art teacher, conceived Color Rush to provide the Plein Air experience to people enjoying Park City's beautiful vistas. No equipment or experience is needed at Color Rush, where individuals or groups are equipped with everything needed to paint their very own personalized mementos. These on-site paintings are finished in one sitting. Color Rush accommodates patron painters by going to the location they choose, if possible. Favorite locations are plentiful in Park City. Color Rush provides oil paint and all tools and materials, including canvas, aprons, chairs, easels, transportation, lunch, beverages and a box for taking the finished painting home. Marquez recommends that painters bring a jacket, hat and sunscreen to allow for unpredictable mountain weather. Destinations and times for outings are flexible. Let Color Rush show you a refreshingly inventive way to enjoy the sunshine and scenery of Park City.

747 Richmond Drive, Park City UT
(435) 940-0202
www.sharonmarquez.com

213

# Deep Blue

Deep Blue Seafood & Grocery is the ultimate source for fresh seafood in the landlocked, desert reaches of the Rocky Mountains. Park City may be far from the sea, but shoppers at Deep Blue feel much closer to the sea when they sample the seafood selections that Deep Blue has flown in overnight from coastal regions. The potentially seafood-starved Park City dweller can choose from such delicacies as cooked and cracked lobsters, steamed crabs plus several catches of the day. Visit the Deep Blue website to learn more about the qualities, cooking methods and storage requirements for such catches as grouper, flounder, sea scallops and salmon. Deep Blue does it all when it comes to seafood, including catering for your business or special event. Don't let a mere mountain range keep you from eating the bounty of the sea. Visit Deep Blue Seafood & Grocery, where you can buy with confidence and leave the fishing to the experts.
1792 Bonanza Drive, Park City UT
(435) 658-1700   www.dbseafood.com

# Blind Dog Grill

The Blind Dog Grill was born in 1998 and named for Rigger, the family's beloved blind black lab. Tucked away in Prospector Square in Park City, the Blind Dog brings a bit of the East Coast to the Wasatch Mountains. Voted Best Casual Dinner by Food and Wine magazine, Best Crab Cakes by City Weekly and Best Steak by Citysearch, the menu at the Dog can tempt even the toughest critics. Oysters, fresh fish, prime steaks, lobster and tons of blue crab make this restaurant stand out. Chef Penny Kinsey's flair for reinventing Old School recipes will leave you satisfied and asking the hostess to book you a table for the next night. The energetic waitstaff's knowledge of the cocktail menu and wine list, a *Wine Spectator* award winner, will shine the light on getting a drink in Utah as it entertains your imagination. You won't be able to find fresher seafood creatively crafted, presented or consumed anywhere in Utah. Japanese cuisine with an East Coast twist and the charms of a newly renovated dining room have earned the loyalty of local residents. The sushi bar, located right next door, offers the freshest and finest quality sushi in town and boasts one of the most extensive wine and cocktail menus in the state. This family-run establishment exudes comfortable class as well as a sense of humor. Where else can you order a sashimi plate or tempura shrimp for starters then finish with fire-grilled New York Strip or Penny's signature Dreamloaf? Let Chef Penny tempt your taste buds while her extremely talented staff provides great service at Blind Dog Grill.
1781 Sidewinder Drive, Park City UT
(435) 655-0800   www.blinddoggrill.com

# El Chubasco Mexican Grill

In Mexico, *chubasco* refers to a storm. El Chubasco Mexican Grill in Park City is true to that description by whipping up a storm of flavors. All of the tastes are so authentic that the restaurant draws natives from Mexico as regularly as it draws a world of customers from everywhere else. The prices here are impossibly reasonable for the amount and quality of food served on each plate and the menu is large and varied. To spice up the chips that come with every order, there are 16 varieties of freshly-made salsas available in the center station. Two of the most popular are the sweet, hot mango salsa made with *manzano* peppers and the sour cream-based chipotle salsa. Entrées are consistently delicious and the service is fast. Meat is trimmed on-site and the house uses only roma tomatoes, romaine lettuce and quality chilies. Added to the standard drink menu is the exceptional house *horchata*. This chilled milk and rice drink with sugar, vanilla and cinnamon cools overloaded tongues. Familiar dishes like burritos, tacos, enchiladas and chile rellenos are served in splendid glory. Selections of exotic dishes shine as well. There is a rich goat stew and the *pozole*, a hearty soup of pork, hominy, onions and cabbage, is a filling meal in itself. Owner Andy Woodard, who acquired the restaurant from his visionary brother, invites you to sample a true taste of tantalizing Mexico. 1890 Bonanza Drive, Park City UT (801) 645-9114

# The Egyptian Theatre Company

The Egyptian Theatre Company presents cutting edge artistic theatrical performances in an intimate theater that has served the community for a century. The Egyptian was built on the ruins of the Dewey Theatre, a popular cultural center in Park City until heavy snowfall caused the roof to collapse. The discovery of King Tut's tomb influenced the building's design, with lotus leaves, scarabs, hieroglyphics and celebratory symbols decorating the structure. It survived some tough times, including a period when Park City was considered a ghost town. When Park City found its niche as a ski destination, the theater continued to function. It was finally renovated in 1998 and became the permanent home of Park City Performances. The Egyptian is a private corporation for serving the greater public good, with Artistic Director Dana Keiter bringing professional live theater to the Park City area. This establishment is one of only four professional theaters in Utah. The Egyptian Theatre seats 266 people and every seat is a good one. Buy your tickets early because this theater draws an audience from across the country. The Egyptian Theatre offers an incomparable after-skiing experience or a memorable summer night on the town.

328 Main Street, Park City UT   Box Office: (435) 645-9371   Business Office: (435) 645-0671   www.parkcityshows.com

# Park City Historical Society & Museum

Park City is well known for skiing, so visitors are often surprised to learn about the town's origins as a silver mining camp. The Park City Historical Society & Museum is housed in the town's first city hall, constructed in 1885. The museum basement still holds the original territorial jail, where many colorful characters were invited to dry out during Park City's rowdy mining boom. The museum displays a wide collection of artifacts from Park City's past, including the restored Kimball Brothers' stagecoach that operated between Salt Lake City and Park City from 1872 to 1890. Exhibits recount the early days of silver mining, when prospectors sought their fortunes and millionaires were made, and celebrate the town's emergence as a world-class ski resort and host of the 2002 Winter Olympic Games. The Park City Historical Society & Museum is a must-see for those seeking to get acquainted with the history of this Utah city.

528 Main Street, Park City UT

(435) 649-7457   www.parkcityhistory.org

# Silver Queen

The Silver Queen in Park City is everything a hotel aspires to be. Jana Potter, artistic entrepreneur extraordinaire, has ensured that a visit to the Silver Queen appeals to all of the senses and not just the physical ones. The location is beyond reproach. It is an easy walk to the town ski lift. Located along historic Main Street, there are incredible art galleries, shopping, restaurants, night life and a host of other entertainment opportunities within walking distance. The nearby transportation stop shuttles passengers all over the city, free of charge. When guests are not on the town, the staff of the Silver Queen provide the exemplary service for which they are highly renowned. Full concierge services include acquisition of tickets, reservations and massages in addition to necessities such as the daily snow report. The Silver Queen has grocery, child-care and dry-cleaning services available also. All of this is provided for guests before they ever get to the luxurious rooms. The rooms are visually, physically and emotionally attractive. All suites offer a fully equipped kitchen. Twelve grand suites and an assortment of one and two bedroom units blaze with personal fireplaces, ski lockers, jetted tubs and steam showers. The icing on the cake is a rooftop garden and hot tub. There is no better view anywhere in the city. Book early and stay late. The Silver Queen will provide an unequaled paradise vacation.

632 Main Street, Park City UT   (435) 649-5986 or (800) 447-6423   www.silverqueenhotel.com

# Christmas on Main Street

Al and Sharron Latimer have been upholding Christmas traditions year-round since 1989. As owners of the festive Christmas on Main Street holiday boutique, the Latimers are able to keep the holiday spirit alive even on the warmest day. Christmas on Main Street has a steady clientele of visitors from around the world who are drawn to the lovely nativities and ornaments that the shop displays. Thanks to consistent tourism and their loyal local customers, the shop remains viable throughout the year. The idea came about when friends of Sharron's encouraged her to open a

business that focused on something she loved, which was Christmas. The shop carries an astounding array of ornaments, many of which are heirloom quality, tree skirts, figurines and holiday home décor. Sharron shops at several gift markets every season, making a special point to visit the Los Angeles outlets while seeking inventory for the shop. These buying trips allow Sharron to select only the finest quality and specialty items for her customers. Christmas on Main Street is the perfect place to discover the spirit of Christmas and take a little piece of it home with you.
442 Main Street, Park City UT
(435) 645-8115

# Zoom

Zoom opened its doors in November of 1995 in the former train depot at the foot of Main Street in Park City. Since that time, and under the direction of Zoom General Manager Steve Solomon and Executive Chef Brian Prusse, the restaurant has evolved as a popular spot for both locals and visitors to Park City. The restaurant was most recently featured on the cover of the January *Bon Apetit* magazine for its extraordinary cheesecake. As one of the Sundance restaurants, Zoom reflects Sundance's commitment to the arts. Its walls are adorned with photos from the annual film festival and the Sundance Institute's film labs. Its name is taken from the zoom of a camera lens. Its chic, but comfortable, contemporary interior sets off the charm of the historic depot. The restaurant is known for its distinctive twist on American Continental cuisine, taking classic dishes and making them their own, turning ordinary mac and cheese into a gourmet comfort food. In the summer of 2004, Zoom introduced a new dining experience with a special dinner and concert featuring renowned singer/songwriters from Nashville's Bluebird Cafe. Guests enjoyed a special three-course dinner and concert on the outdoor patio. The series was an immediate success and will continue in the summer of 2006. Zoom, together with the Tree Room and the Foundry Grill, encapsulate Sundance's commitment to celebrating food as art and the spirit of community. This vision of community devoted to art and nature began in 1969 when Robert Redford purchased the land. Sundance continues to grow and further its mission as a community that fosters dynamic and significant experiences for people. Come see how Zoom is a primary example of the success of this mission.
660 Main Street, Park City UT   (435) 649-9108
www.sundanceresort.com/zoom.htm

# Seasons Day Spa

Seasons Day Spa was created in 1998 when the Sweeney Brothers (Mike, Pat and Ed) helped turn an old mining rail yard into Park City's lower Main Street and brought skiing to Old Town. The locals coined this location "where the mountain meets Main Street." Seasons Day Spa is located just beneath the town lift and is the only ski-in, ski-out day spa on Main Street. You can ski right to Seasons' front door. When it's really time to unwind, relax your mind and experience a complete rejuvenation with the best pampering in all of Park City for your face, body and hair. You will love Seasons' plush, peaceful and private rooms and Seasons can bring its services directly to your room. Seasons brings a little bit of Shangri-la to the active lifestyle of Park City. Among the therapies designed to relax and revitalize guests are a choice of massages including total relaxing massages, a deep tissue massages, hot stone therapy and a special couple's massage. Exfoliate and detoxify your body with wonderful treatments like the Seasons Salt/Sugar Glow or a detoxifying body wrap. Facials are a fabulous way to achieve a refreshing glow and protect your skin from Utah's dry climate. The most popular facial at the spa is the signature Seasons Facial, which cleanses and hydrates your skin. The friendly and courteous staff also offers expert hand and foot care. Other services include hair care, waxing, tinting and sunless tanning, all designed to enhance your own natural beauty. For a day filled with pampering, relax, rejuvenate and revitalize your mind and body at Seasons Day Spa.
825 Main Street, Park City UT
(435) 658-2639 or (877) 578-2639
www.seasonsdayspa.com

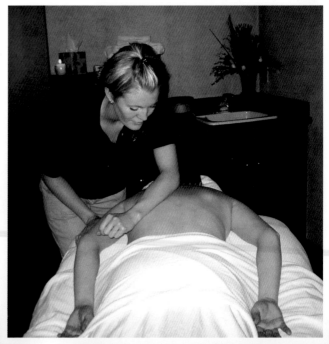

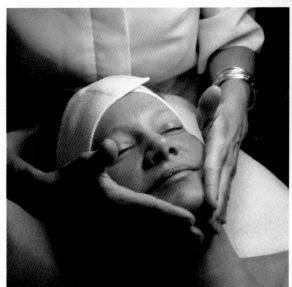

# Java Cow/Cows Ice Cream

Park City has quickly become one of America's favorite destination communities. When it's time for a treat, stop by Java Cow and Cows Ice Cream in this charming community. In 1999, Ken and Marcie Davis purchased Cows Ice Cream parlor and did some extensive renovations that created a more welcoming ambiance and emphasized the cow theme. Ken, a retired corporate executive, knew that people wanted ice cream made from the finest quality, all natural ingredients. The winning recipe for Cows Ice Cream originated in Cavendish, Prince Edward Island. Each of the 32 flavors is produced in Charlottetown, Prince Edward Island and is shipped to Park City. The truly mouthwatering ice cream has a variety of eclectic names like Déja Moo, Wowie Cowie and Obi-Cow Kenobi. In 2003, the Davises expanded into an old Starbucks coffee shop next door and opened Java Cow. Continuing on his mission of excellence, Ken researched and scoured the nation to find exceptional fair-trade coffee. He found what he was looking for at Caffe Ibis, located just an hour and a half away in Logan. The coffee is roasted to perfection by Ibis's master roasters and delivered to Java Cow the very next day. Mornings start early at this dual business. At 5 a.m., the bakery lights are on and the staff is busy whipping up homemade breads and pastries. The menu includes wonderfully thick sandwiches, savory soups and specialty coffees. The Los Angeles Times touted Java Cow and Cows Ice Cream as "a place not to be missed." Enjoy the friendly people and wonderful treats available at Java Cow and Cows Ice Cream.

402 Main Street, Park City UT
(435) 647-7711
www.cows.ca

## Envy a Swanky Boutique

Historic Main Street in Park City is a veritable treasure trove of shops and restaurants. It is a year-round draw for traveling shoppers and Park City residents. Many of the shops are unusual in one way or another. Brigitte Larsen and her sister Erin Price are proprietors of Envy a Swanky Boutique. They carry lingerie and outerwear, jewelry, shoes, accessories and novelties for the chic shopper. Authentic handmade vintage album purses are one of their rare offerings. Designer names hang from the racks, but the merchandise found here is not easy to find anywhere else. Prices are reasonable, and shoppers leave happy. In an area known for its perfect snow and beautiful landscapes, Envy Boutique fits in like a jewel on a velvet cushion.

608 Main Street, Park City, UT
(435) 658-3689

## The Spur Bar & Grill

"Upscale" and "classy" are not terms usually used to describe a Western bar and grill, but in this regard, The Spur Bar and Grill stands apart. The Spur is a saloon with a difference; it's smoke-free, comfortable, casual, and yes, elegant. Its short menu highlights mouthwatering food, simply and deliciously prepared, such as grilled buffalo bratwurst, ham and cheese flatbread and queso fundido (a Mexican fondue). The Spur serves an excellent selection of wines, the best margaritas in town, plus domestic and imported beers for enjoying in the welcoming ambiance. After a long day on the slopes or watching cutting-edge films at the Sundance Film Festival, The Spur is just the place to rest and review the day. Come lounge on elegant leather furniture in front of a rock fireplace or sit at rough-hewn tables around the music stage. If you prefer, take a seat on a leather stool at the polished copper bar that looks like something straight out of the 19th century. Later in the evening, The Spur is the place for dancing! Most nights, The Spur features live music, including acoustic guitar acts, an abundance of blues and bluegrass and rock and roll bands. The Spur Bar and Grill is where locals and guests alike discover good food, good times and good friends!

350½ Main Street, Park City UT (435) 615-1618 www.thespurbarandgrill.com

# Dugins West

Robert Dugins spent years as a full-time professional skier wandering from resort to resort, captivated by the mad rush of fresh powder and the atmosphere of fun and camaraderie on ski vacations. So when Robert left Lake Tahoe and came to Park City in 1984, he wanted to start a business that kept people in touch with the joy of a vacation well-spent. Thus, 21 years ago, the first Dugins West was born. Dugins is Park City's place to go for gifts, souvenirs and resort apparel for the entire family. This venture turned out to be so much fun that Robert opened a second Dugins West with Jim Bradford nine years ago. Together, they get to spend their days with people who are all on vacation and having a fabulous time. The Dugins West at 425 Main specializes in the fuzzy and cuddly with warm après ski wear, cute stuffed animals, toasty Park City socks and gifts that evoke oohs and aahs when opened. The Dugins West at 352 Main caters to the more serious gift-giver and carries western wear, jewelry, collectibles and art, all with Park City flavor. Every memento will evoke a whiff of the cool mountain air and wonderful times enjoyed by all during your travels in Utah. If you haven't been to Dugins West, the souvenir capital of Park City, you haven't finished your shopping.

352 Main Street, Park City UT
(435) 658-5378
425 Main Street, Park City UT
(435) 649-5817

# Tommy Knockers Jewelry

The legend of the Tommy Knockers revolves around mysterious nighttime sounds emanating from the 1000-mile network of mining tunnels that stretch out beneath the streets of Park City. These sounds are attributed to dwarves, elves or ghosts of miners at work. As legend has it, Tommy Knockers only work in fruitful ground and those who track it to the source will find a treasure waiting for them. Such is the case at Tommy Knockers Jewelry in Park City. Owned and operated by Clark Johnson and his wife, Christie, the store opened more than two decades ago. The founder, Clark's father Stan, was an architect and artist who turned his sights on jewelry design. He studied extensively and his keen talent propelled him into the public eye, allowing him to become a full-time jewelry artist. When Clark was a teenager, he joined his father in a silver-smithing class. Clark possessed an obvious affinity for the craft and was soon selling his own creations in a local jewelry store. He continued to apprentice with his father while pursuing his education at the Gemological Institute of America in the Jewelry Manufacturing Arts program, the same institution his father had attended. These days Tommy Knockers continues to offer distinctively crafted jewelry with the resident designer on-site. There is a full-service repair department and an exclusive metal ski pass. Choose your future heirloom at Tommy Knockers Jewelry.

577 Main Street, Park City, UT   (435) 649-8482
www.tommyknockers.net

223

# O.C. Tanner

Almost 30 years ago, Obert Tanner set out to give Salt Lake City one of the finest retail stores anywhere. It would not be just a place to buy jewelry, it was destined to become a landmark. As Park City became one of the most popular resort communities in the world as well as one of the hosts of the 2002 Winter Olympics, O.C. Tanner expanded and opened a second store on historic Main Street. This beautiful new store brilliantly showcases

exclusive lines of jewelry as well as the Olympic medals produced and donated by the O.C. Tanner Company. Today, it too is becoming a landmark store in Park City with celebrated gifts, jewelry and watches from all over the world. Look for watches by Patek Phillipe, Cartier and David Yurman, jewelry by Picchiotti, Scott Kay and Oscar Heyman & Brothers as well as crystal by Steuben, Lalique and Baccarat. You are invited to come and experience the O.C. Tanner tradition.
416 Main Street, Park City UT
(435) 940-9470 or (888) 246-6217
60 E South Temple Street, Salt Lake City UT
(801) 532-3222 or (888) 246-6217

# Village Keepsakes

If you're looking for the perfect souvenir to commemorate your Utah vacation, stop by Village Keepsakes. This fantastic gift shop is filled to the brim with wonderful and witty items that are ideal for a personal keepsake or to give as a gift. Village Keepsakes has been continuously owned and operated in Park City by the Parker family for over thirty years. Dan Parker was the town's pharmacist. As the town grew, Dan knew he had to grow with it and expand his inventory to include more than pharmaceuticals. Village Keepsakes now has two locations that carry a large selection of Park City and Utah-specific souvenirs. The shop also offers a terrific array of fun and funny items, including doormats, baseball caps, t-shirts, toys, collector spoons, bells, thimbles and a huge collection of pins and patches. Village Keepsakes also carries lovely picture frames and Italian charms. While you're at the Main Street location, be sure to pick up some of the finest chocolates that Utah has to offer at the Village Candy Shoppe. Tucked away inside of Village Keepsakes, the candy shop provides decadent candies made on-site to guarantee optimal freshness. Look for hand-dipped chocolates and rich caramels; this is also a great place to get Park City huckleberries and saltwater taffy. Treat yourself and pick up a few things for the folks back home at Village Keepsakes.

314 Main Street, Park City UT
(435) 655-7647
Village Gifts & Store
Top level, Park City Mountain Resort, Park City UT
(435) 649-3418
www.villagekeepsakes.com

# Southwest Indian Traders

Raette Mullen is a third generation Indian trader who learned the trade at her father's side growing up in Four Corners, New Mexico. Backed with a lifetime of on-the-job-training, Mullen has the experience and inherent ability to select quality pieces of traditional, antique and contemporary Native American artwork and jewelry. Using her knowledge and skill, she opened Southwest Indian Traders in Park City. Now, as owner of the largest retail space in Park City, Mullen uses her expertise to bring an extensive selection of antiques, gifts and collectibles to you. This amazing store, one of the most popular during the 2002 Winter Olympics, offers a fantastic collection of Native American pottery from the Navajo, Ute and Pueblo Indian tribes. Enjoy an evocative selection of Zapotec Mexican-Indian woven rugs in a variety of sizes. Southwest Indian Traders is proud to have the largest collection of antique wooden skis, snowshoes, ice skates and sleds in town. Visitors will delight in the vast array of fine Native American jewelry, including a full display case of pawn jewelry. Pawn is a term used to describe well-worn authentic pieces of Indian jewelry, regardless of tribe or origin, that show unsurpassed craftsmanship and remarkable stones or designs. Patrons will be charmed and surprised by the hand-carved wood bears, picture frames, Leanin' Tree Cards, Indian headdresses, bear rugs, and an assortment of bows, arrows and quivers. Stop in and visit Southwest Indian Traders on your next visit to Park City and explore the many treasures that await you.
550 Main Street, Park City UT
(435) 645-9177

# The Crosby Collection

The Crosby Collection is Park City's premier dealer in Native American collectibles. Owners Bing and Vickie Crosby are well known in the field; Bing has been trading in southwestern Indian art and jewelry since the 1950s. Their collection features a wide range of jewelry, including pawn and contemporary pieces in gold and silver and a wide assortment of traditional and modern styles for both men and women. The Crosby Collection specializes in gem quality turquoise from domestic mines, a commodity that is increasingly difficult to find. The gallery also has an extensive selection of Pueblo pottery by matriarch potters such as Maria Martinez, Lucy Lewis, Fannie Nampeyo and Margaret Tafoya as well as their descendants. Other significant offerings are antique and contemporary Navajo rugs, Zuni fetishes, and Hopi kachinas. The Crosby Collection is the exclusive representative for several non-Native American artists, including famed jewelry artists Benny and Valerie Alrich and Kim Yubeta. Be sure to visit both of the Crosbys' Main Street locations, including the gallery in the historic Crosby Collection Building. Built in 1922, it was once part of the most celebrated saloon in town. It is now presided over by Kroz, the Crosbys' Australian Blue Heeler, who has become a fixture on Main Street, welcoming many a return visitor. The inspiring and masterfully-crafted pieces of The Crosby Collection will draw you into the magic of the Southwest and add warmth and beauty to any room.

419 Main Street, Park City UT (435) 658-1813 or (800) 960-8839
513 Main Street, Park City UT (435) 649-6522 or (800) 291-8839

# The Expanding Heart

There are some places that draw you in and keep you enchanted so that you will return again and again. The Expanding Heart is just such a place. Located on historic Main Street in Park City, this unusual shop offers peace and harmony to its customers. Owner Joy Barrett states, "The primary purpose of The Expanding Heart is to hold an energy of awareness and open-heartedness. The things I sell are only supporting that purpose." The warm and inviting ambiance creates an environment that naturally shifts the consciousness of all who enter. The muted natural essence of the store soothes you as you browse through the extensive collection of books, chosen explicitly to help transform consciousness through the heart. The Expanding Heart also carries a fine array of crystals, jewelry, statuary, clothing, accessories and gift items that are affordable and exude the loving intent of the store. Joy feels that her friendly and compassionate staff members are integral to the store ambiance and operations; they certainly excel at putting you at ease while offering exemplary service. Another character you are likely to meet at The Expanding Heart is Sierra. Sierra, an Andalusian mountain retriever, is a living example of how to live with an open heart. Open your senses and renew your spirit with a visit to The Expanding Heart. 505 Main Street, Park City UT (435) 649-1255

228

# Mountain Body Herbal Spa & Body Products

Park City is home to a flagship store featuring an innovative line of skin care merchandise that uses food as the main ingredient. Mountain Body Herbal Spa & Body Products tantalizes pedestrians with colorful displays. Fresh fruits, shea and cocoa butters, sugar, honey, sea salt and other items that might ordinarily fill the shelves in a gourmet kitchen are incorporated into these whimsical premium body products.

Soaps are cut to resemble cheese and are wrapped in deli paper. Masques and scrubs are kept on ice and packed in to-go containers. Mountain Body tests new items with customers before adding them to the catalog, making the shop an intriguing stop for fans wondering what the next new product might be. Massages, wraps and facials are offered at the store as well. The entire cosmetic line is environmentally friendly and all of the products are preservative and additive free. Visitors can take advantage of a complimentary hand treatment and the store is renowned for its ultimate salt glow and honey spa treatment. Superior customer service plus fresh deli cosmetics, mineral makeup and natural and organic face and body products all add up to one delicious sum. Mountain Body Herbal Spa & Body Products knows what to serve to your skin, so stop by for a unique beauty experience.

608 Main Street, Park City UT
(435) 655-9342
www.mountainbody.com

229

# Eleganté

Customers with a desire to create their own personal ambiance in their home décor will find the perfect furnishings and accessories for their individual delight. From elegant contemporary to rustic mountain-esque and everything in between, the designs of Eleganté are uniquely diverse. Eleganté prides itself in searching far and wide to bring items from all over the world, ensuring an eclectic array of merchandise. They also carry the wares and rarities of local artisans, some of whom supply the store with items, found in only 3-4 businesses nationwide, making for truly one-of-a-kind gifts. In addition to Eleganté, Mike Ryan owns two other stores along Main Street: Elements of Eleganté and Xpressions. Branda Northrop manages all three stores where you can talk to an interior designer on staff that will assist you in every detail of embellishments. Eleganté's experienced designers have designed home interiors all over the U.S. so they're sure to help you express your very own decorating ideas and create a style for your home that's truly personal. The richness of diversity in the furnishings and accessories Eleganté carries will surely amplify your personal style. Visit the knowledgeable staff for your next decorating project and you'll be glad you did.

364 Main Street, Park City UT
(435) 647-0288
www.elegante-online.com

# Red Banjo Pizza

For more than 40 years, Mary Lou Toly and her family have been serving great pizza and friendly smiles at Red Banjo Pizza in Park City. Mary Lou started the business in June of 1962 as a bar called Red Banjo Saloon. The name changed in 1974 and now stands as the oldest business on Main Street. Mary Lou co-owns the local favorite with son Scott Toby Toly and three generations of family currently work there. The building was originally constructed in 1900 and the décor is a welcoming cross between an old west saloon and the modern pizza house it actually is. A huge antique mirror dominates the space behind the bar and an old-fashioned piano occupies the back wall. Red Banjo also doubles as a gallery for the interesting and entertaining napkin art that has accumulated over the years. The dining area is usually abuzz with the chatter of resident teens and Park City families. This charming restaurant has a long history of being a gathering place for local Italian immigrants and the embracing warmth of camaraderie lingers and invites folks to come in, relax and enjoy a meal. Red Banjo's brick oven bakes wonderful pizzas dripping with cheese. The crisp but chewy crust is an ideal canvas for fresh, tasty toppings. The Red Banjo also offers fiery jalapeño poppers and fabulous cheesy bread sticks. To wash down your meal, they offer soda and beer on tap. When it's time for pizza in Park City, it's time for Red Banjo Pizza. 322 Main Street, Park City UT   (435) 649-9901

# 350 Main Brasserie

At 350 Main Brasserie in Park City, guests enjoy the finest contemporary global cuisine created by Chef Michael LeClerc. The lofty, earth-toned dining room gets its warmth and welcoming ambiance from a massive fireplace, cozy booths and beautiful original artwork, allowing you to indulge your other senses while the incomparable cuisine delights your palate. Menu options change by season and include steak and game, seafood and vegetarian fare. An international traveler, Chef Michael LeClerc reflects his global experience in his menu. Trained at the famous Culinary Institute of America, he has an amazingly diverse gastronomic repertoire. Michael has practiced his culinary art in such places as Maui, Thailand, Deer Valley, Geneva, New York and Paris. He uses his classic continental foundation as a base for blending Italian, Asian, Mediterranean, South American and French influences, creating an extraordinary and exciting global dining experience. Try an appetizer of scallop and crab ceviche with enoki mushrooms, wasabi aioli, seaweed salad and daikon sprouts. Follow it with an entrée of venison medallions crusted with black pepper and served with a blackberry-shitake jus, roasted beets and cranberry-orange marmalade. Top it off with tropical fruit fantasy, a heavenly concoction of passion fruit, rum and coconut mousse; your mouth will think it has gone on vacation. Spend some time in 350 Main's elegant bar with its extensive wine list, recognized annually with a *Wine Spectator* Award of Excellence, and fruit-infused vodkas, the basis of the restaurant's creative signature cocktails. It is no wonder that 350 Main Brasserie has become not only a must-try restaurant in Park City, but also a long-time favorite of legions of faithful diners, who visit again and again.
350 Main Street, Park City, UT (435) 649-3140 www.350main.com

# La Casita

Park City was founded on silver and Park City was founded on silver and bathtub gin but both are now gone. Actor Robert Redford put the town back on the map when he transformed a failing ski resort into the Sundance Film Institute, drawing artists and nature lovers to its miles of biking and hiking trails, summer films, art shows and music performances. Luckily, all these visitors can feed their hunger at La Casita, where Alberto Martinez serves up sassy Mexican fare. Alberto moved to Park City from Veracruz, Mexico because he loves the snow and the excitement of the resort town. In this city of diverse travelers and mountain locals, he found an opportunity to share his mother's great cooking with the world. In his beautiful, casual establishment in the Summit Watch Plaza, the Martinez recipes are rediscovered. Here, the customer is king and the fabulous service is geared to please. Alberto's legendary salsas are made daily and the homemade mole sauce is his grandmother's recipe. She also gets credit for the world-famous Mexican hot chocolate and Mexican flan. This is exotic, robust Mexican food at its best and is impossible to get anywhere else, except in Alberto's mother's kitchen. Meals are reasonably priced and take-out is available. For a genuine taste of Mexico, La Casita is a sublime discovery.
710 Main Street, Park City UT   (435) 645-9585   www.lacasitaparkcity.com

# No Name Saloon and Grill

The home of the buffalo burger in Park City is the No Name Saloon and Grill. This prime example of the Old West, owned by Jesse Shetler and Radu Dugala, wants you to know that because "beer makes you smart, you'd better have a couple." This is only one of a list of saloon rules to abide by at the No Name. Here you will find plenty of wild west humor, a selection of tasty burgers and possibly the ski patrol winding down after a day on the slopes. The No Name staff will substitute beef for buffalo, but not willingly. Various popular sandwiches like Philly steak, turkey and hot pastrami on rye are offered alongside chicken and veggie burgers, too. There are seafood selections for fish lovers and buffalo chili served in a sourdough bread bowl. This is also the only place you can get the signature house-made buffalo chips and the No Name Saloon Southwestern style salsa to accompany them. The salsa is available for sale in the souvenir collection, along with an assortment of hats, t-shirts and hoodies. There are also tank tops and fitted t-shirts for the ladies as well as posters and stickers.

Pint glasses and beer steins are available for purchase at a reasonable price. Your meal at No Name Saloon and Grill is sure to be an enduring memory of your Park City experience.

447 Historic Main Street, Park City UT

(435) 649-6667

www.nonamesaloon.net

# Wasatch Brew Pub

Wasatch Brew Pub offers award-winning hand-crafted beers and a menu full of succulent creations for any palate to savor. For over 10 years tourists and locals alike have chosen this as the place to stop in for a beer and a bite to eat. The fish and chips are true English style, and Utah trout and pine nut crusted salmon are top menu favorites. Other fare served includes Louisiana barbecue style shrimp, buffalo burgers, and chicken pesto pizza. Wasatch's micro brew beer is noted for avoiding the heaviness and yeastiness of many microbrews, having a clean finish on the palate. Their Porter is considered by many to be their best beer. A dark, medium bodied ale, its inviting chocolate and malty flavors give it a slightly dry yet silky smooth finish. Wasatch's Hefe-Weizen is a wheat beer brewed in the traditional, unfiltered German style, using a hybrid Bavarian yeast strain & Hallertau hops. This particular brew garnered Wasatch's Brew Pub the First Place Blue Ribbon in the Wheat Beer Category at Idaho's Beer Festival in June 1998. Newly remodeled, the pub is inviting year-round. In the winter you can choose the table with two-sided window views, while in the summer, you might want that patio table with the perfect view of Park City. Upstairs, the cantina, a private club for members, features a fantastic top-shelf tequila bar and the best margaritas in town. Wasatch Brew Pub is the perfect place to unwind, dine, and savor that special brew.

250 Main Street, Park City UT
(435) 645-9500 or (435) 649-0900
www.wasatchbeers.com

# Down Under Dreaming

For nearly 20 years Queensland's Down Under Dreaming has offered customers quality Australian opal at affordable rates. Owning mines in northeast Queensland, they are able to supply their stores with the finest Bolder, Crystal, Koroit and Yowah opal found in the world today. In 2004, Down Under Dreaming opened their first American store in the popular destination community of Park City. Owners Ron and Traci Wooleg cut and design many of the stunning pieces of jewelry featured, and so are able to offer these pieces at unbelievable prices. Furthermore, Down Under Dreaming has many Australian connections that allow them to offer patrons collector pieces, many of which have been featured in numerous opal books around the world. The jewelry you will find at this wonderful shop are all original pieces set in 14- and 18- carat yellow or white gold, platinum or silver. They also feature unique jewelry designed by a young artist from India, Sonali Zaveri, who has entered many pieces of her work in jewelry competitions around the world. In addition, Dreaming Down Under carries a fine selection of Aboriginal art including didgeridoos, sheep skin rugs from Tasmania, leather works and pieces by 2004 artist of the year Colin Wightman. Other intriguing items to be found are kangaroo fur apparel and accessories, walking sticks and boomerangs, and Australian soaps. Explore the wonders of Australia at Down Under Dreaming in Park City.

614 Main Street, Park City UT
(435) 658-0058
www.downunderdreaming.com

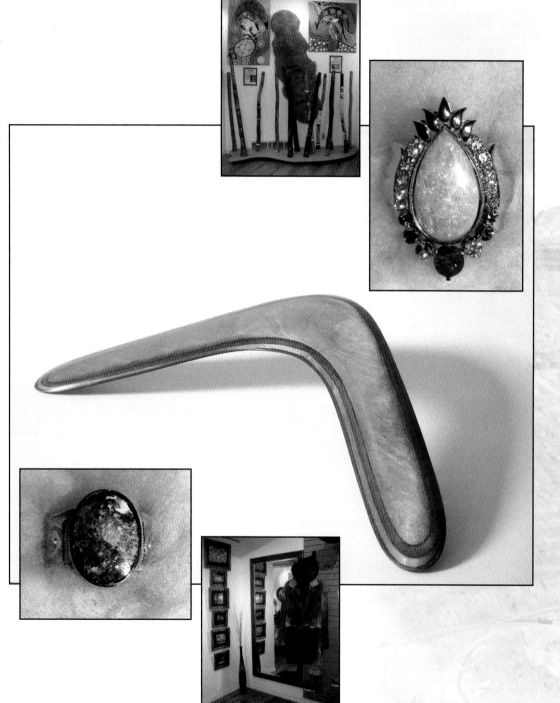

235

# Bandits' Grill and Bar

If you wander into Bandits' Grill and Bar on a Tuesday night, you're likely to find yourself in the middle of an old western shootout and bandit chase, so be sure to look both ways! Tuesdays are Kid's Night at Bandits and shootouts are part of the menu. It's not just kids who'll be clamoring to make a stop at this terrific family restaurant on Main Street's restaurant row in Park City. If you want the very best in Western barbecue, the *L.A. Daily News*, *AAA Dining* and *Los Angeles* magazine all agree that Bandits' Grill and Bar is the place to go. Their smoked ribs, rotisserie-style chicken and brisket pulled pork are just about legendary. This says a lot for owners Shane and Jenifer Barber. In two short years, they've managed to realize Shane's childhood dream of owning his very own barbecue joint. Back in 1978, the eatery was known as Texas Red's Barbecue, but even then, Shane had his eye on it. In 2001, he bought it, tore it down and started all over again. Shane and Jenifer have put their heart and soul into remodeling the restaurant and it shows. Stop into Bandits' Grill and Bar for a gunfight, the best barbecue in the west and a chat with Shane. He loves to come out of the kitchen every night to shoot the breeze with his guests and make sure everybody's happy!

440 Main Street, Park City UT

(435) 649-7337

www.banditsbbq.com

# River Horse on Main

A shining star among the prime eateries of Park City is the award-winning River Horse on Main which opened on New Year's Eve of 1987. The restaurant quickly became highly regarded by both the local public and the area's restaurant critics. The 1993 arrival of Executive Chef Bill Hufferd helped the River Horse on Main achieve an even higher level of acclaim. In 1995, River Horse received national recognition as a recipient of the coveted DiRoNA award, which is dedicated to excellence in dining. The award was given to only 335 restaurants from all across North America, and River Horse has maintained the honor every year since originally earning it. Further praise came to the River Horse in January of 2000 when it became the first eatery in Utah history to be named by Mobile Travel Guide as one of the top 233 restaurants in the United States, Canada and Mexico. This is considered to be the ultimate hospitality industry honor and River Horse on Main is the only restaurant in the state to hold both a DiRoNA award and a Mobile Four Star Award. The diverse menu offers something for everyone with menu favorites ranging from grilled Honduran lobster tail with shiitake mushrooms in white wine sauce to crispy half-duckling with cranberry-hoisin glaze. River Horse further features a distinguished wine list and an excellent dessert menu. Whether you're planning an intimate evening for two or a gala for 300, make your reservations for River Horse on Main.
540 Main Street, Park City UT   (435) 649-3536   www.riverhorsegroup.com

237

# Mother Nature's Nook

If the natural spirit of the wilderness moves you and you also relish an original shopping adventure, visit Mother Nature's Nook for an escape from the ordinary. Owner Julee Nichols recognized the need for a centralized place where local Utah artists and craftspeople could sell their handmade wares. Julee, an artisan herself, started out by traveling to art festivals and craft fairs to sell her jewelry and florals. After 10 years, her inventory became too large to cart around so she opened a 4000 square foot store in Heber City with a second location on Main Street in Park City. With all the cabins and vacation homes in the vicinity, Julee found a niche for her locally made rustic and woodsy home décor, mountain furnishings, accessories and artwork. Not only are the items at Mother Nature's Nook an incredible joy, they are useful too. You'll find extraordinary articles such as beds with twists and gnarls, distinctive three-legged chairs, one-of-a-kind lamps with handmade lampshades and antler chandeliers. If you're looking for something more traditional, discover original art, custom florals, jewelry, quilts and even handmade candy. If you still can't find what you're looking for, one of Julee's 300 talented artists can create it for you at Mother Nature's Nook, so pay Julee a visit and find what you're looking for today!

608 Main Street, Park City UT
(801) 319-4793
155 N Main Street, Heber City UT
(435) 654-9900
www.mothernaturesnookonline.com

# Sterling Real Estate

Sterling Real Estate in Park City is committed to keeping the interests of its clients forefront. The company, located in the Silver Queen Hotel, is owned and operated by Jana Porter, a 25-year real estate veteran who has been active in the Park City area for 20 years. Jana specializes in residential, commercial and investment properties. She also owns Silver Queen Management, a property management firm that specializes in nightly rentals and long-term leases of commercial and residential properties. Her diversity ranges into design and development with the further ownership of Sterling Design and Development. These diverse specialties allow her to bring a wealth of practical knowledge to her customers. When you do business with Sterling Real Estate, you can expect integrity, hard work and attention to personal detail. Jana and her team do their best to help you achieve your real estate goals at Sterling Real Estate.

632 Main Street, Park City UT
(435) 649-1266 or (800) 447-6423
www.sterlingparkcity.com

# Le Bar Bohème

*All that jazz* is what you will find at Le Bar Bohème, located downstairs from Easy Street Brasserie in the historical Utah Coal and Lumber building, constructed in 1925. This snazzy club offers a little something for everyone. A Park City hot spot, Le Bar features intimate seating along with a stylish, antique copper bar, framed by a 1000-thousand bottle, climate-controlled stone wine cave. Guests can warm themselves by the fire while enjoying a great selection of wines and spirits. Those who would like to have a bite to eat can order a gourmet delight, prepared by Master Chef Neville King, from the upstairs brasserie. During the summer, enjoy the live concerts outside on the patio. Experience the best that the French have to offer, without having to fuss with a passport, at Le Bar Bohème.

201 Heber Avenue, Park City UT
(435) 658-2500
www.easystreetbrasserie.com

# Easy Street Brasserie

If you are looking for fine French cuisine with a touch of posh attitude, consider Easy Street Brasserie, located in popular Park City. Sample incredible dishes created by Master Chef Neville King and prepared in Easy Street's open kitchen. Using a classic French rotisserie, Chef Neville transforms herb-crusted chickens and fresh fish into scrumptious meals fit for Napoleon himself. Chef Neville also serves delicate potages, like onion soup gratinee, baked with gruyère cheese, and white bean soup with bacon and pistou. Salad lovers will rejoice in crisp and piquant creations, like the heirloom tomato and goat cheese with tapenade vinaigrette and fried basil. To finish off your peerless repast, Easy Street turns out a decadent selection of desserts that will weaken your knees. Three luscious flavors of crème brulee or the tasty, almost sinful soufflé will tempt you into sweet submission. In keeping with the tradition of famous French restaurants in the motherland, Easy Street features seasonal dishes that showcase the best of local and regional cottage food producers and farmers. East Street is located in the restored Utah Coal and Lumber building, built in 1925. The elegant interior of Easy Street allows guests to come in and relax, while the warm ambiance flows around them to create a decadent atmosphere for enjoying what is sure to be a truly satisfying meal. Maitre d' Gordon Montana, and his highly trained staff provide patrons with exemplary service in the old-world style. Make plans to come and see for yourself that Easy Street Brasserie is truly trés magnifique.

201 Heber Avenue, Park City UT
(435) 658-2500
www.easystreetbrasserie.com

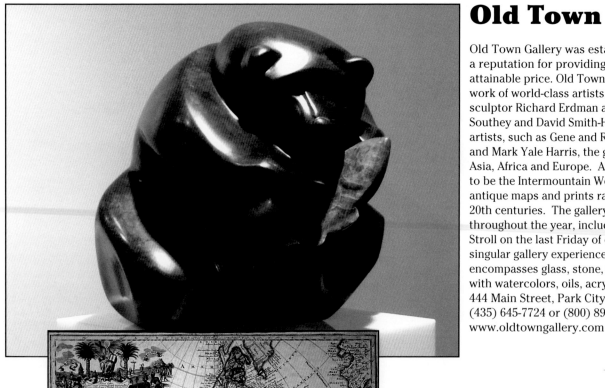

# Old Town Gallery

Old Town Gallery was established in 1980 and has achieved a reputation for providing unique contemporary art at an attainable price. Old Town Gallery continues to feature the work of world-class artists, such as the famed American sculptor Richard Erdman as well as Utah artists Trevor Southey and David Smith-Harrison. Along with regional artists, such as Gene and Rebecca Tobey, Marlene Lenker and Mark Yale Harris, the gallery represents artists from Asia, Africa and Europe.  And now, Old Town Gallery is proud to be the Intermountain West's exclusive dealer of original antique maps and prints ranging in age from the 16th to 20th centuries.  The gallery hosts and participates in events throughout the year, including the Arts and Eats Gallery Stroll on the last Friday of each month. Old Town Gallery is a singular gallery experience. Its extensive and varied collection encompasses glass, stone, wood and bronze sculpture along with watercolors, oils, acrylics and engravings.
444 Main Street, Park City UT
(435) 645-7724 or (800) 891-7085
www.oldtowngallery.com

# Images of Nature

"Photographer Thomas Mangelsen creates wildlife images with an eye for splendor, a passion for conservation and principled notions about artistic ethics," says American Photo Magazine Author David Gonzales. No man's life can be summed up in just one sentence, but Gonzales' words come close. For more than thirty years, Thomas D. Mangelsen has been driven to express the beauty and intricacies of the wilderness and its inhabitants in award-winning photography. Visitors to the thriving community of Park City can view his works at his gallery, Images of Nature. The gallery features a selection of limited edition photographs, posters, calendars, and art cards, all with Mangelsen's stunning photography. Mangelsen has a background in wildlife biology and uses both cinematography and still photography to touch people on an emotional level and inspire them to love and protect these fragile wild environments and their inhabitants. American Photo magazine named him one of the 100 most important people in photography.. His work has been featured in several leading magazines, including *National Geographic*, *Life* and *Wildlife Art*. He has also been a guest on programs such as *Good Morning America* and *CNN's World News*. Additionally, Images of Nature supports many environmental organizations including The Nature Conservancy, the African Wildlife Foundation and Polar Bears International. Discover nature through the eyes of Thomas D. Mangelsen with a visit to Images of Nature.
364 Main Street, Park City UT (888) 238-0233
www.mangelsen.com

# Montgomery Lee Fine Art

Taminah Gallery is now Montgomery Lee Fine Art, but its mission to showcase the finest in realistic and impressionistic paintings and sculptures by award-winning 20th century artists remains the same. "We're not a gift shop and we're not a glitzy kind of gallery," says Linda Lee, the mother half of the mother-daughter team that owns and runs Montgomery Lee. "We are a fine art gallery." Linda and daughter Jennifer are bringing Montgomery Lee into its 11th incredibly successful year, replete with change of name. Montgomery Lee Fine Art is truly a traditional gallery showcasing museum quality artists with national and international reputations as well as those who are just emerging. Their subject matter covers a wide range of genres including Western art, wildlife sculpture, still life, figurative pieces and contemporary and traditional landscapes. Some of the gallery's award-winning sculptors and painters include Sandy Scott, Ed Fraughton, Mike Malm, Joe Alleman and Jim Wilcox. The establishment also specializes in monumental bronze commissions for residential and commercial spaces. A life-long collector herself, with a degree in fine arts, Linda is inspired by the opportunity to find incredible artists and showcase their work. Montgomery Lee Fine Art is a wonderful place for people to buy their first painting and Linda takes pride in both educating and guiding clients in their first steps toward building a collection. Whether you're a novice or an art aficionado, Montgomery Lee Fine Art is definitely the place to witness the artist at work.

608 Main Street, Park City UT

(435) 655-3264

www.taminah.com

# Mountain Trails Gallery

Housed inside the historic bank building on Main Street is Mountain Trails Gallery. With a focus on providing something for everyone, Owner Adam Warner oversees an eclectic collection of works ranging from oil paintings to bronze sculpture. Half of the gallery is dedicated to the largest collection of Western art in Utah. Recently, Warner has extended his collection to include young and emerging Utah artists as well as established favorites. Some of the artists presently featured in the gallery are internationally recognized, such as work from Alan Wolton and an award-wining sculpture by Corinne Hartley. Mountain Trails Gallery originally opened in 1999 under the ownership of renowned sculpture artist Vic Payne and was purchased by longtime friend and gallery manager Adam Warner in 2005. The magnificent oil paintings, stunningly real sculpture and beautiful native-influenced pottery will draw you in and leave you feeling rewarded and inspired. The gallery hosts several exhibits, gatherings and special events throughout the year. Experience the beauty of the West through the moving collections at Mountain Trails Gallery.

301 Main Street, Park City UT
(435) 615-8748
www.mountaintrailsgallery.com

# Stanfield Fine Art

Park City flourishes with enough excellent art galleries and studios to keep art-loving visitors to this favorite destination town happy for days. Among these is the elegant Stanfield Fine Art. With many area galleries focused on western art and showcasing only regional artists, owner Devon Stanfield wanted to offer the community something different. He decided on the global approach. Stanfield travels Russia, Europe, South America and the far reaches of the United States to bring his patrons stunning, hand-selected pieces created by internationally renowned artists. Stanfield specifically searches for those hidden treasures of the art world and takes the time to display museum quality pieces designed by masters. He began pursuing art as a career directly after high school in 1987. Through extensive travel and study, he has learned several languages that he now speaks fluently. He later developed a degree for Arts Promotion at the

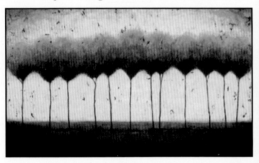

University of Utah. Stanfield also studied and worked in Laguna Beach, Carmel and San Francisco. His distinctive perspective and style is influenced by his time in California combined with his globe-trotting experiences. The gallery opened in 1997 with a focus on talented emerging artists as well as the representation of known artists. The gallery is housed in two separate locations within the Main Street building. The first, larger space allows for the more comprehensive collections and the second, smaller gallery is suited to more intimate pieces. Stanfield Fine Art presents a wonderful mix of cosmopolitan and contemporary art that will leave you breathless. Exhibitions change frequently so there is always something new and inspiring to view at Stanfield Fine Art.
751 Main Street, Park City UT
(435) 658-1800 or (877) 657-1800
www.stanfieldfineart.com

# Terzian Galleries

Though Karen Terzian is new to Park City, she's not new to the world of art, artists, and art collecting. Her family's Armenian heritage is known for their love of culture and the arts, so Karen believes passionately in the necessity for art in life and vice versa. A retired professional skier who traveled the world, she was naturally drawn to the gallery business, where she's been working for more than 20 years. Both she and her staff are experienced collectors themselves and their focus is on friendly and knowledgeable service.  Terzian Gallery is a very approachable, fun gallery, with a light, airy and open feel and colorful, well arranged displays. Karen is drawn to art that speaks to her, and shows many regional and Utah artists who are working in mixed medias. Oil, acrylic and watercolor painting, eclectic glassworks, and metal, marble, and stone sculpture are all represented here. She focuses on artist's whose work is contemporary and unique with an interesting and edgy feel. She doesn't do prints or limited editions, so every piece is an original one-of-a-kind work. In keeping with her philosophy that art is for the people and people need art, her pieces are priced so there's something unique for all budgets. Stop into Terzian Gallery and see what Karen is showing today. Chances are you will  find that special piece of work that speaks to you in a way you can't live without.
309 Main Street, Park City UT   (435) 649-4927   www.terziangalleries.com

# Phoenix Gallery

A visit to Park City's Phoenix Gallery feels similar to a life-sized kaleidoscope filled with a riot of color, texture and wondrous treasure. This contemporary gallery has an eclectic array of paintings, sculpture, blown and fused glass, furniture and multi-media work, all fabulously displayed to both surprise and delight visitors. Curator and Co-owner Judi Grenney displays many of Utah's most prominent artists along with work by other accomplished regional artists. The result is a harmonious blend of mediums, styles and influences. Some of the featured artists include Salt Lake City Olympic Painter Susan Swartz, Abstract Artist Curtis Olson, Sculptor Wayne Salge and Metal Artist Elis Gudmann. This collection is housed in one of Park City's most beautiful historic three-story buildings at the heart of Main Street. Original wood floors, exposed brick walls and upbeat music create a cozy, comfortable atmosphere that is anything but your typical stilted museum feel. Friendly sales associates encourage you to chat about the art or enjoy a moment of respite on one of the inviting leather couches or chairs scattered throughout the space. Phoenix Gallery's tag line states they have "accessible, attainable, collectible art," which allows both new and established collectors to feel at ease when browsing and purchasing artwork. Throughout the year, the gallery highlights artists with art receptions, events that foster the relationships between collectors and the artists whose work they admire. Phoenix Gallery is also a hotspot for the local performing arts post-production parties, Sundance Film Festival parties and other special events. All of these factors make Phoenix Gallery an inspiring gallery; one of the not-to-be-missed finds in Park City.

508 Main Street, Park City UT   (435) 649-1006   www.phoenixparkcity.com

# West Light Images

When West Lights Images' Owner David Schultz was advised at an early age that his diabetes could cause loss of vision, it fostered a passion to see all that he could. A native of Michigan, David began his career as a professional fashion photographer in Dallas, Texas. An assignment in the Utah Mountains prompted him to focus on nature and the remarkable outdoor scenery, and he moved to Utah to revel in it. He has since traveled throughout the United States, Alaska, Canada and South America, and is currently preparing a trip to Antarctica. His work reflects the wonder of a world that often goes unnoticed by the casual onlooker. Schultz' nature photography adorns the walls of this Park City gallery and is featured in private and public collections worldwide. David's photographs are hand-signed limited editions, each printed on Fuji Crystal Archive paper. Each piece is matted with acid-free, museum mat board colored in a light gray, with a dark gray border. These measures insure the vivid colors and sharp details for which his work is noted will be enjoyed for generations to come. Aside from the brilliance of color found in Schultz' images, quality and craftsmanship are important aspects of finishing a framed piece. Every piece receives special care and attention, as orders are often filled by the photographer himself. Stop in at West Light Images to enjoy the warm, casual gallery environment and the dramatic visual experience.

738 Main Street,
Park City UT
(435) 645-8414
or (800) 713-9474
www.westlight.net

# Thomas Anthony Gallery

Thomas Anthony Gallery is located in the heart of historic Main Street in the visually stunning and highly popular year-round mountain resort of Park City. Surrounded by three major ski resorts (Deer Valley, Park City and the Canyons Resort), the gallery features a beautiful selection of paintings and sculptures by national and internationally acclaimed artists as well as regionally up-and-coming artists. Showcasing such an array of quality artists from many different countries allows the casual viewer and the serious collector a visual delight unmatched in the resort gallery experience. Featured artists include Vilanova, Royo, Javier, Rieder, Frederick Hart, Pujol, Samerjan, Alvar, Arkhipov, Barbara McCann, Liu Miao Chan, Adam Stewart, Martin Greer, Sottil, Farrar, deDecker and Pierre Bedard. Thomas Anthony Gallery takes great pride in offering Old World service to its collectors while utilizing new world technology to facilitate their passion for collecting fine art.

340 Main Street, Park City UT   (435) 645-8078   www.thomasanthonygallery.com

249

# David Whitten Gallery

Drawn by a love of skiing, photographer David Whitten came to Park City at the age of 19. He was soon enrolled in The University of Utah, where he took a wide variety of classes and discovered his love of photography. Over the next several years, David went on to hone his skills and worked in many area galleries. Through the 1990s, he worked for the Kimball Art Center in Park City, where he taught both color and black and white photography classes and became sort of a Jack-of-all-trades for the Center. David opened his own gallery in the spring of 1996. For more than 20 years, David has been taking captivating pictures that capture the natural beauty of Utah, Wasatch County and North America. Many of David's pictures are taken with his Pentax 6x7 camera as the large film size lends itself beautifully to large prints filled with exquisite detail and depth. Each photograph is individually printed using only the highest quality and longest lasting photographic papers available. Additionally, each piece is a signed and numbered limited edition. The David Whitten Gallery frames and mounts all works on-site, using the highest quality conservation-grade materials, designed to give each photograph optimal protection and provide a lifetime of enjoyment. Enjoy David Whitten's spectacular imagery, beautifully displayed at the David Whitten Gallery in Park City.
523 Main Street, Park City UT
(435) 649-3860 or (866) 649-3860
www.davidwhittenphoto.com

# Meyer Gallery

Since 1965, Meyer Gallery on Main Street in Park City has been catering to the discerning collector. Situated in the historic 1890 building that formerly housed the First Bank of Utah, this well-established gallery has long fostered a reputation for exquisite artwork and exemplary service. The building itself still exudes turn of the century elegance, and the Meyers have maintained the original character of the architecture over the years. The Meyer Gallery was founded by Darrell and Gerri Meyer and later purchased by Daughter Susan Meyer Jones. Meyer Gallery specializes in bronze sculpture as well as representational and impressionistic work by regional and national artists. With both modern and traditional paintings, watercolors and wax-based encaustics on display, this engaging gallery offers something that will appeal to the art lover in all of us. The gallery additionally features an astounding array of mixed media, carvings and traditional sculpture. The Gallery has displayed works by all of the major contemporary artists working today. Meyer Gallery performs other services for their patrons in conjunction with finding and displaying fine art. These services include installation or hanging of artwork for the purchaser and providing a delivery upon approval service. Find the artwork that best suits your tastes and complements your lifestyle at the full service Meyer Gallery.

305 Main Street, Park City UT
(800) 649-8180
www.meyergallery.com

# Mother Nature's Nook

If the natural spirit of the wilderness moves you and you also relish an original shopping adventure, visit Mother Nature's Nook for an escape from the ordinary. Owner Julee Nichols recognized the need for a centralized place where local Utah artists and craftspeople could sell their handmade wares. Julee, an artisan herself, started out by traveling to art festivals and craft fairs to sell her jewelry and florals. After 10 years, her inventory became too large to cart around so she opened a 4000 square foot store in Heber City with a second location on Main Street in Park City. With all the cabins and vacation homes in the vicinity, Julee found a niche for her locally made rustic and woodsy home décor, mountain furnishings, accessories and artwork. Not only are the items at Mother Nature's Nook an incredible joy, they are useful too. You'll find extraordinary articles such as beds with twists and gnarls, distinctive three-legged chairs, one-of-a-kind lamps with handmade lampshades and antler chandeliers. If you're looking for something more traditional, discover original art, custom florals, jewelry, quilts and even handmade candy.

If you still can't find what you're looking for, one of Julee's 300 talented artists can create it for you at Mother Nature's Nook, so pay Julee a visit and find what you're looking for today!

608 Main Street, Park City UT
(801) 319-4793
155 N Main Street, Heber City UT
(435) 654-9900
www.mothernaturesnookonline.com

*Vernal Temple (below), Unknown Temple detail (right)*

# Guitars & More

On the west side of the Jordan River stands the thriving, growing city of West Jordan, home of Guitars and More. Here, Owner Adam Ohlwiler is committed to providing products that cannot be found at other shops. Quality personal service helps customers browse through the largest variety of guitars possible for the space, and the staff is expert at buying, selling and trading merchandise. If you don't see what you want, they can get it for you at the lowest prices in town. Lessons and repairs are also available at the shop and the owner loves to teach. Ohlwiler finds satisfaction in watching his students become good players. He started playing at the age of 13, progressing from playing in bands into teaching and providing instruments, music and industry connections that students can't find anywhere else. Guitar packages often include the instrument itself as well as a stand, a gig bag, amp, microphone and stand, cables, a strap and picks. Drum packages can include cymbals, throne, hardware and sticks. Lessons are so reasonably priced that you'll want several. Come in and try the special offer of four guitar or drum lessons or purchase them as a gift for your own budding musician. At these prices, you can even purchase the instrument to go along with the lessons!

7211 S Plaza Center Drive # 170, West Jordan UT   (801) 282-6736
1218 N Main, Tooele UT   (435) 843-9822
www.guitarsdrumsandmore.com

# Utah Firefighters Museum & Memorial

In 2000, the Utah State Firemen's Association saw the realization of 25 years worth of effort when the Utah Firefighters Museum & Memorial was dedicated. Since its opening, it has quickly become a popular destination for Utahans and visitors from throughout the West and around the world. Conveniently located at the Desert Peak Complex in beautiful Tooele Valley, the Museum's 30,000 square feet of display space features more than 35 different fire trucks and vehicles, as well as uniforms, artifacts and apparatus covering well over a century of heroic struggle against the scourge of fire.

Designed as a living museum, the complex includes an auditorium for presentations, and fire safety training is offered to school groups and scout troops. When you visit, be sure to take time to pay your respects to the memory of the Utah firefighters who sacrificed their lives on behalf of their fellows; each is honored by a plaque on the Memorial wall. The Utah Firefighters Museum & Memorial is currently open to visitors on Fridays and Saturdays and by special arrangement. You can contact the curator, David Hammond, for more details.

2930 State Route 112, Grantsville UT
(435) 843-4040 or (435) 830-6556
www.utahfiremuseum.com

254

# Daynes Music

Imagine that it's 1873. A Steinway & Sons piano is being shipped from Germany. It comes through San Francisco, then up over Donner Pass in a wagon, through Nevada and on to Salt Lake City. That piano is still in service at Daynes Music in Midvale, the oldest music store in the West and second oldest in the United States. Established in 1862, Daynes is also Utah's first retailer and the 76th oldest family-run business in the entire nation. When Utah became a state, Daynes Music was already 34 years old. Gerald R. "Skip" Daynes, president and chairman of the board, is among the fourth generation of Dayneses who have taken care of customers at this store. He considers it part of his business to sponsor great music throughout the intermountain west. To that end, Daynes Music has been instrumental in the establishment and promotion of the Utah Symphony, the Utah Civic Ballet (a.k.a. Ballet West) and the Utah Opera Company. The store once carried a variety of musical instruments but now concentrates on piano sales and is Utah's only Steinway dealer. If you'd like some history with your new piano, head to Daynes Music in Midvale.

6935 S State Street, Midvale UT
(801) 566-6090
www.daynesmusic.com

*Courtesy of Newman Photography*

## Tuscan Garden Works

About eight years ago, Jim and Kathy Lillywhite went to work in their garage because Kathy needed an arbor for some climbing roses. She hadn't been able to find anything suitable in the area, and with Jim's background in engineering and Kathy's skill at design, they ended up creating not only an arbor but a business, Tuscan Garden Works. At first they were just providing custom designed structures for their neighbors' gardens. As their reputation grew, they went from selling items out of their garage to selling on consignment out of local garden supply stores. Later they opened their own showroom. They quickly outgrew this first facility and now are in a much larger indoor facility, which displays multiple old world garden settings, including garden structures, benches, splashing fountains, all surrounded by greenery with serene classical music playing in the background. Tuscan Garden Works provides an enchanting setting for Jim and Kathy's creations. In addition to designing arbors, trellises, gazebos and all manner of structures for the garden, The Lillywhites have branched out into interior design. You can also find beds, rockers, bistro style iron chairs and tables, baker's racks, decorator items, gifts and more. Tuscan Garden Works also features garden sculptures, including the largest selection of Nativity scenes available in the area.
468 W 9160 S, Sandy UT (801) 233-9434 www.tuscangardenworks.com

# Great Models

The story of Great Models reflects the combining of traditional and modern business techniques. It all started with Douglas Models. One of the country's oldest hobby shops, it had operated in Utah since 1934. A typical example of a brick and mortar hobby shop, it was very successful due to the passion and experience of its staff and owners. Then, in the 1990s, the dot com world met the old-fashioned industry when GreatModels.com was created in the basement of a hobbyist. Both companies merged in 2004 to make one of the world's largest plastic model companies. It offers over 24,000 hobby-related products on its website and about 10,000 plastic and remote control products at its storefront, located at 7700 S. Redwood Road in West Jordan. The Internet company, based in Sandy, has spread its wings with other websites like KitLink.com and now ships to over 100 countries. For all your modeling desires, head to Great Models in Jordan or on the world wide web!

8385 S Allen Street, Suite 140, Sandy UT    (801) 565-0634 or (800) 619-3402

www.greatmodels.com

# Tiburon Fine Dining

Tiburon Fine Dining has quietly become one of Utah's premier restaurants. Tiburon is located in an unassuming building that formerly housed a fruit stand in the south end of the Salt lake Valley. Don't be fooled by the location, Tiburon serves award winning cuisine ranging from beef tenderloin with foie gras and a sweet madeira syrup to black sesame crusted ahi tuna with honey and soy marinated carrots. The crab cakes consistently win best in the state and the salads are raved about by the locals. It doesn't end with the food, service is always top notch. Led by a staff that has been with Owners Ken and Valerie Rose since its opening, guests at Tiburon always feel welcome in the warm and friendly atmosphere. In the Summer with its patio dining, Tiburon is the place to eat in the South Valley.

8256 S 700 East, Sandy UT

(801) 255-1200

# Heritage Gardens at The Deveraux

Heritage Gardens provides classic, quality catering in a magnificent setting that was created to provide clients with the ideal location for their wedding and reception.  This exquisite business, owned by Scott and Jan Gatrell, was designed specifically to fill a particular niche in the Salt Lake City wedding market. That market is for the bride who wants the caliber of wedding/reception that the more traditional Utah "punch and cookies" reception center can't offer, at a more affordable price than the grand ballroom of a luxury hotel, country club or fine restaurant.  Their friendly and knowledgeable staff will help you with all of the infinite little details to make your special day absolutely perfect.  The catering that Heritage Gardens provides is delightful, high-quality cuisine with a variety of menu items to select.  Heritage Gardens can also assist you with selection of the cake, flowers, invitations and photography services. Let the specialists at Heritage Gardens do what they do best—make your wedding and reception a beautiful and memorable experience.

2050 E Creek Road, Sandy UT

(801) 944-4575

www.heritagegardens.com

# Castle Creek Inn

Conveniently located in the center of Salt Lake Valley lies an authentically-designed Scottish castle just waiting to make you feel like royalty. The Castle Creek Inn Bed and Breakfast has been a treasured getaway spot for Utah visitors and locals for 12 years. Owners Lynn and Sallie Calder invite you to come and experience the magnificence of Castle Creek Inn for yourself. Sit in the charming gazebo while listening to the soothing strains of a bubbling rock waterfall or enjoy the beauty of the dense grove of oak trees that surround the castle walls. Several individually-themed rooms are available for guests to choose from. One popular choice is the sunny Romeo and Juliet Room which features a romantic balcony. Another option is Rupunzel's Tower Room with its stunning stone wall and elegant fainting couch. It's just the right room to unwind and let down your hair. A more masculine alternative is the bold Excalibur Room where you will find ancient weaponry dashingly displayed on the walls and antique furniture beautifully accented by rich brocades and velvets. Each comes complete with private bath and jetted-whirlpool tub, gas fireplace and television with DVD player. In the morning, guests may choose between a scrumptious, two-course breakfast in the dining room, or a lighter, just as delicious meal enjoyed in-room. Based on its centralized location, Castle Creek Inn is the ideal place to escape for business or pleasure while experiencing all Salt Lake Valley has to offer.

7391 S Creek Drive, Sandy UT
(801) 567-9437 or (800) 571-2669
www.castleutah.com

# 1887 Hansen House Bed and Breakfast

The 1887 Hansen House in Sandy is a charming bed and breakfast located just south of Salt Lake City. This wonderful inn offers all of the elegance one would expect of a vintage Victorian home along with all of the modern conveniences that make our lives more comfortable and relaxing than that of our pioneer ancestors. This beautiful home has been painstakingly restored to its former glory and proudly displays its stunning woodwork and hardwood floors, which blend harmoniously with stained glass windows, period wallpapers and crystal chandeliers. The parlor and the library, popular with guests, are each warmed by graceful period fireplaces. Owners and Innkeepers Ed and Fran Hansen have beautifully designed and decorated several themed rooms each with its own bath. For instance, the Blue Lagoon Room features a king-sized round bed and Jacuzzi tub, and the English Fox Hunt Room is ideal for retreats and family reunions. Guests of the Hansen House are treated to hearty and delicious breakfasts in the morning and are provided with an in-room tea tray in the evenings. The Hansen House is a non-smoking facility, and pets are not allowed within the home; however, outside accommodations are available for four-footed guests. The 1887 Hansen House is an ideal place to stay while touring nearby historical sites, checking out the shopping in Salt Lake City or enjoying one of numerous ski slopes or recreational trails. The Sandy area is also home to several performing arts centers, where you can enjoy the symphony, opera or ballet. Make your Utah vacation complete with a stay at the 1887 Hansen House.
8586 S Center Street, Sandy UT   (801) 562-2198   www.hansenhouse.com

# Brighton Resort

In an age of competition and hustle, Brighton Resort stands with one foot in the peaceful past and one in the accommodating present. Brighton is all about skiing and snowboarding, pure and simple. Three of the seven lifts are high-speed quads. There are 1,050 ski-able acres above 8,750 feet and an annual average snowfall of 500 inches. Brighton's diversity extends beyond retaining the personal, family-owned feeling of the past, it is also a nationally top-ranked resort year after year. On the mountain, Brighton offers something for everyone. Throughout its 70-year history, Brighton has been known as a family-friendly place. With a superb ski and snowboard school and a balance of beginning, intermediate and advanced terrain, Brighton caters to all ages and abilities. This is also a mecca for pro-skiers and boarders with backcountry access to the greatest snow on earth and a top quality pipe and park. Daily guests rave about the grooming, with impeccable corduroy to be found off the top of every lift. With 200 acres lit at night and serviced by three lifts, Brighton's night skiing offers the most variety in the region. An ancient glacier carved out Brighton's weather-producing bowl. It is devoid of condominiums and offers the well-stocked Brighton Mountain Sports retail shop and Molly Greens, a private club with après ski drinks and sit-down dining. Guests also can find sustenance at the Alpine Rose cafeteria, the Milli Chalet café or the Brighton Village Store café. More lodging and restaurants are available in a five to 30-minute drive. A visit to Brighton will make you want to return again and again.
12601 E Big Cottonwood Canyon Road, Brighton UT
(801) 532-4731 or (800) 873-5512
www.brightonresort.com

# La Caille

Beyond the subdivisions and stoplights of Utah's Salt Lake Valley is a 20-foot-tall cast iron gate marking the entrance to La Caille restaurant. As you pass through the gate, the restlessness of the world fades. The air gets cooler, the trees seem greener and the geraniums look brighter. Once you make your way up the red brick lane, magnificent buildings await. Recalling the French chateaus and European gardens of 200 years ago, La Caille is also distinctly fresh. The menu could deliver you to a bucolic farmhouse for roasted duck or swing you east and into the 21st century with a progressive dish of ahi tuna prepared with tempura and wasabi. Dining at La Caille is a sensual experience, one of the last bastions where people believe that a meal should be a relished, pampering and intoxicating experience. La Caille, with its 22 acres of vineyards, dining rooms, ponds, barns and overnight cottages, has been owned by the same family for 30 years. A living, breathing entity, this establishment is constantly changing and evolving, yet always feels the same. Year after year the same families, businesses and travelers faithfully return to La Caille. There aren't amusement parks for connoisseurs, artists and those who delight in grace and elegance, but if anyone needs a blueprint for such a place, La Caille is it. La Caille is as accommodating to a table of two as it is for a wedding or corporate party of a thousand.
9565 Wasatch Boulevard,
Little Cottonwood Canyon UT
(801) 942-1751
www.lacaille.com

# The Bingham Canyon Lions Club Gift Shop

The Bingham Canyon Lions Club Gift Shop features many specialty items relating to the area's historic and still-productive Kennecott's Bingham Canyon Mine. The Bingham brothers settled in the area in 1848 with cattle on their minds, but it wasn't long until the rich deposits of metal brought attention to the region. Around 1906, low-grade copper ore began to be mined from the mountain in Bingham Canyon. Now the mine is the largest man-made excavation on Earth. It is the only man-made structure other than the Great Wall of China that can be seen by astronauts in outer space. The mine is currently about two and a half miles across and three-quarters of a mile deep and it is estimated that it will be about 500 feet deeper by 2015. Seventeen million tons of copper have been taken from this mine, more than any other mine in history. It has also produced 23 million ounces of gold, 190 million ounces of silver and 890 million pounds of molybdenum. Bingham Canyon Lions Club Gift Shop offers gifts inspired by local ore in the forms of jewelry, t-shirts, copperware and many shelves full of other eye-catching items. All the merchandise is sold to benefit the children of Copperton and across the nation, in keeping with the Lions Club's vision. Funding goes to Guide Dogs for the Blind and the Moran Eye Center. To help in this quest, the Lions Club also collects registration fees for swimming, dances and sports activities over the holidays.
12400 South 4-111, Copperton UT
(801) 569-6251

*Photos courtesy of KUC*

# South Jordan Leisure, Aquatic & Fitness Center

South Jordan, an agrarian community along the Jordan River, stands alone among cities of comparable size. This is a city that caters to family life. In keeping with that spirit, the South Jordan Leisure, Aquatic and Fitness Center is an impressive glass and brick structure full of activities for every age and temperament. This recreation destination boasts the largest indoor swimming pool in Utah, containing 190,000 gallons of water. The center plans to install an Ozonator, which will drastically cut the amount of chlorine needed by as much as 60 percent. A great deal of care went into the details for this large-scale pool. For instance, the main support pillars on the west side have been placed at specific angles to provide more sunlight in the winter and less in the summer, and the developers didn't stop with the pool. There are three full-size basketball courts, a weight room, jogging track, dance rooms and a spinning room. For the young and young at heart, there is an indoor slide, water toys, a lazy river and a kid's pool. Extreme sports lovers will find an outlet as well at the competitive skate park with a 15-foot bowl for skateboards and roller blades. Come on by when you need some fun action. The South Jordan Leisure, Aquatic and Fitness Center is bound to make your heart race.

10886 S Redwood Road, South Jordan City UT
(801) 253-5236   www.sjc.utah.gov

# Sweet Briar Hollow

In the heart of Draper is a 150-year-old home that has become a popular place to purchase gifts, furniture and accessories for the home and garden. The house, originally owned by Joshua Terry, was renovated and upgraded to meet commercial codes in 1992. Once known as the Pioneer House Bed and Breakfast, Karen and Lee Warren purchased the establishment in 1997 and turned it into the present Sweet Briar Hollow. The Warrens were able to expand their retail offerings, thanks to the addition of the Potting Shed in 1998 and the Guest House in 2000. The historical charm and beauty of the buildings and the grounds provides a pleasurable shopping experience, bound to put you in the mood to shop for home décor. The staff at Sweet Briar Hollow provides in-house design consultation services to help you find just the right florals, lamps, furniture, house and garden accessories. The neighborhood has changed some since Joshua Terry's days. Look for Sweet Briar Hollow just west of Draper City's new roundabout and the entrance to its historical district and just up the street from the new city hall and the new library. When you need just the right item for a gift or for yourself, visit Sweet Briar Hollow.

1229 E Pioneer Road, E 12400 S, Draper UT
(801) 572-5971

# Hemstitched Lullabys

Jenny Sedgewick's goal is a modest one: she just wants to bring hemstitching back to the world. Her personal mission is to revive what is almost a lost art so that today's parents, grandparents and babies can experience this loving tradition that is rich in history. Hemstitched Lullabys specializes in beautiful baby gifts, blankets and bibs that you can buy or create yourself. Hemstitching is a method of decorative hand-stitching that was used in the early 1900s to make elaborate designs and patterns around the edges of expensive linen, tablecloths, parasols and baby articles. The custom was to wrap a new baby in a warm flannel receiving blanket that had been edged by a family member with its own unique, hand-crocheted stitching. At Hemstitched Lullabys, a new generation is now learning the joys of this time-honored domestic art. With an array of over 300 warm and cozy quality flannels to choose from, you can design your own combination or choose one of Jenny's best sellers. Jenny and her dedicated staff will give you free instruction and help with customizing that special gift for the newborn in your family. Initially, Jenny started working out of her home. With the renaissance of the art of hemstitching, she transformed this family-run home business into a full retail store in Draper. Drop by and see for yourself how wonderful a return to the past can be at Hemstitched Lullabys.

584 E 12300 South, Draper UT   (801) 816-1880   www.hemstitchedlullabys.com

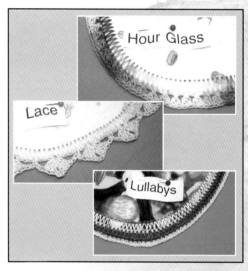

# Access Motorsports

Do you want access to the appropriate toy for every season? Do you want to avoid the headaches, breakdowns, and costs associated with owning those toys? Access Family Recreation is a dealership and Timeshare for recreational vehicles including: RVs, boats, ATVs, motorcycles, snowmobiles and watercraft. They are also recreational consultants for vacation homes, condos and properties. Access Recreation purchases the machines and pays taxes, license and registration fees, storage, maintenance and insurance. Access absorbs the depreciation and the expense, leaving you with fun! Fun! Fun! Your membership gives you access to family recreation at less than the cost of a new waverunner or ATV. Access Motor Gear also provides rock bottom prices on all parts and gear for Bombardier, Ski-doo, Suzuki and Sea-doo.

Dealership: 13200 S 48 East, Draper UT   (801) 495-3278
Rental facility: 11585 S State Street, Draper UT   (801) 561-9601
www.accessrec.com

# King Arthur Self Storage

The city of Draper is surrounded by the impressive Rocky Mountains, and located between Provo, the home of Brigham-Young University, and famed Salt Lake City. It is also the site of a self-storage facility like no other. This winner of the 2003 storage facility of the year award carries its theme beyond logos. The building is a castle, complete with fireplace, round table conference room, and plush surroundings. There are three locations, all owned by visionary Owner Mitch Huhem and his partners, James and Jay Mitton. The stone facility is as secure as King Arthur's court, with state of the art security ranging from 24-hour video surveillance to perimeter beams, and keypad entry with resident managers on site. A free 15-foot moving truck complete with side panel mural is available for the use of clients to move their belongings into the facility. A full line of moving supplies is available for purchase. The Draper and West Valley locations also offer some climate-controlled units for temperature-sensitive items. Offices for rent are located on the upper level of the building. Manager Annie Coyle rules the day-to-day activities. The opposition encountered in the owners' struggles to build provides inspiration for countless future entrepreneurs, and is a part of the community's history. The resulting convenient, economical, secure and safe facility is a model of self-storage with flair! The royal hosts will greet you with cookies upon your arrival at King Arthur Self-Storage.

14039 S Minuteman Drive, Draper UT
(801) 619-1999   www.kingarthurstorage.com

# Johnson Mill Bed & Breakfast

Johnson Mill Bed & Breakfast in Midway is an inn with everything you could imagine for a romantic getaway, honeymoon destination or restful retreat. A gazebo accessed by a pier is the perfect location for viewing the sunset or watching swans float serenely on the magnificent four-acre lake. Guests can even take a canoe ride for a closer view. Each room has a distinctive perk, evidenced by its name, and all rooms share certain luxuries such as rock fireplaces and oversized tubs. The Moroccan-style honeymoon suite has a waterfall faucet in the bath. Three rooms feature unique views of either Mt.Timpanogos, an adjacent 40-foot waterfall or the picturesque Provo River. Another room features a private entrance opening into the courtyard. Choose from eight magical rooms, or rent the entire inn for a special occasion. Johnson Mill is an enviable site for a wedding or group event. Rentals of the full facility, including the grounds and kitchen, must be for a minimum of three days. A stay at Johnson Mill includes a full breakfast, but this is far from a typical bed and breakfast. Enjoy 26 acres of wooded pathways, streams and ponds, plus opportunities for world-class fishing and cross-country skiing. If you are looking for amazing, out-of-the-ordinary lodging, this is it. Drop off your bags and fall into an outdoor hammock. Choose a package for that special vacation because Johnson Mill Bed & Breakfast will convince you that it doesn't get any better than this.

100 Johnson Mill Road, Midway UT
(435) 654-4466 or (888) 272-0030
www.johnsonmill.com

264

# Invited Inn

The Invited Inn Bed & Breakfast in Midway offers guests the rare, coveted experience of total relaxation. Bill and Susi Stern own and operate the inn, and as their motto states, they aim to spoil you rotten. The five elegantly themed rooms all boast of private bathrooms with steam showers and European towel warmers, fireplaces, featherbeds and down comforters. In addition, the four deluxe rooms offer double whirlpool tubs, private saunas and private patios or balconies. But the real difference at Invited Inn is the level of comfort enjoyed here, where a guest is free to throw on a provided robe and slippers and wander downstairs to enjoy a movie on large screen television while munching on fresh popcorn and specialty beverages. The ambience is relaxed and intimate, like visiting friends and family. You can play games or strum a guitar, eat cookies off the endless cookie plate or help yourself to sodas, water or juices in abundance. This bit of paradise has the added benefit of being situated in a prime location where everything is virtually a country stroll away. The inn is on the second tee of one of five local golf courses. Nearby attractions include mineral pools, a full-size outdoor ice rink and the largest ski resorts in Utah. This town is also host to the Sundance Film Festival, Swiss Days and the Cowboy Poetry Festival. Active guests can enjoy outdoor activities, including hot air balloon rides, horseback riding, hiking, mountain biking and fishing. At the end of the day, return to one of five themed rooms; bask in the firelight and fall asleep in a log bed or under a romantic, draped canopy. For a home away from home with fun and fine dining around every corner, visit the Invited Inn. It's more than a stay; it's an experience.

1045 N Homestead Drive, Midway UT
(435) 654-7075 or (866) 654-7075
www.invitedinn.com

*Kolob Canyons*

# Inn on the Creek

Planning a wedding, vacation or team-building retreat? Perhaps you are looking for a romantic interlude for two? No matter the reason, make your reservation for the Inn on the Creek in Midway. Centrally located between the Sundance Ski Resort and Park City's Deer Valley Resort, this elegant, contemporary inn provides all the amenities of a big hotel with friendly and exemplary service in an intimate atmosphere. The inn features 40 oversized rooms that have been designed with luxury in mind. Each beautifully decorated guestroom has a private bath with jetted tub and separate shower area, televisions with VCR, coffee maker and triple sheeting on the beds. Most of the rooms have fireplaces and private decks or balconies. Dining at Inn on the Creek is a delicious experience, and the inn's impressive on-site restaurant boasts one of the largest and most comprehensive wine cellars in the state. Here, Utah native Chef Cody and his dedicated staff create one fabulous meal after another. Cody has honed his skills in kitchens around the world and presents an eclectic and inspiring menu of dishes from all across Europe and the United States. This stellar restaurant has received many awards for its cuisine and wine selection. Inn on the Creek is also known for its elegant banquet dinners. Guests of Inn on the Creek can renew their mind, body and spirit without ever leaving the inn with a visit to the full-service day spa. Only minutes away from several area golf courses, galleries and ski spots, a stay at Inn on the Creek will make the most of your next getaway.

375 Rainbow Lane, Midway UT
(435) 649-0892
www.innoncreek.com

# Heber Valley Historic Railroad

The journey begins with the unmistakable sound of the whistle and familiar call of all aboard, as Utah's 100-year-old train prepares for departure. The excitement builds as engine 618, a 1907 Baldwin Steam locomotive, pulls out from the Heber Depot for a spectacular scenic ride through the farmlands of Heber Valley. The Heber Valley Historic Railroad dates back to 1899 when trains served the pioneers who first settled the valley. Today, vintage coaches are pulled over this beautiful vista by two 1907 Baldwin steam locomotives and three vintage diesel electric locomotives. Over 77,000 passengers ride the train each year, and that number is steadily growing. The dramatic route meanders along the shoreline of Deer Creek Reservoir, plunges into glacier-carved Provo Canyon and follows Provo River to Vivian Park. Sightseers enjoy dramatic views of the Wasatch Mountains and majestic Mount Timpanogos. In 1970, the community rallied for support to keep the rails alive by introducing a scenic tourist line called the Heber Creeper. Named for its leisurely pace, it's still fondly referred to by this name today by all who rode the train during that era. Today, the Heber Valley Railroad operates scenic rides, entertainment trains and private charters. Special events include comedy murder mysteries, dances and the barbecue dinner train. Look for ghosts and goblins aboard October's Haunted Canyon Train or ride The Polar Express during the month of December. Heber Valley Historic Railroad is dedicated to keeping the history of Utah and the West alive by lovingly restoring railroad equipment back to operating condition. Come experience a classic treasure of Utah.
450 S 600 W, Heber City UT (435) 654-5601 www.hebervalleyrr.org

# Two Sisters Fine Art Gallery

Two Sisters Fine Art Gallery may be a new venture (its doors opened in 2003), but its origins date back to the childhood days of Lynn Farrar, when her sister Cynthia Stott remembers watching Lynn sketch everything in sight. She drew Peggy Fleming at the 1968 Winter Games, horses, trees and ballet dancers, among other things. "You might say the gallery is a marriage of the minds or right and left brain," says Gallery Owner Cynthia. Along with her sister's work, Cynthia represents 12 other substantial local Utah artists in the gallery. Visitors will find everything from the whimsical sculpture of Jack Morford to traditional landscape paintings by Lynn Farrar and Karrie Penne. Come see fused glass sculpture and found object assemblages by Dennis Smith plus still life and equestrian art by Lonni Clarke, whose work is collected by Ralph Lauren. Two Sisters Fine Art Gallery is located in the charming village of Heber Old Town, next to the famed Snake Creek Grill. For a fresh take on fabulous art, visit Two Sisters Fine Art Gallery.
6500 W 100 S, Heber City UT   (435) 654-6250   www.twosistersfineartgallery.com

Bryce Canyon

# Southern Utah

# Thanksgiving Point

Karen Ashton's dream of a garden weaved its way into her heart at an early age when she read the wonderful children's novel, A Secret Garden. She had discovered for herself the miraculously restorative effect natural landscapes and gardens have on the human soul. And, like little Mary Lennox of the novel, Karen longed for a bit of earth. Karen's bit of earth became reality in 1995 when she and her husband, Alan, were blessed with unexpected abundance and purchased an alfalfa field – lush, green and isolated. Then, as an expression of untold gratitude to a kind and gracious Creator, the Ashton's established Thanksgiving Point. A nonprofit institute, Thanksgiving Point is dedicated to the idea that knowledge through first-hand experience is one of the greatest gifts one can offer. Today, Thanksgiving Point has become the gathering place for the community, promoting the renewal of mind and spirit in a beautiful and family-friendly setting. It has grown to include a 55-acre botanical garden, a world-class museum, a working farm, courses in a variety of arts and sciences, restaurants and retail shops, not to mention one of the region's best golf courses. Thanksgiving Point is home to hundreds of private and public events each year. Fairs, festivals, corporate events, exhibits, banquets and weddings are all traditional fare at Thanksgiving Point. Music, ballet, film and art are also mainstays with performances held regularly at the Show Barn, Electric Park and the spectacular Waterfall Amphitheater. Providing a one-of-a-kind, hands-on opportunity for discovery and an entertaining, educational experience is the driving force at Thanksgiving Point. In short, it is a place to experience – to touch, to taste, to feel and to discover.

# Thanksgiving Point Gardens

Karen and Alan Ashton created Thanksgiving Point Gardens as a refuge from everyday life—a unique destination that would showcase the beauty and majesty of nature and as a literal expression of their gratitude. One of Utah's most amazing escapes, Thanksgiving Point Gardens features 55 acres of beauty and relaxation, an impeccably designed masterpiece with 15 uniquely themed gardens and the largest man-made waterfall in the western hemisphere. The gardens are organized like rooms of an immense estate, with thousands of trees, shrubs and grasses serving as living barriers between spaces, creating a sense of wonder as guests pass from room to room along nearly 4 miles of pathways. Walking the gardens is just part of the experience; you can learn to make your own garden thrive by attending the many of Thanksgiving Point Garden classes.

Within Thanksgiving Point Gardens are 15 separate themed gardens.

**Shepard's Hill**
**Grand Allee**
**Creek Garden**
**Monet Garden**
**Rose Garden**
**Koi View Pier**
**Vista Mound Garden**
**Fragrance Garden**
**Secret Garden**
**Butterfly Garden**
**Italian Garden**
**Prairie Garden**
**Parterre Garden**
**Waterfall Amphitheatre**
**Mountain Garden**

# The Children's Discovery Garden

Located adjacent to Thanksgiving Point Gardens, The Children's Discovery Garden is a child's dream of exploration and educational diversion. The Bear Cave, Eco Pond, and Mineral Mound, await young adventurers seeking to discover more about Utah's environment and provide fertile ground for young naturalists. A central feature of the Children's Discovery Garden, Noah's Ark is a watery work of art that, along with the nearby Hedgerow Mazes, provide hours of entertainment for the young and young at heart. Home to the Bug Stage and Discovery Station Classrooms, The Children's Discovery Garden is also a place to enjoy musical and lyrical performances or participate in unique activities and classes covering a wide variety of topics.

# Museum of Ancient Life

Take a giant leap back in time for a super-sized, hands-on, prehistoric experience. While the air buzzes with insect chirps and dinosaur growls, explore a Carboniferous Forest, dive deep into a Jurassic Ocean and traverse a valley packed with breathtaking reptiles. This is no ordinary museum. There are so many things to touch and feel and do, your hands won't know where to begin. Dig your own fossils, design your own colorful dinosaur, make charcoal fossil etchings, or build an entire sand valley at the Erosion Table (complete with tiny dinosaurs and trees) then watch as gushing rivers wash it away.  When it's time to give your busy hands a rest, stroll beneath the behemoth Supersaurus, dodge dueling T-Rexes or gaze into the toothy jaws of the giant Megalodon, the largest shark in the history of, well, history.  The Museum of Ancient Life is the most impressive and astounding dinosaur museums on the planet, not to mention the world's largest. With more than 60 skeletal displays, 50 touch-and-feel exhibits, and a 3D movie theater with a 60-foot screen, it's a world-class facility and a community treasure.

# Farm Country

When the rooster crows, things get going at Farm Country. After all, this is a real, honest-to-goodness working farm.  It's also a great way to get up close and personal with all your favorite farm critters from geese and goats to cows, pigs, horses and everything in between. It seems there's even an ostrich or two wandering around.  Farm Country, with its display of domestic farm animals, serves as a tribute to farming and demonstrates the impact of the American Farmer on modern life. It is also a favorite destination for educators and students from area elementary and middle schools; tens of thousands visit each year for field trips and other educational opportunities.  Families love the hands-on one-on-ones, with plenty of opportunities for petting, feeding, and general quality time. When you're all tuckered out, you can relax with a pony ride or a wagon ride and a trip to the gift shop.

# Thanksgiving Point Golf Club

 A championship caliber course, the Golf Club at Thanksgiving Point is 7,728 yards long and covers more than 200 acres, making it the largest golf club in the state. Ranked in the top 10 new courses in the country by *Golf Digest* in 1997, the Golf Club at Thanksgiving Point was recently named the number one public golf club in Utah by Golf Digest and one of 15 "hidden gems" in the country by *Links Magazine*. This Johnny Miller Signature Golf Club cradles the most spectacular gardens in Utah, and creatively uses the natural mountain desert landscape to enhance the overall golf experience. The course features a beautiful clubhouse, spacious practice facilities, premium rental clubs, the Hall of Fame Grill and is home to the Annual Champions Challenge and the Johnny Miller Golf Academy, truly making it a world-class facility.

280

Even shopping and dining are unique
experiences at Thanksgiving Point.

**Shops**

*Cobblestone Design*

*Candy Shop*

*Chambrey's*

*Cobblestone
Kitchen*

*Discover Utah
General Store*

*Tulips & Tadpoles*

*The Village Toy*

**Dining**

*Harvest Restaurant*

*Deli*

*Soda Fountain*

# The Village
# at Thanksgiving Point

With its distinctive water tower and proximity to Interstate 15, The Village at
Thanksgiving Point is perhaps the most recognized venue on the entire property
as well as a landmark for travelers. The Village offers a unique shopping
experience featuring many specialty shops, tasty food and beverage at the
Deli, old-fashioned ice cream treats at the Soda Fountain and an elegant dining
experience at the unforgettable signature restaurant, Harvest.

Nearby, the impressive Show Barn stands ready to accommodate up to a thousand
guests, and is used for concerts, dinners, corporate events, dances and other special
events. Just around the corner is Electric Park, an expanse of more than 12 acres
of green grass, an 800-seat pavilion, volleyball and basketball courts, ample parking
and gated entries, which make it the location of choice for large outdoor events like
the Utah County Fair, the Scottish Festival, the Brazilian Festival, Holiday Lights and
more. Electric Park is also available to rent for corporate and family gatherings.

281

# Harvest Restaurant

Located in the Village at Thanksgiving Point, Harvest Restaurant features regional American dishes with Mediterranean influences. Harvest's grand entrance and three masterfully hand-painted dining rooms create a perfect gathering place for a business lunch or a romantic getaway. Harvest features a variety of steaks, chops, fresh seafood, pasta, salads and seasonal soups with desserts made fresh daily in the Thanksgiving Point bakery. In addition to serving lunch and dinner, Harvest offers Saturday Breakfast served weekly, along with lunch favorites off the menu. Experience the simple elegance of Thanksgiving Point's signature restaurant, Harvest.

Reservations: (801) 768-4990

# Thanksgiving Point

*3003 North Thanksgiving Way*
*Lehi, UT*

*(888) 672-6040*
*www.thanksgivingpoint.com*

# Sundance

The pastoral simplicity of the Sundance Resort is graced by 6,000 acres of protected wilderness at the base of 12,000-foot Mt. Timpanogos. Only an hour's drive from Salt Lake City, and 45 minutes from Park City, Sundance was ranked 6th by *Conde Nast Traveler*'s 2005 Reader's Choice Awards. Founded by Robert Redford in 1969, Sundance is committed to the balance of art and nature. Mountain recreation includes year-round, world-class fly-fishing in the Provo River; skiing, snowboarding and cross country skiing in winter; hiking, biking and horseback riding in summer. Discreetly tucked into the mountainside, Sundance's rustically elegant mountain cottages are designed to echo the purity of the natural setting, featuring rough sawn beams, stone fireplaces or wood stoves. Guests may choose to stay in a mountain home, mountain suite, Sundance suite or studio. Sundance features award-winning cuisine in the Tree Room, Sundance's fine dining restaurant, the Foundry Grill, noted by Zagat's for its brunches to die for and Zoom in Park City. The Tree Room features seasonal mountain cuisine at its best in a romantic atmosphere, with candlelight and soft illumination accenting the Native American Art and Western memorabilia from Robert Redford's private collection. The Foundry Grill is a casual, three-meal-a-day restaurant with an incredible view of Mt. Timpanogos.

The hearty, down-home seasonal flavor is achieved through cooking techniques that center around the restaurant's open Foundry kitchen, which features a wood-burning grill, oven and rotisserie. Zoom puts its own distinctive twist on American Continental cuisine. Sundance provides the perfect blend of art, nature and recreation. In addition to mountain activities, explore the other treasures of Sundance. Whether creating your own piece of jewelry in the Art Shack, or enjoying a hot stone massage in our Native American-inspired spa, your trip to Sundance will be filled with memorable opportunities.

(801) 225-4107 or (800) 892-1600

www.sundanceresort.com

# Brätt Water Features

What do all of the following places have in common—the Brigham Young Historic Park, McKay Dee Hospital, Thanksgiving Point, the American Express Corporate Office, Suncrest Welcome Center, Sherwood Hills Resort, the I-15 Pleasant Grove Interchange and the LDS Conference Center? The answer is waterfalls, fountains, streams, ponds or other water features designed and built by Brätt Water Features Inc. of Pleasant Grove. "We've built most of Utah's largest water features," says Brätt President Derk Hebdon. Derk has owned the business for five years; Brätt has been in business for over 40 years and has been nationally recognized several times for its superior workmanship. Brätt is a fully licensed and fully insured builder, a John Deere preferred dealer and a member of the Better Business Bureau of Utah. Brätt can build a water feature on any landscape. Water gardens, rock retaining walls, waterfalls or water gardens large or small – Brätt has done it and has the expertise to satisfy you as well. Come in and experience the difference that a master water feature builder can make. For a better idea of what Brätt can do, check out Brätt's demonstration features at the Cottonwood Mall (next to the food court) and at Trolley Square (next to the theatre entrance). 754 W 700 S, Pleasant Grove, UT
(801) 785-8100 or (866) 485-8100
www.brattwaterfeatures.com

285

# Brigham Young University

Brigham Young was known as an expert craftsman, colonizer, territorial governor, and the President of The Church of Jesus Christ of the Latter-day Saints. In 1875, as part of a drive to provide opportunities for self-growth and development, Young established Brigham Young Academy, now known as Brigham Young University. A forerunner for its time, Brigham Young University encouraged women as well as men to seek continuing education. Today, the university continues to embrace students who have the capacity and desire to continue learning and serving others throughout their lifetimes. Additionally, the university retains its focus on excellence and remains well-known for both its inspiring faculty and its academically-minded and diverse student body. Brigham Young University is further renowned for its spectacular performing arts ensembles and its extensive language program. Students of BYU are also exposed to an excellent athletics program, which features 10 men's and 11 women's teams and is considered to be one of the top programs in the country. BYU offers courses for 11 different colleges including a School of Education along with Nursing and the Ira A. Fulton College of Engineering and Technology. They also offer continuing education and graduate studies along with three general undergraduate programs including religious education. The picturesque Provo campus features two libraries, four astonishing museums and five concert halls and theaters, along with several auditoriums. Achieve your personal, spiritual and academic goals at Brigham Young University, where their aims are achieved when you achieve yours.

Brigham Young University, Provo UT   (801) 422-4636   www.byu.edu

Photo by Jaren Wilkey/BYU

Photo by Mark Philbrick/BYU

Photo by Steven Walters/BYU

Photo by Mark Philbrick/BYU

Photo by Steve Walters/BYU

## Seven Peaks Water Park

What better way to beat the summer heat than to make a splash at Provo's Seven Peaks Water Park.  Seven Peaks is Utah's largest water park with slides, pools and activities sure to delight every member of the family.  Tad Pole Pond and Adventure Bay are just right for the little ones and feature kiddy-sized slides, interactive play structures and waterfalls. Adventure seekers can take on the extreme challenge of the 30 foot Boomerang, six-story Slide Tower, or Wave Pool while those just looking for a chance to kick back and relax can float along the quarter mile Lazy River.  Seven Peaks showcases a huge variety of activity pools, tube runs and speed slides to fill your day with excitement.   Over 24 shaded cabana areas around the park are available for reservation and are ideal for parties or family gatherings.  Pavilion style tents can accommodate small or large corporate and private groups and a full catering menu is available to make your celebration complete.   If the combination of swimming and dancing sounds intriguing, Seven Peaks plays host to pool parties and movie nights to offer visitors a unique and wholesome environment for family recreation.  Seven Peaks Water Park is the perfect destination for good clean water fun.
1330 E 300 N, Provo Utah
(801) 373-8777
www.sevenpeaks.com

## Hines Mansion
## Bed and Breakfast

Welcome to Hines Mansion Bed and Breakfast, a quiet place to relax and enjoy the natural beauty of Utah County. This Victorian mansion has played an active role in the life of Provo since its construction in 1895, Built by Russell Spencer Hines after Provo's recovery from a major boom-and-bust period, the mansion later became an apartment house, a boys' school, a number of restaurants and an antique shop. In 2002, John and Sandy Rowe purchased the Hines Mansion and turned it into a comfortable lodging. Guests can choose from nine bedrooms and read or play games in the Victorian parlor with its imported Italian marble fireplace. All rooms are equipped with a private bath and two-person spa tub, comfortable robes and cable television with a VCR and complementary video library. Business travelers will appreciate the wireless Internet access. Each day, the Rowes treat guests to a gourmet breakfast with such specialties as strawberry-stuffed French toast. During the day, look for fresh-baked cookies and cakes set out in the kitchen. The Hines Mansion Bed and Breakfast has a special ambiance conducive to small weddings and summer lawn receptions. It's a memorable getaway for a vacation or private celebration and sits within walking distance of several downtown restaurants and theaters.
383 W 100 S, Provo UT    (801) 374-8400
www.hinesmansion.com

# Center Street Musical Theatre

In March 2004, Gavin and Sharilyn Grooms fulfilled a lifelong dream and opened Center Street Musical Theatre in the heart of historic downtown Provo. Provo's only dinner theatre, Center Street Musical Theatre performs musicals and features a live orchestra with most productions. The Grooms and their seven children work as a team to create a family oriented atmosphere for all to enjoy. Gavin and Sharilyn have a combined 60 years of experience in theatre and music in New York, California, Idaho and Utah. In just a year's time, they created a large following of patrons who come back again and again. Their theatre can seat just under 300 people for the show and up to 175 for dinner at one time. Local restaurants cater the before-show dinners. Center Street Musical Theatre takes a strong interest in involving youth and young adults in theater by offering workshops, summer camps, dance lessons, voice and music lessons. The Theatre has plans to start both jazz and children's choirs. 177 W Center Street, Provo UT (801) 764-0535 www.csmtc.com

# McNaughton Fine Art Gallery

Picture yourself walking through open gates that lead to lush garden paths, quiet streets, charming homes and poetic landscapes. Mesmerizing scenes will captivate you at the McNaughton Fine Art Gallery. This gallery and studio features the impressionistic art of Jon McNaughton, an established Utah artist whose popularity is increasing among collectors from across the country. Painting from the heart, McNaughton focuses on his memories of nostalgic places in his own mind's eye rather than looking at a photograph. The effect is pure serenity with his softly painted landscapes that use subtle tones of color. Each of his paintings seems to speak with familiarity, as if you've seen it before, yet the image stands alone. Today, few artists paint in the style of the French Barbizon School, popular from 1830 to1875. Artists such as Monet, Van Gogh and Renoir as well as McNaughton found their inspiration from the Barbizon painters. Visitors to the McNaughton Fine Art Gallery can watch the artist as he works on his newest masterpiece and can select from original paintings, giclee prints on canvas and limited edition reproductions. McNaughton teaches his technique at workshops to help aspiring painters develop their own talents. Owners John McNaughton and Lee Freeman invite you to gaze at the beauty of soft Impressionism and traditional landscapes.
Provo Towne Centre Mall
1200 Towne Centre Boulevard,
Provo UT
(801) 319-7219
www.mcnaughtonart.com

*River Color*

*Day's End*

290

# The Window Box Gallery

Owned by the esteemed Judi Harding and her daughter Cori Olsen, the Window Box Gallery has exhibited distinctive artwork for over a decade. Located in historic downtown Provo, the gallery carries paintings and prints by Utah artists and is also a Greenwich Workshop and Mill Pond Press dealer. The Window Box Gallery specializes in Latter-day Saints art and works by the eminent James C. Christensen. Latter-day Saints artwork depicts themes prominent in the history and beliefs of the Church of Jesus Christ of Latter-day Saints, though these artists of merit are not necessarily members of the LDS Church. Artist James C. Christensen lives in Utah and is world renowned for his personalized style of whimsical fantasy art. Christenson has published several successful and widely acclaimed books and has won innumerable awards for his work, which is often referred to as having a Shakespearean influence. Christenson's works depict an imaginative world of graceful actions and the symbolic manifestations of human emotions. U.S. Art magazine recently inducted him into their Hall of Fame. He is a designated Utah Art Treasure and has received the Governor's Award for Art in recognition of his significant contribution to the culture of Utah. As a represented artist at the Window Box Gallery, you will find

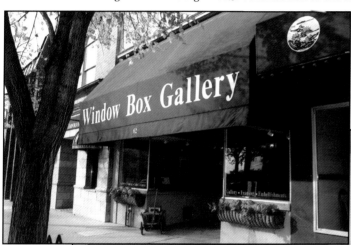

signed works by James Christensen and, perhaps, a personal appearance by the artist himself. Browse the Window Box Gallery's many display-ready pieces or create your own signature look with the Gallery's expert archival quality matting and framing. Whether you are looking for that special piece to highlight your collection or just looking for an opportunity to experience Utah's artistic culture, you'll discover it at the Window Box Gallery.

62 W Center Street, Provo UT

(801) 377-4367

# Springville Museum of Art

The Springville Museum of Art is Utah's oldest and most beautiful museum for the visual fine arts. The history of the museum began in 1903, with the donation of art work to Springville High School by founders Cyrus E. Dallin and John Hafen. When the current building was erected, it was dedicated as "a sanctuary of beauty and a temple of meditation" by David O. McKay, Today, the museum houses over 1,900 works, 1,400 of which are Utah art. Twentieth Century Russian-Soviet Socialist Realism, an impressive array of 150 years worth of Utah fine art and American Realist art comprise the permanent collection. With an average of 15 visual art exhibitions annually, the museum is a key promoter and contributor to the arts in Utah. The collection and exhibitions are displayed throughout 29 galleries in this 45,000-square-foot facility. The museum seeks to fulfill its mission by refining minds and building character through fine art. As the official State Wide Art Partnership (SWAP) headquarters, the museum is home for visual art educational outreach programs for the schools of Utah. A variety of exhibitions, concerts, programs and special events are offered throughout the year. The museum annually serves 80,000 plus visitors on-site, 35,000 off-site and is available for rentals. For a history lesson of Utah, through the imagination of its artists, visit the Springville Museum of Art.

126 E 400 South, Springville UT   (801) 489-2727   www.sma.nebo.edu

# Krishna Temple

An enriching cultural experience awaits you with a peaceful visit to the Krishna Temple. For five years, the temple has openly welcomed everyone to tour the beautiful grounds, explore the cultural center, feast at the vegetarian buffet or peruse the gift shop. Visually stunning, the temple is modeled after a famous devotional palace in India called Kusum Sarovar, which means temple on a lake of flowers. The structure, perched on an elevated 15-acre plot in rural Utah, features a 50-foot-tall main dome, 108 arches and columns, magnificent sculptures and murals, open patios, gardens and fountains. The main temple shrine is embellished with ornate black teakwood and gold leaf altars. Serenity abounds as you take a stroll to see the koi pond. This 200,000-gallon lake even has a lovely waterfall and shaded picnic area and a grand outdoor stage and amphitheater holds many festivals throughout the year. Visitors are delighted by the resident llamas, peacocks and parrots and are surprised to find that they can lease a llama for camping, trekking, pack trips and parties. Located just 45 miles south of Salt Lake City, the Krishna Temple is an all-encompassing sanctuary filled with peace and beauty. Step into a world of tranquility not often found in today's busy society at Krishna Temple.

8628 S Main Street, Spanish Fork UT
(801) 798-3559

**Young Living Essential Oils**

# Young Living Lavender Farm

Driving on highway I-15 through the stark, high-desert area of central Utah, it is difficult to envision anything but sage brush and pinion pines growing in this isolated area. Yet suddenly, large squares of deep purple appear on the desert landscape. Curiosity beckons and leads you to an unexpected herb farm, the Young Living Lavender Farm.

While large herb farms are common in France, Italy, Great Britain, and Spain, they are a rarity in the United States—particularly in the deserts of Utah. Yet, in a sparsely populated town called Mona lies the largest therapeutic lavender farm and distillery in North America. This particular parcel of land, however, is not new to cultivated herbs. As early as 1871, Howard and Martha Jane Corey, Mormon homesteaders, settled this remote area. While Howard raised livestock, Martha gained a reputation by selling fine liniments and medicines made from herbs that she gathered and grew on some of the very same land.

Today, the Young Living Lavender Farm in Utah consists of 1600 acres of farmland filled with lavender and other aromatic plants that are destined to become some of the finest essential oils available. Several large farm greenhouses protect thousands of tender young seedlings, all waiting for the perfect growing season. A restored farmhouse, complete with a healthy food restaurant and gift shop, also acts as Visitors Center for the farm. There, you can inquire about a variety of seasonal activities that include viewing the distillation process, herb garden strolls, wagon excursions, paddle boat rides, and an occasional wild-west shootout or medieval jousting contest. Young Living also has lush herb farms in Idaho and France.

# Gift Shop and Visitors Center

The scent of premium essential oils greets you at the door of the farm's gift shop and Visitors Center. Your mind tries to identify the dominant aroma that changes as you browse from room to room. This beautifully restored home was originally owned by Howard and Martha Corey.

Warm and inviting, this attractive, brick building sells only the best essential oils and essential oil products. Though they may be used as perfumes, bath fragrances, or room fresheners, these oils are therapeutic-grade and are highly prized by skilled professionals to use as powerful healing agents. You can't help but know that Martha Corey would be pleased with the modern use of her lovely home.

The store, built near the center of the farm, houses oils extracted from herbs grown in the very fields that surround it. The cheery atmosphere is partly due to friendly clerks with a solid knowledge of essential oils. They inform you of activities to enjoy while visiting the farm. They can also schedule corporate events and family gatherings, such as weddings and reunions.

The mingled aroma of the oils are captured in your hair and clothing, and it lingers with you long after you leave. You also notice that you feel a little more peaceful and relaxed. All shopping should feel this good.

# Whispering Springs Grill: A Healthy Steak House—Why Not?

A truly unique eating experience, the Whispering Springs BBQ Smokehouse Grill, located in back of the Visitors Center, combines healthy, primarily organic foods with the great taste of familiar, home-cooked meals flavored with essential oils—a rare commodity in our fast-paced, fast-food society.

Whispering Springs BBQ Smokehouse Grill serves homemade potpies, stews, fire-grilled beef or buffalo steaks, and perfectly seasoned, roasted chicken, all range fed and hormone-free. These mouthwatering entrées are complimented with fresh salads and roasted vegetables, many of which are grown right on the farm. On the lighter side, the grill offers delicious sandwiches and a variety of freshly made wraps—a wide selection for every member of the family.

The in-house specialty is an agave-sweetened, New York style, wolfberry cheesecake. Agave, a mild tasting, low glycemic, golden nectar is made from the agave cactus. And if you haven't heard about the legendary wolfberry from Ningxia China, you are missing out on one of the most powerful antioxidant and longevity foods on the market. This is one of the few sinfully delicious desserts that you can eat without having to worry about empty calories or your health.

This fabulous restaurant offers a highly appetizing menu at affordable prices. Eat healthy, eat hearty, and enjoy it at the Whispering Springs BBQ Smokehouse Grill. Please call ahead for availability, as the restaurant is only open seasonally.

# History of Young Living Essential Oils

In 1989, from the humblest of beginnings, D. Gary Young started what would grow into the world's leading essential oil company on a one-quarter acre farm in Spokane, Washington. On this small plot of ground, Gary cultivated herbs for essential oils. He also built his first distiller by welding two pressure cookers together with a swan neck of copper pipe. It was placed on the kitchen countertop, and the water for the cooler came from the kitchen sink.

Three years later, in 1992, Gary bought 160 fertile acres in St. Maries, Idaho, and planted lavender exported from France.

In 1993, Young Living Essential Oils was established in Riverton, Utah.

In the summer of 1994, Gary designed his first stationary distiller. It was stainless steel with a decompression chamber and manifold to produce low-pressure, low-temperature steam.

In 1996, the Young Living farm in Mona was increased to 1,600 acres, making it the largest herb farm for the distillation of essential oils in North America. This same year, the Young Living corporate office was moved from Riverton to Payson, Utah.

Business grew rapidly, and in 1999, Young Living opened the Australian and Japanese markets. The distillery at the Mona Farm added more cookers, owning a total of thirty.

In 2003, Young Living purchased a farm in France. The corporate headquarters moved from Payson to a large, modern office building in Lehi, Utah.

Today, Young Living is the world leader in the marketing and distribution of essential oils and related personal care and nutritional products.

# D. Gary Young

The Founder, D. Gary Young, formed the company after realizing the need to share with the world his incredible discovery of the power of essential oils. As a young man, Gary suffered a crippling injury that nearly cost him his life. This launched him on a personal health odyssey that transformed him both physically and emotionally. Traveling the world to study essential oils and alternative health care, Gary has become a foremost authority in natural health and has become intensely committed to sharing his knowledge and expertise on essential oils with others.

Today, Gary continues traveling across the continents, investigating both traditional and modern uses of essential oils and gaining insights on every facet of essential oil production—from distillation and harvesting to seed selection and crop management. The company owns the largest, most technologically advanced distillery for the production of essential oils in North America. Our proprietary distillation process preserves the fragile integrity of pure essential oils.

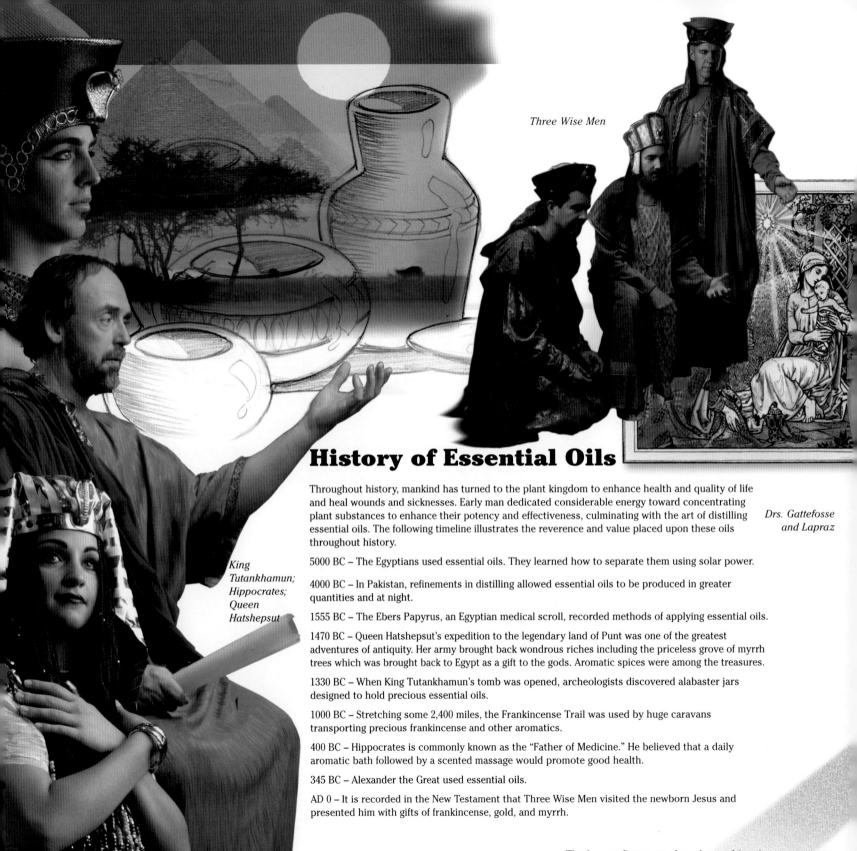

*Three Wise Men*

# History of Essential Oils

*Drs. Gattefosse and Lapraz*

Throughout history, mankind has turned to the plant kingdom to enhance health and quality of life and heal wounds and sicknesses. Early man dedicated considerable energy toward concentrating plant substances to enhance their potency and effectiveness, culminating with the art of distilling essential oils. The following timeline illustrates the reverence and value placed upon these oils throughout history.

*King Tutankhamun; Hippocrates; Queen Hatshepsut*

5000 BC – The Egyptians used essential oils. They learned how to separate them using solar power.

4000 BC – In Pakistan, refinements in distilling allowed essential oils to be produced in greater quantities and at night.

1555 BC – The Ebers Papyrus, an Egyptian medical scroll, recorded methods of applying essential oils.

1470 BC – Queen Hatshepsut's expedition to the legendary land of Punt was one of the greatest adventures of antiquity. Her army brought back wondrous riches including the priceless grove of myrrh trees which was brought back to Egypt as a gift to the gods. Aromatic spices were among the treasures.

1330 BC – When King Tutankhamun's tomb was opened, archeologists discovered alabaster jars designed to hold precious essential oils.

1000 BC – Stretching some 2,400 miles, the Frankincense Trail was used by huge caravans transporting precious frankincense and other aromatics.

400 BC – Hippocrates is commonly known as the "Father of Medicine." He believed that a daily aromatic bath followed by a scented massage would promote good health.

345 BC – Alexander the Great used essential oils.

AD 0 – It is recorded in the New Testament that Three Wise Men visited the newborn Jesus and presented him with gifts of frankincense, gold, and myrrh.

*The human figures are based upon historic reenactments.*

AD 100 – Pliny, a Roman historian, wrote a book titled Natural History that describes the uses of herbs and essential oils.

AD 1000 – An Arab physician named Avincenna advanced the science of essential oils by developing steam distillation.

AD 1400 – During the Medieval Plague, four thieves in Marseilles, France, robbed the dead without becoming sick. When captured, the men revealed a mixture of aromatics they used to protect themselves against the deadly plague.

1930 – A terrible accident in his laboratory caused Dr. Rene-Maurice Gattefosse, a cosmetic chemist, to be burned severely. He covered his burns with lavender essential oil. Amazed by the positive effect of the lavender, Gattefosse focused his research on the healing powers of essential oils. He coined the term "aromatherapy."

1940 – Using Gattefosse's research, Jean Valnet, a French doctor during World War II, successfully treated wounded soldiers with essential oils.

1980 – Dr. Jean Lapraz, a student of Dr. Valnet and a member of the prestigious phyto-aromatherapy research team in Paris, discovered that microbes could not survive in the presence of some essential oils.

1985 – On a personal quest to discover the keys to health and longevity, Gary Young traveled through Europe in search of lost essential oil knowledge.

1989 – Returning to the United States, Gary Young was determined to restore the forgotten therapeutic secrets of essential oils.

*Avincenna and Dr. Valnet*

*Above: terra cotta distiller (4000 BC); Petros along the Frankincense Trail (1200 BC to AD 200); Ebers Papyrus from Egypt circa sixteenth century BC.*

*Four thieves*

*Young Living Lavender Farm in France*

# Young Living Essential Oils Worldwide

Young Living Essential Oils is an internationally established company that is renowned for its high-quality products, which include therapeutic-grade essential oils, dietary supplements, personal care products, and other unique solutions for healthy lifestyles.

Recognized as a global leader in natural health products, Young Living has perfected the art and science of essential oils and continues to be the foremost leader in aromatherapy. For well over a decade, Young Living has been leading the way in unlocking the health secrets of antiquity. The most advanced civilizations of the ancient world—the Egyptians, Greeks, Romans, and Chinese—relied upon the vast power of pure plant essential oils to regain, increase, and maintain a healthy body and a strong mind.

Adding to this ancient knowledge with advanced scientific research, Young Living is restoring this lost wisdom to the world and is providing practical solutions to today's health care needs through its therapeutic-grade essential oils and oil-enhanced products. Young Living empowers individuals and families to achieve their highest potential and enjoy increased physical, mental, emotional, and financial health.

The essential oils in Young Living's collection, which are freshly cultivated and steam distilled, are life-enhancing gifts from the plant kingdom. Essential oils have been revered for centuries for their restorative properties to body, mind, and spirit and are now re-emerging as a key solution to the wellness challenges facing our modern lifestyles.

To meet today's dietary needs, Young Living manufactures and sells the highest-quality food and dietary supplements, which are enriched with our pure therapeutic-grade essential oils. All Young Living food products contain nutrient-dense, natural, whole ingredients and are free of artificial sweeteners. Our company prides itself on the quality and performance of its products.

As a global leader in the research and development of innovative essential oil and health-related products, Young Living continues to set the pace for the alternative health care industry. Using the highest-quality, therapeutic-grade essential oils and leading-edge technology, Young Living has developed a new line of products designed to help people of every age live healthier and happier lives. Our high-tech laboratory and cutting-edge production facility ensure that every Young Living product consistently leads the industry in purity, quality, and effectiveness.

Young Living's products are distributed worldwide by more than 100,000 independent distributors.-Come visit us and find out what makes our products so unique!

# Tarahumara Humanitarian Project

Young Living and its employees are anxiously engaged in doing much good within the community and globally. For example, Young Living President and Founder D. Gary Young led a team of Young Living corporate leaders and company distributors on a weeklong humanitarian expedition to the Tarahumara Indians in the rugged Sierra Madre Mountains of northern Mexico.

The Tarahumara Indians live in the remote regions of the Sierra Madre mountains in the Mexican state of Chihuahua. The Tarahumara are northern Mexico's largest Indian tribe and are a nomadic people who typically live in several different dwellings during the year, including caves. In today's world, the Tarahumara retain their ancient, aboriginal way of life.

The humanitarian expedition provided the Tarahumara village of Coyachique with food, children's school kits, and the building materials for a small schoolhouse. After erecting the support structure and roof on the schoolhouse in Coyachique, the Young Living team cleared the land for a second schoolhouse in the village of Wimaivo.

While in Coyachique, Gary Young sought out the source of the village's water supply. Discovering the entire village received their water from one very small and inadequate seep, Gary left for Chihuahua, a city located more than four hours away, to purchase a water pump and supplies for a new water system for Coyachique.

Every team member on the Young Living Tarahumara expedition described the experience as "life-changing."

303

# Places To Visit & Things to Do

There are a number of fun and educational activities that may be enjoyed when visiting the Young Living Essential Oils corporate office and the Young Living Lavender Farm. Our company is especially interesting to individuals who enjoy plants, herbs, healthy lifestyles, luxurious aromas, and nature. Make plans from the following list of things to do and places to visit.

### Herb Farm—Mona, Utah

From spring until fall, Young Living Lavender Farm provides an array of useful information and demonstrations centered on herb farming and distillation. Learn alternative farming techniques used to produce herb crops without the use of chemical fertilizers and harmful pesticides. Call ahead to set appointments for in-depth planting and farming demonstrations.

### Annual Herb Harvests

Observe annual herb harvests, scheduled from the end of June until the beginning of September. Of particular interest is the yearly lavender festival. This harvest-time celebration includes not only lavender and distillation demonstrations but also samplings of unusual foods made with lavender, fun games, and a lot of hard work. Call the Visitors Center for dates and activity lists.

### Distillation

After the herb harvests, our unique distillation process begins. Watch as large amounts of raw herb material are transformed into small amounts of valuable essential oils. Call ahead to the Visitors Center for a schedule of planned harvest and distillation times, which vary according to the season.   Essential oils may be purchased in the Visitors Center along with other alternative health care products.

### Family Park

This restful oasis is the perfect place to escape from a hectic lifestyle. Bring a picnic lunch or call ahead for catering from the Whispering Springs BBQ Smokehouse Grill. The large, park pavilion is perfect for individual family outings, family reunions, parties, dances, wedding receptions, and corporate getaways. Children can ride paddleboats on the duck pond, scale the rock-climbing wall, or enjoy the on-site playground. Another point of interest is the pretty herb garden that grows near the Visitors Center. If you are in the mood for exploration, wander down through the Old English Village to the reservoir. There, you may see a bald eagle or a graceful blue heron.

### Special Occasions

Several events are planned throughout the year. During these times, you can experience wild west shoot-outs, wagon rides and races, jousting tournaments, and other lively activities. Check with the Visitors Center for possible dates of upcoming events.

**Corporate Office—Lehi, Utah**
Tour the place that keeps it all happening, the corporate office in Lehi, Utah. Scheduled tours allow you to visit points of interest, such as our Creative Services and Media departments, Distributor Network Services, Research and Development, our research lab, and other departments that keep our business humming. While there, visit our Will Call store and purchase the purest essential oils and essential oil products available.

**Contact Info:**
**Young Living Lavender Farm, Visitors Center, and Whispering Springs Grill**
3700 North Highway 91
Mona, UT 84645
1-435-623-7911
www.younglivingfarms.com

**Young Living Essential Oils Corporate Office**
Thanksgiving Point Business Park
3125 West Executive Parkway
Lehi, UT 84043
1-801-418-8900
www.youngliving.com

# St. George Art Museum & Dinosaur Discovery Site at Johnson Farm

The St. George Art Museum hosts fine art traveling exhibits and the work of local artists. Housed in what once was a sugar beet storage facility, the St. George Art Museum is part of the historic Pioneer Center for the Arts complex located in the downtown area. The city of St. George's mission is to establish a quality collection of art that features Southwest Utah. Within one mile of the museum, visitors also have the chance to go back in time to the Jurassic Period thanks to the Dinosaur Discovery Site at Johnson Farm. In 2005, while leveling a hill on his property, Sheldon Johnson found dinosaur tracks fossilized in sandstone. A visit to this prehistoric wonderland, which attracts visitors and scientists alike, includes the world's largest collection of swim tracks made by dinosaurs swimming in ancient Lake Dixie. Fossil tracks made by a theropod dinosaur, as well as a 52,000-pound single track block with 14 dinosaur trackways on its surface, are among the other unique finds. Combined with the museum's family-friendly Discovery Center, a trip to St. George is an amazing, educational and memorable adventure for all ages. Whether you like art or history, you'll get plenty of both at the St. George Art Museum & St. George Dinosaur Discovery Site at Johnson Farm.

St. George Art Museum & Store
47 East 200 North, St. George UT
(435) 634-5942 ext. 117
www.sgcity.org/arts
St. George Dinosaur Discovery Site at Johnson Farm
2180 East Riverside Drive, St. George UT
(435) 574-DINO (3466)
www.dinotrax.com

306

# City of St. George Golf Courses

The City of St. George offers more golf courses per capita than just about anywhere else in the country. Nestled in a beautiful desert setting with towering red sandstone cliffs off in the distance, you are sure to find a course that perfectly fits your game. All told, there are nine public courses and one private course in the area. Of those, the City of St. George manages four. Dixie Red Hills offers a relaxing round of golf on nine scenic holes. It's a favorite of those who like to walk the course because it is known as one of the most player-friendly courses in the area and has hundreds of mature trees for shade in the warmer months. Southgate Golf Club, a favorite of the local players, offers 18 scenic player-friendly holes in a relaxing atmosphere. Sunbrook Golf Club has to be the premiere golf course in the area as *Golf Digest* named it the number one publicly-owned course in the state. Three distinct nines offer a total of 27 championship holes you can play. Finally, St. George Golf Course offers 18 challenging holes and boasts some of the best greens in the state. It's the home of the St. George Amateur, has some difficult par three's, and is an easy course to walk. Be sure to stop, visit, and play golf in the beautiful City of St. George.
175 E 200 N, St. George UT
(435) 986-4418

# Rosenbruch Wildlife Museum

The world-class Rosenbruch Wildlife Museum is a beautiful way to experience over 300 wildlife species from around the world in their natural habitats. Guests carry a self-paced radio that narrates their personal journey through the museum, complete with a visit to a two-story mountain with two live waterfalls, ambient animal sounds and sporadic thunder and lightening storms. Some of the species exhibited at the museum are extinct in their native countries. Managed sport hunting aids governments in providing protection for critical habitat and wildlife resource management. The large mammals on display at Rosenbruch have been collected over the past 40 years by means of legal hunts, providing revenue for protecting habitats and for anti-poaching efforts in developing countries. The museum offers a variety of community programs for youth, including a fun and educational Saturday Kids Club for children ages three to12. At Rosenbruch Wildlife Museum, family nights and school tours encourage education as well as offering a rollicking good time for all participants. Wild birthday party packages and a generous scholarship for one Washington County high school senior each year illustrate some of the many inspiring ways Rosenbruch Wildlife Museum interacts with the community. The Rosenbruch family also operates yacht-based sport fishing, touring and hunting excursions for the public. To inquire into these trips, go online to www.glacierguidesinc.com. Visit Rosenbruch Wildlife Museum to take advantage of the rare opportunity to glimpse nature at its finest. 1835 Convention Center Drive, Saint George UT
(435) 986-6619
www.rosenbruch.com

# Sun River Golf

At SunRiver St. George Golf Club, you're bound to have one of the best golfing experiences imaginable. This breathtaking, 18-hole championship course is nestled in a beautiful valley next to the Virgin River. Surrounded by colorful desert landscape, wide-open blue skies and impressive sandstone cliffs, you'll find the finest greens on which to putt, and the only bent grass tees in the southern part of the state. Surrounded by the planned home-site community of SunRiver St. George, you'll find a course that was constructed in such a way as to take full advantage of the area's natural terrain.

The 6,700-yard course perfectly preserves and captures stunning vistas and was designed with the area's 55-and-older population in mind. The area also boasts of some of the most amazing natural scenery in the world. You're also near many national parks like Zion, Bryce and the Grand Canyon. Even though the area attracts millions of visitors each year , you'll find yourself playing golf in a quiet, relaxed and rural setting. St. George has been recognized as one of the premier places to live in the nation. You're invited to come and spend a day on this amazing course, and have a golfing experience that's bound to keep you coming back again and again.
4210 S Bluegrass Way, St. George UT
(435) 986-0001 or (877) 986-0131
www.sunrivergolf.com

# SunRiver St. George

Imagine yourself living in a part of the country that boasts wide-open spaces, crystal blue skies, and breathtaking sandstone cliffs. Now imagine yourself living in a premier master-planned, active adult lifestyle community. At SunRiver St.George, you can find all this in a quiet, rural, unspoiled location. The community as a whole was constructed with the idea of creating a unique lifestyle, while at the same time providing homes built with top quality construction. In addition, all the amenities usually found only in larger metropolitan areas are included and designed to enhance the lives of active adults. In this community, however, you'll find no high-density crowded neighborhoods or other stressful urban settings. Enjoy playing a round of golf on the beautiful 6,700-yard course. It boasts stunning vistas of the area and the layout is perfect for the community's age 55 and better residents. There are plenty of other activities available too, such as swimming, biking and lawn bowling. Another important and appealing part of the community is the Community Center. At 30,000 square feet, some of its features include an indoor/outdoor pool and spa, computer and card rooms, and a New Life Fitness Center. Eight model homes are on display and there's a Vacation Villa available. Stop by and see for yourself all that SunRiver St. George has to offer and why the area is considered to be one of the nation's premier places to live.

1887 W Magenta Mist Circle, St. George UT

(435) 688-1000 or (888) 688-6556

www.sunriver.com

# Blue Bunny Ice Cream Parlor

Wells Dairy got going in 1913 when Fred H. Wells purchased his horse and wagon and a few milk cans. It is now the largest family owned dairy processor in the United States and the face behind the multitude of beloved Blue Bunny ice cream treats. The Blue Bunny Ice Cream Parlor in Saint George is not just another ice cream parlor. Not only is the ice cream exceptional, but the parlor experience makes a treasured memory. Guests enjoy a choice of tables, booths or a counter to-go service. Staff members do much more than provide excellent service; they also sing, dance and engage in activities designed to encourage customer participation. Interactive lights, giant ice cream sculptures and a lively décor make the parlor a popular place for groups, families and special events. The gift shop carries original Saint George gift. Blue Bunny t-shirts and stuffed animals. After you visit Blue Bunny Ice Cream Parlor, you may want to plan a trip to Le Mars, Iowa, home of the Wells' Dairy and the Ice Cream Capital of the World Visitor Center. Bring your ice cream appetite to the Blue Bunny Ice Cream Parlor.

20 N Main Street, Suite 100, Saint George UT
(435) 674-9425
www.bluebunny.com

# Larsen's Frostop

Larsen's Frostop has been a good old-fashioned car-hop service with fresh-cooked food since the 1960s. They never freeze their meat and they never compromise the exceptional service and mouth-watering taste of their traditional menu. Larsen's Frostop shines in the burger department, but they also win points for the rest of their extensive menu. They provide a long list of shake flavors, in addition to a variety of smoothies, freezes and floats. For the slush aficionado, there are the regular flavors, as well as the glacier variety, which is a slush with ice cream. Big appetites are put to rest with foot long hot dogs or quarter pound cheeseburgers. Long-time fans delight in the tasty sides of Piccadilly chips and onion rings. Much of the menu is unwritten, except in the minds of frequent diners, and commemorates some of the diners past. Customers still ask for the Larry burger or Larry sauce for their fries. Larry was a former cook. The Joe burger is named after a friend of the owner. Larsen's Frostop makes a top-notch, original signature sauce. For a real delicious burger, an out-of-the-ordinary cold drink, a fry sauce or tartar sauce like no other and the ambiance of all great car hops, don't miss Larsen's Frostop.
858 E Saint George Boulevard, Saint George UT
(435) 673-2216

# Cowboys and Indians

Gabe Collett manages Cowboys and Indians in Saint George. He knows the store's artistic treasures thoroughly. Gabe grew up acquiring this knowledge on adventurous explorations with Carl Ray Collett, Gabe's father and the owner of C & C Indian Art. The business was a natural outgrowth of the passion the Colletts shared for Native American culture, art and artifacts. The Saint George shop is located in the Zion Factory Mall, but its influence is felt much further. In exciting new partnerships with home designers and other industry professionals, design planning is drawing on Native American and western culture with the result that this functional and beautifully decorative artwork is being incorporated into many more homes. The shop is a rich mix of rare collectibles, one-of-a-kind jewelry, hand-crafted furniture and too many glorious finds to list. Cowboys and Indians proudly features the softly gleaming bronze sculptures of acclaimed artist Jerry Anderson. The Colletts and their capable staff offer a wealth of information on the pieces they offer for sale, as well as the stories they've acquired on the art and culture represented in the shop. Come in and tell them what you're looking for. If they don't have it, the crew at Cowboys and Indians are experts at successfully hunting down the rare and elusive.

250 N Red Cliffs Drive, Suite #18, Saint George UT
(435) 673-0636
236 E Maine Street, Vernal UT
(435) 789-8447

# Bit & Spur Restaurant and Saloon

The Bit & Spur Restaurant and Saloon is not tucked away anywhere. It stands bold and proud at the entrance to Zion National Park in Springdale. Famous for its spicy Mexican food, large portions and live music, this former watering hole and 1940s pool hall enjoys a long, rich history with a lively atmosphere befitting local legend. At the Bit & Spur, the menu is loaded with fare to awaken the taste buds, such as bistek asado, a chile-rubbed, grilled rib eye steak, served with port wine demiglace and shoestring onions. If white meat is your preference, try the pollo relleno, consisting of a baked chicken breast stuffed with flavorful basil pesto and goat cheese, topped with a chile-honey glaze and served with pineapple salsa, black beans, rice and salad. The delightful Asian pear salad mixes pears with field greens, blue cheese, candied pecans, avocado and a champagne vinaigrette. The menu's full page of house favorites features such classics as chile verde, mushroom-stuffed poblano peppers and chile rellenos. Beyond great food, expect terrific service, art exhibits and a patio with sunset and garden views. You are invited to join the fun and have a rousing good time at the Bit and Spur Restaurant and Saloon.

1212 Zion Park Boulevard, Springdale UT
(435) 772-3498
www.bitandspur.com

# Painted Pony

The beautifully artistic Painted Pony Restaurant is located on the second floor of the Tower Building in Saint George's Ancestor Square. Rave reviews of this highly rated restaurant are glowing for a reason. The food is unparalleled for its appearance, originality and exquisite taste. Owned by Executive Chef Randall Richards and his wife, Manager Nicki Pace Richards, the two have maintained the gracious, casual ambience imparted by former partner June Pace. The wait staff performs with cheerful professionalism, and they have reason to smile. The meals they serve are flawless. Randall is aware of the advantages of using local, seasonal fresh produce and supports organic gardeners in the area. Mouthwatering dinner entrées include specialties such as a sesame-crusted escolar prepared with sweet potato green onion hash, cilantro and ginger sauce or an exotic, seared ahi tuna mixed in pan-fried soba noodles, with tangy wasabi aioli and a luscious orange mango sauce. One of the many delicious luncheon sandwiches is the barbecued pulled pork sandwich with poblano aioli and grilled red onions. Incredible salads and gourmet style appetizers are served for both lunch and dinner. The sage smoked quail is served with apricot glaze, mushroom risotto and creamed spinach. A fresh, mixed green salad is tossed with toasted walnuts, apples and bleu cheese, and topped with a balsamic vinaigrette. The house-made desserts are delightful and exotic enough to warrant saving room for them. The restaurant has won over locals and travelers alike. Visit Painted Pony Restaurant and find a new favorite.
2 W St. George Boulevard, St. George UT   (435) 634-1700   www.painted-pony.com

312

# La Soirée

La Soirée translated into English could mean an evening, a party or an evening performance. All three meanings describe this wonderful fondue/creperie in St. George. Managers Justin and Jessica Lanoue combine the arts with the culinary world by presenting a casual fine dining restaurant that also serves up live entertainment and an art gallery. The menu features savory crepes for lunch and a variety of fondues for dinner. La Romantique is an offering of a four-course dinner for two comprised of any one of the entrées of seafood, wild game or vegetarian fare followed with the grand finale of a delicious dessert fondue.

La Soirée Dining Experience brings such acts as a jazz ensemble or a string quartet onto the restaurant's center stage. A local potter, sculptor or painter is invited to add their creations to the ambience. Dinner theatre is also an essential part of the restaurant's desire to treat guests like royalty. The first ever interactive dinner theater program in St. George is La Soirée's production of The Ghosts of Christmas Past, a comedic murder mystery. Other special events include a Masquerade on New Year's Eve and a black and white party for Valentine's Day. While in St. George, try something different and elegant, book reservations to find yourself an unforgettable experience at La Soirée.

20 N Main Suite 105, St. George UT

313

# Earth and Light Gallery

Earth and Light Gallery, located in the fabulous Coyote Gulch Art Village in Ivins, offers a wonderful selection of fine art and landscape photography that captures the qualities of land and light found in the desert Southwest. Owner Charles Wood and his wife Kathleen have created a warm and welcoming atmosphere that is the ideal backdrop to Charles' magical photography. Earth and Light Gallery allows you to browse through the intimate setting while quietly enjoying inspiring romantic and scenic vistas of the West. Charles is an extremely popular photographer whose work is predominantly done inside the American Southwest, with an emphasis on the Red Rock and desert regions of Utah and Arizona. His imaginative photographs have been featured in numerous travel and trade publications, and several of his pieces have gained permanent exhibition space at various museums. The Earth and Light Gallery offers a plethora of fine art photography, including nature and landscape prints, high resolution virtual drum scans, fine art custom archival digital printing and personalized architectural photography. Experience the magnificence of the Southwest through the eyes of Charles Wood at the Earth and Light Gallery.
880 Coyote Gulch Court, Kayenta (Ivins) UT
(435) 673-2805  www.earthlightgallery.com

# Treasures of
# *Utah*